T0120129

TALKING TO THE DEAD

TALKING TO THE DEAD

KATE AND MAGGIE FOX
AND THE
RISE OF SPIRITUALISM

BARBARA WEISBERG

HarperOne
An Imprint of HarperCollinsPublishers

HarperOne

HarperCollins books may be purchased for educational, business, or sales promotional use. For information, please e-mail the Special Markets Department at SPsales@harpercollins.com.

HarperCollins Web site: http://www.harpercollins.com

HarperCollins®, 📖®, and HarperOne™ are trademarks of HarperCollins Publishers.

FIRST HARPERCOLLINS PAPERBACK EDITION PUBLISHED IN 2005

Library of Congress Cataloging-in-Publication Data is available upon request.

ISBN 978–0–06–075060–2

HB 08.15.2023

FOR DAVID

CONTENTS

PART III
DARLING LITTLE SPIRIT, 1852–1857

PART IV
WORLDLY TRIALS, 1857–1888

PART V
AFTERLIFE, 1888–TO THE PRESENT

*Lithograph courtesy of the Department of Rare Books and Special Collections,
University of Rochester Library.*

I asked these spirit figures if I was seeing them or if I was seeing what was in my own brain. They answered, "both."

—EILEEN GARRETT,
twentieth-century medium

INTRODUCTION

I N LATE MARCH 1848 two young sisters excitedly waylaid a neighbor, eager to tell her about the strange sounds they had been hearing at home nearly every night around bedtime. The noises, the girls confided to Mary Redfield, seemed to have no explanation. Their father had failed to discover the source of the raps and knocks. Their mother was exhausted from worry and lack of sleep.

Ghosts, Mary Redfield thought wryly. As she later told a newspaper reporter, what she really suspected was a childish prank.

She didn't know the girls well. Along with their parents, they had just moved to Hydesville, a quiet community of farms and fields in western New York State, the previous December. Margaretta, nicknamed Maggie but sometimes called Margaret, like her mother, was a pretty, saucy fourteen-year-old. Eleven-year-old Catherine, called Cathie or Kate, was black haired and pale, more delicate in appearance than her sister. The two children were outgoing, polite, and friendly, and they were almost always together.

A few nights later, on March 31 at about 8 P.M., Mary and her husband, Charles, heard a sharp knock—a human one—on their own front door. John Fox, the girls' father, was standing in the snow with a bizarre story to tell. Raps had broken out in his house more loudly than ever, and his wife, Margaret, had determined that they were caused by the spirit of a murdered man whose remains lay buried in the cellar.

Would the Redfields come immediately? Margaret urgently wanted their opinion.

Charles Redfield declined, but Mary agreed to go, teasing John that she would "have a spree with it, if it was a ghost." Humor, however, wasn't one of dour John's strengths. He grimly led Mary to the house, a nondescript frame structure on a neatly fenced plot, and headed straight to the bedroom that he and Margaret shared with the girls. Margaret Fox, a comfortably plump, generally cheery woman, though now highly agitated, met Mary at the door.[1]

Glancing inside the room, which was lit by a single candle, Mary recognized in an instant the seriousness of the situation. Kate and Maggie were huddled on their bed, clinging to each other in terror.

Margaret drew Mary down beside her on the other bed in the room, then began to speak into what must have seemed like thin air.

"Now count five. . . ." Margaret Fox commanded. Five knocks followed, seeming to indicate an intelligent presence.

"Count fifteen," Margaret ordered. The invisible noisemaker did so. She asked it to tell Mary Redfield's age, and Mary later remembered with wonder that it "rapped thirty-three times so we all heard it."

"If you are an injured spirit," Margaret Fox continued, "manifest it by three raps."

Knock, it answered.

Knock.

Knock.

There was no sign that anyone in the room was making the noise.

"By this time," Mary Redfield candidly confessed, "I became much interested. . . ."

She decided that she wanted her husband, Charles, to size up the situation for himself, but before leaving the Fox household she paused for a moment to comfort Kate and Maggie. She tried to reassure them that if indeed a spirit was present, it had no intention of hurting them.

One of the girls—like most people, Mary had a habit of referring to the sisters as if they were interchangeable—answered with emotion: "We are innocent—how good it is to have a clear conscience."

Forty years later, on an autumn night in 1888, a bespectacled Maggie Fox, wearing a red flowered hat and black dress, stepped onto the stage of New York City's Academy of Music to a cacophony of hisses, cheers, and boos. Standing in front of the packed house, she glanced nervously down at her prepared speech and started to speak in an excited voice. She was about to make a stunning—and to some members of her raucous audience devastating—pronouncement.

In the four decades since the first raps at Hydesville, she and Kate had become world famous. When the eerie sounds continued, word had spread that spirits made them and that the girls were talking to the dead. Soon Kate and Maggie were delivering otherworldly messages to friends, then strangers, then large public audiences. Debates about the authenticity of spirit communications had riveted the nation.

Before long, other mortals discovered that they too could serve as intermediaries between this world and the next. By the mid-1850s tens of thousands of Americans—the curious, the skeptical, and the converted alike—were flocking to seances to contact the departed. A journalist had called the movement Modern Spiritualism, and it swiftly had acquired an international following.

It was Modern Spiritualism, the fervor of which she had helped to create, that Maggie now, trembling visibly in the footlights' glow, set out to destroy: she had come to announce to the overflow crowd at the Academy of Music that the spirits of the dead never return to communicate with the living. The raps that had sent Mary Redfield hastening to find her husband on that long-ago night in 1848 had been a fake, as had so many other alleged spirit manifestations through the years.

Front-page headlines shouted news of Maggie's confession: she had dealt a death blow, reporters wrote, to Spiritualism.

But the headlines, as it turns out, were premature. The Fox sisters' story wasn't over, and the Spiritualist movement hadn't been destroyed. A year later Maggie recanted her confession of fraud. Asserting that she had been under the sway of the movement's enemies and overwhelmed by financial pressures when she falsely confessed, she adamantly reaffirmed her faith in the spirits. And Modern Spiritualism, a religion and social force that has dramatically influenced our ideas about immortality, remains very much alive today.

Faith in the power of good and evil spirits is ancient, although ideas about the nature of these entities differ from culture to culture. It was—and is—Modern Spiritualism's central tenet that death does not exist. Instead, the state commonly called death is only a transition, a shedding of the body, and the spirits of individuals not only survive beyond the grave but also communicate from the other side. A related belief holds that mediums, men and women who are able to receive and transmit spirit messages, can help other, less finely attuned, mortals establish contact at seances. The word *seance*, French for "session," now almost exclusively denotes a gathering held to commune with spirits.

Formed by many different influences, Modern Spiritualism as a popular movement began with the Hydesville raps. In defiance of Judaeo-Christian theologians who argued that alleged spirit visitations were either demonic manifestations or delusions, Americans in the third quarter of the nineteenth century crowded into seance rooms, seeking wisdom and comfort in what they perceived as tangible evidence of immortality. Many believers were men and women struggling to reconcile religion with science at a time when geologists were questioning the very age and origins of the earth and its creatures. Whether by design of the spirits or inadvertently, Kate and Maggie Fox served as the catalyst for what believers in spirit communication called the dawning of a new era.

The passionate interest of the mid-nineteenth century is in fact a mirror of our own. Since I began my research on the Fox family, books on the afterlife by mediums and psychics have appeared consistently on the *New York Times* best-seller list, and several of the authors have become television celebrities, as widely sought after in our day as Kate and Maggie were in theirs. In movies and TV dramas, individuals whose spirits survive death routinely return to help with the problems encountered by the living.

Opinions about Kate and Maggie vary, of course (as they do about today's mediums). There are debunkers—among them some, but by no means all, magicians and historians—who delight in or abhor the sisters as one more example of humbug in a society famous for it. Several decades after the sisters' deaths, two particularly memorable antagonists contributed to the debate over Spiritualism: the magician Houdini and the author Arthur Conan Doyle, creator of the master detective Sherlock Holmes. In the 1920s Houdini tried to convince Doyle that Spiritualism was a fraud by unmasking fake mediums, while Doyle persisted in holding tight to his Spiritualist beliefs.

Controversy about the Fox sisters accounts in part for the frequent retelling of the girls' story through the years: there are so many possibilities and versions. For Spiritualists, the saga has the resonance of a sacred story, one that helps illuminate the origins or at least an aspect of their continuing faith. Others find the sisters' story intriguing because it reads like a classic ghost yarn or because it triggered such a widespread and colorful inquiry into the nature of life after death. Still others are interested in exploring how the girls might have faked their spirit manifestations.

I first encountered Kate and Maggie Fox in a book about mystics and mediums, Peter Washington's *Madame Blavatsky's Baboon: A History of the Mystics, Mediums, and Misfits Who Brought Spiritualism to America.* The two Fox sisters jumped off the page and seized me with a grasp as firm, if as invisible, as a ghost's. I was consumed with curiosity to learn more about these nineteenth-century children. What actually took place that March night in Hydesville? Had the girls pulled off an elaborate hoax, mischief that might have started innocently? If so, how could they have perpetuated such a fraud for forty years? Alternatively, were they in the grip of some powerful, shared delusion? Or, as some theorists suggest about teenagers in general and about those who trigger strange phenomena in particular, had the stresses of puberty released unconscious forces, sexual energies capable of turning the most ordinary household into a horror?

Or were Kate and Maggie spirit mediums, as many reputable people of the day believed?

I began my exploration into the sisters' lives with a focus on the paranormal and otherworldly. My curiosity led me not only to bookstores and libraries but also to Hydesville, for the hundred fiftieth anniversary of

Modern Spiritualism in 1998, and to Lily Dale, a Victorian town located near Buffalo, New York, that's now inhabited almost entirely by mediums and other Spiritualists.

Somewhere along my route, however—and much to my surprise—my interest in Kate and Maggie shifted from the paranormal to the normal or at least to the social and cultural aspects of life in the nineteenth century. I became less absorbed with the elusive question of whether the Fox children invented the spirits, and I grew more curious about who the girls were and what kind of world they lived in. What factors in the Fox family and the culture helped produce these two strikingly original young women? Faced often with derision and scorn, forced to undergo grueling investigations of their powers, why did Kate and Maggie continue to hold seances? And in an age when almost no one achieved the celebrity status that our athletes, movie stars, and mediums take for granted today, how did these two unknown country children manage to seize the public's imagination to such an astonishing degree?

Over the last three decades, historians have produced a significant body of work that explores Spiritualism as both a reflection and expression of the tensions inherent in nineteenth-century America. Following their lead, I became intrigued by the saga of this particular nineteenth-century family—John and Margaret Fox and their children—navigating, with resilience and invention though not always with success, a rapidly changing culture.

Ordinary Americans in the 1800s had great opportunity for social, economic, and geographic mobility. They faced a number of questions that perhaps can be summed up in a simple query that had rarely been so pressing in the past: "Where are we going?"

Shall we pack our worldly goods and journey westward? Or leave the farm behind and head for the city?

Are our struggles moving us upward on the social ladder, or have our risks only pushed us down a notch?

Is our society advancing toward utopian perfection? Or under new pressures such as urbanization, is it descending into chaos?

Those of us who are women—will we stay placidly at home or step out into the street, into the labor force, into public life?

Those of us who are enslaved—will we remain in bondage or march forward into freedom?

For many Americans of the time, each of these questions was coupled with an older, deeply personal one: am I bound for heaven or hell?

And all these questions were shadowed by a pervasive concern: what control do we have over any of our destinations?

The more I thought about the Fox sisters, the more it seemed to me not only that Kate and Maggie sparked a movement, but that their lives epitomized the conflicts and urges that helped fuel its blaze. The question of the other world aside, the girls' appeal surely stemmed in part from the ways they embodied—and intuited—their culture's anxieties and ambitions.

Not that the two of them can be viewed simply as emblematic of their times. Charismatic individuals in their own right, they were as different from one another as most siblings are. They've often been treated as a unit and portrayed flatly either as frauds or martyrs.

I approached Kate and Maggie primarily through the narratives written by their contemporaries. Few of the mediums' own unpublished letters seem to have survived, although the ones included here allow an intimate, if often oblique, glimpse into each sister's emotional life. But there's no scarcity of books, pamphlets, and letters in which to find the girls' nineteenth-century visitors registering violently different opinions about them.[2]

Not surprisingly, little documentation exists for the period before Kate and Maggie rose to fame. Their oldest sister, the thrice-wed Leah Fox Fish Brown Underhill, wrote a useful but frequently unreliable and self-serving memoir, which has to be read with care. For anyone interested in the Fox sisters, there are many discoveries yet to be made.

Kate and Maggie are the protagonists in this true story, but other major players appear as well. Leah, a formidable woman who wielded immense influence over her younger siblings and on the course of Modern Spiritualism, became her sisters' impresario and a medium herself. The audience attracted by the sisters, composed of doubters and believers alike, served as a collective force that helped define and spread Spiritualism's concepts and practices. And, whether inventions of the mediums or immortal visitors, the spirits themselves were compelling figures.

When all is said and done, however, I always circle back to the impulse that first drew me to Kate and Maggie. The Fox sisters' story—of spirits and conjurers, skeptics and converts—remains a puzzle, a maze. I hope that readers will experience their story as I do, as a drama filled with emotion and surprise but one that also provokes questions in an unusually vivid and concrete way about how we *know* what we know and how secure we are in our knowledge.

As I read conflicting nineteenth-century accounts, I still feel that I'm in much the same position as the participants in the sisters' seances were one hundred and fifty years ago, asking the same questions, watching tables levitate, and struggling to understand inexplicable sounds.

E. E. Lewis, a writer who interviewed the Fox family in the 1840s, ended his introduction with an invitation I now extend to you: "Let them step forward and solve this mystery, if they can."[3]

PART I

EARTH AND THE WORLD OF SPIRITS
1789–1849

ONE

"A LARGE, INTELLIGENT AND CANDID COMMUNITY"

T WO WEEKS BEFORE Christmas 1847 a blacksmith named John David Fox, accompanied by his wife, Margaret, and their two youngest daughters, Kate and Maggie, moved to the rural community of Hydesville, New York. One of the worst winters in recent memory was pummeling the region, a windy, fertile plain in the northwest corner of the state.[1]

"The almost unparalleled bad weather which we have experienced since 'cold December' set in," complained the *Western Argus*, a local newspaper, "nearly diverted our attention from the fact that Christmas is almost at hand." The writer regretted that residents were staying home by the fire instead of venturing out, by wagon or sleigh, to make the customary holiday calls.[2]

The weather not only dampened good cheer, it also stalled construction on the new home that John and Margaret were building two miles from Hydesville, next to their son David's farm. Since work wouldn't resume until spring, the couple had rented a modest, one-and-a-half-story frame house to wait out the winter.

Today Hydesville has vanished from all but the most detailed local maps, but it was—and is—part of the township of Arcadia, located in New York's Wayne County. Farmhouses, barns, and steeple-capped villages dot the surrounding countryside; here and there flat-topped hills, called drumlins, rise up like ancient burial grounds. The county's northern boundary is Lake Ontario, which separates western New York from Canada. In August, fields of peppermint, a major crop, blossom with pink flowers that release a faint, delicious scent, but winters like the one of 1847 bring month after month of slate skies and snow.

Slight but sturdy, a country girl, Maggie was an ebullient fourteen-year-old with glossy dark hair, a broad-boned face, and frank brown eyes. Black-haired Kate was slim and soulful, at ten years old still very much a child, with compelling eyes that struck some people as deep purple and others as black or gray.[3] The girls were the youngest of six children, the only two still living at home with their parents, and they were often thrown back on each other for company. Their four siblings, Leah, Elizabeth, Maria, and David, were already adults with families of their own.

The girls' father, John, was a wiry man who peered out at the world through brooding eyes, his spectacles balanced on his hawk nose. Sometimes considered disagreeable by people other than his children, he was intense and inward, an impassioned Methodist who knelt each morning and night in prayer.

His wife, the former Margaret Smith, was in most respects his opposite. A kindly matron with an ample bosom and a double chin, she was as chatty and sociable as her husband was withdrawn. In the uncharitable opinion of one Hydesville neighbor, sweet-faced Margaret was superior to John "in weight and good looks" and in personality "the best horse in the team by odds."[4]

Already in their fifties, the weary survivors of economic reversals and marital crises, John and Margaret undoubtedly hoped that when their new home was finished it would be their last: a permanent, comfortable place to complete the tasks of child-rearing. They even may have looked forward to help from their grown children who lived nearby.

Raising two young daughters was a responsibility that must have weighed increasingly on them as they aged. What would happen if they fell ill? Or if they died? How would Kate and Maggie manage, and who would care for them?

The couple had accumulated little in the way of land or money, and girls who grew up without either eventually needed to find a devoted husband or a decent livelihood. Teaching was one alternative for a young woman, the drudgery of factory labor another. It was possible to slip down the ladder of opportunity as well as to climb up it.

A close-knit family, however, could provide refuge in times of trouble, and despite a history of geographical dislocations and separations, John and Margaret's six children had remained remarkably attached to one another. With the exception of Elizabeth, who lived in Canada with her husband, they had settled down within an easy radius of one another, having forged what Maggie called "tender ties" to western New York.

Twenty-seven-year-old David Smith Fox, a farmer, lived in Arcadia with his wife and three children in the house that had once belonged to his maternal uncle, John J. Smith. Surrounded by the peppermint fields, filled with good conversation and well-thumbed books, the farm was a place where friends and family liked to gather.[5] Maria, who lived only a few miles from her brother, had done her part to solidify family bonds by marrying one of her cousins, Stephen Smith.

Leah, the oldest of the six Fox siblings, had settled farther away, thirty miles west of Arcadia in the thriving young city of Rochester, New York, but she too retained close ties to her family. Her adolescent daughter, Lizzie, spent almost as much time in Hydesville with her young aunts, Kate and Maggie, as she did with her mother in Rochester.

Officially a hamlet within Arcadia's borders, Hydesville was an ordinary little cluster of farms and establishments that served the farmer: a sawmill, gristmill, and general store, along with a few artisans' workshops such as the cobbler's. The hamlet had been named for Henry Hyde, a doctor who arrived in Arcadia by wagon in 1810, in the days before physicians needed either a license or formal training.

Death was a constant fact of life. The reaper struck with fire and drowning; typhus, malaria, yellow fever, and a host of other diseases;

accidents that ranged from the swift shock of a horse's kick to a slow-spreading infection from a cut finger; and suicide and murder. More than one-fifth of the children born died before their first birthday; at birth the average life expectancy for an adult was little more than forty.[6] Medicine at best could offer a patient little help and at worst was lethal, an excruciating matter of bleeding, blistering, and purging with potions such as laudanum, a mixture of opium and alcohol.

Dr. Henry Hyde discovered a tonic that worked for him if not for the sickly; he opened a public house at a busy crossroads, where migrants heading west paused to gamble, drink, and race their horses. Hydes Tavern became the nucleus of the new settlement, and he became a rich man.

Within a decade or two of the doctor's arrival, clapboard houses had replaced log cabins; soon several wealthier residents had built fine brick homes. By 1847 Hydes Tavern had disappeared, and its owner had passed away. His son, however, remained a well-to-do landowner, and it was from Artemus Hyde that John Fox rented the small frame house for his family of four.

The house had been occupied by a string of tenants. Although Hydesville boasted some second- and third-generation families, like other communities in western New York it attracted most of its inhabitants from elsewhere—adjacent counties, the East Coast, and other countries. Prospective residents came in search of new opportunities, and many families needed temporary lodgings until they either settled permanently or moved on.

While not large, the house was serviceable, with a good number of windows and two stoves. The front door opened directly into the south-facing parlor. The kitchen was set back, on the northwest side, and had its own door to the yard. On the east side, a buttery—sometimes used as a second bedroom—connected to the kitchen, and the main bedroom adjoined the parlor. An enclosed staircase between the buttery and main bedroom led up to a large attic, while another staircase led down to a dirt-floor basement. In back of the house flowed the Ganargua River, commonly known as Mud Creek, a popular spot for night fishing.

The rental's location on the busy corner of Hydesville and Parker

Roads offered everything that Margaret might have wanted for her family. There was a Methodist church within walking distance, next to a district school where Kate most likely studied her three Rs and geography. Maggie, who could already read and write, was beyond the age when school was considered necessary. Both girls ably expressed their thoughts and feelings in letters to friends, and if their punctuation and spelling were erratic, it was a flaw shared by even the most educated of their day.

The girls were smart and full of fun. One former schoolmate of Kate's remembered them as adept mimics.[7] But they weren't always so lively, since they also suffered on occasion from severe headaches that left them weak and depressed.

In late winter Kate and Maggie probably joined other children in going sugar mapling, and the sisters were likely kept busy helping their mother with household chores such as laundry, sewing, quilting, cooking, canning, and cleaning. Local newspapers of the day urged young women to govern their passions—anger and excitement could spoil the complexion—and practice reason, prudence, and virtue through devotion to education and domestic duty. One education expert warned parents that the "first appearance of stubbornness" in their daughters needed instantly to "be checked and resisted." The result of immediate discipline, he promised, would be "tempers sweet and placid."[8]

Heightened emotion potentially posed another threat more serious than bad skin: hysteria. Doctors diagnosed the condition as a woman's disease, believed to originate in the womb and to demonstrate female frailty and fallibility. Girls around puberty were particularly susceptible, doctors worried, to the fits and seizures hysteria could induce. How important it was, then, for a young woman to exercise self-restraint and to remain in a limited arena: the home.

John Fox was an abstracted man, his mind focused on sin and redemption, financial worries and practicalities, rather than on the more subtle matters of his youngest daughters' behavior. And Margaret Fox was probably a more lenient mother than many others. She was a farmer's daughter who had grown up before women were relegated to such a limited, domestic sphere; moreover, in the 1820s she and John had made the hazardous journey westward across New York State to build a new life. With past adventures of her own to remember and current worries to distract her, Margaret on occasion may have looked the other way when her bright, lively children found ways to escape the boredom and confinement dictated by current thinking. Or she may not always have known what diversions her daughters had discovered or what troubles (or visions) were haunting (or inspiring) them, all hidden beneath the pattern of their visible, everyday lives.

In March 1848 an unseasonable lightning storm flashed over Hydesville, followed by fresh snow. Otherwise, life went on much as usual. The Whigs battled the Democrats. Women baked cookies for a town festival. A farmer reported a stray cow. Fire left a family homeless. Kate's eleventh birthday was celebrated, if it was marked at all, on March 27.

In the newspapers, national and international events were duly noted: the end of the Mexican War, which wrested California from Mexico; the abdication of Louis Philippe, the French king, a fall that prefigured the democratic uprisings that swept across the rest of Europe later in the year. The news, however, had to fight for space with product advertisements, many for patent remedies such as Sand's Sarsaparilla and Brant's Indian Pulmonary Balsam, pious advice columns, amusing anecdotes, sentimental poems, and uplifting or shocking stories. One writer reported word of a haunting: the ghostly return of a sixteen-year-old Baltimore resident, murdered by her overbearing father, who had been aiming at her poor but honest suitor.

"The neighbors now a days"—so readers were told—"occasionally see the young lady, falling to the earth, the flash of the gun dispelling the darkness—disclosing her uplifted hands, radiant face, and disheveled hair. . . ." The writer added ruefully that neither philosophy nor reason had been able to dispel the locals' belief "in the ghost of the martyr of love and fidelity."

During the cold months of the year, houses in Hydesville often moaned and shrieked in the harsh winds. Tree branches snapped from the weight of ice. Loose boards smacked against the sides of houses. Small animals burrowed into kitchens, scurrying and scratching in search of food and the warmth of stoves and fireplaces. Sounds such as these were familiar. But in the last two weeks of March 1848, the Foxes' rented house began to resound with eerie knocks at night: thumps on the ceiling, bumps on doors or walls, sometimes raps sharp enough to jar bedsteads and tables.

In statements made in April 1848 to an enterprising journalist named E. E. Lewis, family members and friends described the new and seemingly inexplicable noises that had suddenly disrupted the Fox household. Lewis subsequently published these interviews in a forty-page pamphlet titled *A Report of the Mysterious Noises Heard in the House of Mr. John D. Fox, in Hydesville, Arcadia, Wayne County, Authenticated by the Certificates, and Confirmed by the Statements of the Citizens of That Place and Vicinity.* The voices of the Fox family and their neighbors rise from the page like ghostly echoes.

"It sounded like some one knocking in the east bed-room, on the floor," Margaret told Lewis. She added that the noise sometimes "sounded as if the chair moved on the floor; we could hardly tell where it was."[10]

The knocking always started in the evening, just after the family had gone to bed.

"The whole family slept in that room together, and all heard the noise," Margaret stated, then added that there were four of them in the family "and sometimes five." The fifth person—most likely Leah's daughter Lizzie—may have been visiting her grandparents that March, but Margaret wasn't explicit.

"The first night that we heard the rapping," Margaret continued, "we all got up and lit a candle; and searched all over the house." As they searched, the sound continued in much the same spot.

"It was not very loud," she noted, "yet it produced a jar of the bedsteads and chairs, that could be felt by placing our hands on the chair, or while we were in bed. It was a feeling of a tremulous motion, more than a sudden jar."

The knocks continued night after night.

On Friday, March 31, a fresh snowstorm blanketed the fields just as everyone was beginning to look ahead to spring. Making his way by wagon, David Fox managed despite the weather to stop by for a visit with his parents and little sisters. Sweet-tempered and practical, David tried to reassure them about the rapping by providing a dose of common sense.

"I told them that if they searched," he said, "I guessed they would find a cause for it, as it must be something about the house."

He later testified to E. E. Lewis that the house, as houses should, had remained quiet and well behaved throughout the whole afternoon.

That night, the eve of April Fool's Day, Margaret decided that raps would no longer rule her family's life. She resolved that "if it came, we thought we would not mind it, but try and get a good night's rest." The sky had hardly turned dark when she sent the girls—perhaps Lizzie, too—to bed early.

"We went to bed so early," she said, "because we had been broken so much of our rest that I was almost sick."

Although John wasn't yet in bed, Margaret lay down. The raps "commenced as usual," but what followed had never happened before.

"The girls, who slept in the other bed in the room, heard the noise, and tried to make a similar noise by snapping their fingers. The youngest girl," Margaret explained, "is about 12 years old;—she is the one who made her hand go. As fast as she made the noise with her hands or fingers, the sound was followed up in the room. . . . it made the same number of noises that the girl did."

When Kate stopped, the noise stopped. But the strange game continued.

"The other girl," Margaret said—neglecting to use specific names— "who is in her 15th year, then spoke in sport and said, 'Now do this just as I do. Count one, two, three, four,' &c., striking one hand in the other at the same time. The blows which she made were repeated as before. It appeared to answer her by repeating every blow that she made."

It was Maggie's turn to be—or act—surprised.

"She only did so once," Margaret recalled of her daughter. "She then began to be startled. . . ."

Rather than taking a moment to question or soothe the girls, however, Margaret pressed forward and asked the noise to " 'Count ten,' and it made ten strokes or noises."

What were her children's successive ages? When the raps responded accurately, Margaret quickly concluded that an invisible intelligence was at work, and she set out to confirm its nature.

"I then asked if it was a human being that was making the noise," she continued, "and if it was, to manifest it by the same noise. There was no noise. I then asked if it was a spirit? and if it was, to manifest it by two sounds. I heard two sounds as soon as the words were spoken. I then asked, if it was an injured spirit? to give me the sound, and I heard the rapping distinctly. I then asked if it was injured in this house? and it manifested it by the noise. If the person was living that injured it? and got the same answer. I then ascertained by the same method that its remains were buried under the dwelling, and how old it was."

Would the spirit continue to rap if Margaret summoned the neighbors? It tapped the affirmative.

The children, Margaret admitted in her statement, were now clinging to one another in terror. She seems to have been oblivious to the possibility, soon trumpeted by the local newspapers, that her daughters were teasing her with an April Fool's Day joke. If so, the girls might have been frightened, not by an unseen presence, but by the unexpected success of their prank.

But Margaret remained confident that her instincts that night were appropriate to the situation. "I was as calm, I think," she assured Lewis, "as I am now."

On Margaret's command, around eight o'clock that March evening John hurried to summon their neighbor, Mary Redfield. As it turned out, the children had already reported news of the sounds to her several days before. After hearing the raps for herself, Mary left the Fox household and returned almost immediately with her husband.

"Then Mr. Redfield called in Mr. Duesler and wife, and several others," Margaret remembered. "A great many questions were asked over, and the same answers given as before. Mr. Duesler then called in Mr. and Mrs. Hyde; they came, and also Mr. and Mrs. Jewell."

The men who were night fishing in the Ganargua River heard the hubbub and arrived to investigate. By nine o'clock, a dozen or more curiosity seekers had packed the house.

William Duesler, an aggressive, athletic man who had moved to the area from a neighboring county, had rented the Hydesville house briefly seven years before. After initially dismissing the haunting as pure nonsense, he soon seized the lead in the questioning, extracting the rest of the spirit's tragic tale.

With some admiration, Margaret reported that Duesler ascertained "that it was murdered in the bed room, about five years ago, and that the murder was committed by a Mr. [Bell], on a Tuesday night, at 12 o'clock; that it was murdered by having its throat cut with a butcher knife; that the body . . . was taken down cellar, and that it was not buried until the next night . . . that it was buried ten feet below the surface of the ground."

The rapper claimed to be the spirit of a peddler, brutally murdered for the small fortune he had been carrying: five hundred dollars, more than a laborer's wages for an entire year. In response to a litany of past and present neighbors recited by Duesler, the sounds also identified the alleged murderer: John Bell, a former resident of the house who had since moved to a nearby town.[11]

The peddler's story was riveting, but witnesses were perhaps most amazed by the spirit's thorough knowledge of themselves and their community.

"I then asked the number of children in the different families in the neighborhood?" Duesler said, "and it told them in the usual way, by rapping. Also, the number of deaths that had taken place in these families? And it told correctly."

In a transient community, the spirit's gossipy omniscience must have seemed not only uncanny but also something more: intimate. People weren't strangers to *this* rapper; they were known to it. And by the end of the evening, after they had huddled together and listened to the spirit answer questions about their lives, they were undoubtedly better known to one another as well. As the long, cold winter (when even the mills, traditional gathering places, were closed) wound down, the peddler was drawing neighbors together.

Throughout the evening the spirit responded primarily by rapping only to yes-or-no questions, with an affirmative indicated by a rap and a negative by silence. But at one point Duesler, through a laborious process of calling out the alphabet and asking the spirit to rap on certain letters, learned that its initials included a *C* and a *B*.

Charles Redfield, Mary's husband, descended, candle in hand, into the cellar's pitch darkness to search for the murdered man's hidden grave. Duesler's voice from above and raps from an unspecified location directed Redfield to return again and again to the same suspicious spot in the dirt floor.

Around midnight, the exhausted Margaret and her daughters abandoned the house. She went to Mary Redfield's but added rather vaguely that "my children staid [sic] at some of the other neighbors." John Fox and Charles Redfield stood guard in the house all night.

By the time Duesler returned at seven the next evening, Saturday, April 1, the raps had resumed, and several hundred people—half the population of Arcadia—had gathered to gape and listen, crowding the house and milling in front of it. Committees had staked out different areas to monitor, but the main action continued to be centered in the east bedroom. Duesler entered, only to be quickly asked to leave.

"Some of those in the room wanted me to go out and let some one else ask the questions," he admitted. "I did so and came home."

David Fox and his wife, Elizabeth, also visited the house that Saturday night.

"I did not stay in the room but a few minutes," Elizabeth remarked. "There were so many there that they kept going out and in every few minutes, so that they could all have a chance to hear the noise."

Once the crowds dispersed, David led a small crew of men downstairs to dig up the dirt floor in search of the peddler's grave. The workers had reached a depth of about three feet when they hit a stream of underground water, which forced them to stop.

The next few days were hectic ones for Hydesville. The digging continued on and off, the effort always thwarted by rising water. The crowds and the raps persisted, peddler and people alike noisily vying for attention.

Some of the queries addressed to the spirit turned to matters of theological and philosophical importance. Duesler asked if Universalist doctrine was true but received no raps. After asking the same question about Methodist doctrine, he heard raps—appropriately enough, since the spirit was a guest in a Methodist household.

Mary Redfield asked the most urgent questions of all, ones that foreshadowed later interest in spirit communication.

"I went into the bed-room with others, and knelt down upon the floor by the side of the bed," she said, "and asked if there was a heaven to attain? And got three raps—is my child Mary in heaven? The knocking was heard in answer. These questions, and others," Mary explained, "were asked while in the attitude of prayer to the Supreme Being for a revelation of these mysterious noises to me. Another lady in the room remarked that she was afraid," Mary remembered. "I told her that God would protect her, and at that moment we heard several distinct *raps*. . . . I asked if it was a spirit from God? And it rapped,—are the spirits of our departed friends now around us? The rapping was heard."

It seems that the rapper was behaving in a restrained and dignified manner rather than in the vengeful way its unhappy story might have justified.

Not everyone returned the courtesy. In the weeks following, many of Wayne County's residents came to witness a miracle, others to excoriate the Fox family for fraud or blasphemy. John Fox, beside himself with distress, swore that he had no idea what caused the raps.

"We have searched in every nook and corner in and about the house, at different times, to ascertain if possible whether any thing or any body was secreted there, that could make the noise," he tensely informed Lewis, "and have never been able to find any thing which explained the mystery."

The local newspapers relished the situation.

"The good people of Arcadia, we learn, are in quite a fever, in consequence of the discovery of an 'under ground' *ghost,* or some unaccountable noise," the *Western Argus* reported on April 12. "Picks and bats were at once brought into requisition, and on digging down about four feet, a stream of pure water gushed forth and filled up the 'ghost' hole."

Some of the curious went away awed. Others departed as they had arrived: doubting. More than seventy years later, Andrew Soverhill, a retired attorney who had been a neighbor of the Fox family, described a gathering he had witnessed as a boy.

"We . . . found the small house pretty well filled," Andrew Soverhill wrote in the *Syracuse Herald.* "There were 15 or 20 in the rooms. . . . After we had been there for a while Mrs. Fox went into the bedroom and occupied a chair near the head of the bed. I followed her in with boyish inquisitiveness to see everything that could possibly happen, and sat down beside her.

"The girls, Margaret and Catherine, sat on the bed. They invited me to climb on with them and I did. There was no light in the room at all, but a gleam from a tallow dip in the living room illuminated it enough so that it was possible to distinguish one person from another."

That small beacon was too bright for the girls' mother, Margaret, who worried that light might scare the spirit. With the door closed, proceedings continued.

"To some questions there were answering raps," Soverhill recalled, "to others none at all. I couldn't tell where the raps came from."[12]

The daughter of the Fox family's physician, Mrs. Henry P. Knowles, recalled how her father had been summoned to the house to see Kate, who had "taken ill." The doctor said that he had found "great commotion in the room of his patient; snapping, cracking noises all about the bed . . . as fast as he changed places the raps would do the same." He couldn't account for the noises, he told his daughter, but he thought that Kate was "in some way manipulating the joints or muscles of the fingers, toes, and knees."[13]

E. E. Lewis himself tried to defend the puzzled residents of Hydesville in the newspapers, but other reporters accused him instantly of commercial exploitation.

"Knowing that if the excitement should subside, or people abroad be apprised that the story was a hoax (as every intelligent person would of course pronounce it), it would materially injure the sale of his contemplated work, he has taken the above course . . ." sneered the *Newark Herald*.[14]

The Weekmans, who had lived in the house the year before the Fox family, came forward. They too had been terrorized by raps, they told Lewis. Their adolescent boarder and part-time servant, Jane C. Lape, went further. In her statement she claimed to have seen a man who "had on grey pants, black frock coat and black cap."

She was sure it had been a specter.

Nineteen-year-old Lucretia Pulver completed the story. Several years before, she confided, when she had worked for the accused John Bell, a foot peddler had called at the house.

"This pedler [sic] carried a trunk—and a basket, I think, with vials of essence in it," she remembered. "He wore a black frock coat, and light colored pants."

The Bells had sent Lucretia away for a few days. When she returned, Lucretia testified, there was no sign of any peddler, but Mrs. Bell asked her to mend two coats that had been suspiciously ripped to pieces. Although Lucretia never saw the peddler again, Mrs. Bell claimed that he still visited. She occasionally showed her young boarder silver thimbles and other items likely to have been found in a peddler's trunk.

Questions such as the ones Mary Redfield addressed to the murdered peddler of Hydesville—inquiries about the power of divine beings to protect (or punish), about the survival of the mortal individual's spirit after death, and about the nature of the afterlife—have been common to most cultures. So too have been efforts to understand and on occasion to try to harness supernatural forces.

Americans of the 1840s, whatever their religion or social class, were no strangers to spirits, both the spooky sort and the beatific. Some spirits were conceived of as independent entities, others as the manifestation of a person who had died. Although most inhabitants of the young United States prided themselves on their rationality and boasted of living in an age of material progress, in fact a wealth of beliefs about the supernatural, derived from Christian and non-Christian traditions, permeated mainstream religion, folklore, and popular culture.[15]

Whether or not an unfortunate wanderer lay buried beneath the Fox family's cellar, peddlers were not only familiar figures in New York State but also well-known ghosts in local folklore. Arriving by wagon or on foot, these itinerant salesmen were perennial outsiders and so ideal candidates for tales about unexpected arrivals and mysterious departures, greed and retribution. In many tales, peddlers threatened to pull something over on the buyer—only to receive a comeuppance. In others, they were themselves innocent victims. One story lamented the fate of a peddler at a village inn: "At three o'clock in the morning, half a dozen revelers dragged the peddler down to the well-head in the cellar, murdered him, and cast his body into the well."[16]

From then on the peddler's ghost stalked the spot.

Ghosts and poltergeists—a word that means "noisy ghost" in German—traveled far and wide, borne less by their fearsome powers than by word of mouth and by newspapers that borrowed freely from one another. Even John Bell wasn't the only man by that name—common though it was—to have grappled with the supernatural. In Tennessee in the early 1800s, a witch was said to have driven another John Bell to death. His travails, which began with raps, may have been known in the North by the 1840s.

John Wesley, founder of Methodism, had pondered the issue of witchcraft, and his own family had experienced what may have been a supernatural visitation. In 1726 Wesley wrote that his father's household had been disrupted by raps and knocks, footsteps, groans, and crashes. The behavior was characteristic of a poltergeist, a spirit distinguished by its mischievousness from other more doleful and passive sorts of wraiths. Wesley's parents and his sisters had named the invisible troublemaker "Old Jeffrey."

This episode was reported in the *Memoirs of the Wesley Family*, a book published in 1823 and reissued many times. A new edition was reviewed for the *New York Tribune* in the 1840s by the critic Margaret Fuller and presumably provoked lively discussion in Methodist circles and parlors.

The ideas and practices of Anton Mesmer, an eighteenth-century Austrian healer, had spread to the United States and by the 1840s held the nation in thrall. According to one theory, everything in the universe, including the human body, was composed of an electro–magnetic fluid. Proposing that an imbalance of this essential substance caused illness, Mesmer claimed to cure patients by readjusting the flow of electro–magnetism to the body's diseased or injured part.

Adapting his methods, healers known as mesmerists accomplished their work by placing a patient into a trance, called a magnetic sleep, while waving their hands gently over the subject's body. Whether or not the cure took, the subject was said to have been mesmerized or magnetized in a process now viewed as a precursor to hypnosis.

By the mid-nineteenth century, mesmerism had evolved into a form of entertainment as well as of healing. In parlors and at parties, amateur mesmerists displayed their skills on willing volunteers to amuse the other guests. Professional mesmerists and their subjects also gave public demonstrations for curious—and paying—audiences. In some cases, in which a female subject seemingly fell sway to a male mesmerist's control, the situation resonated with erotic tension. Those who had been mesmerized often awoke believing that they had experienced visions of spirits or attained clairvoyant powers.

The ideas of the eighteenth-century Swedish philosopher and mystic, Emanuel Swedenborg, who wrote extensively about his conversations with God, Jesus, spirits, and angels, had also crossed the Atlantic. Swedenborg's followers had founded the Church of New Jerusalem, but aspects of his writings appealed to other groups as well.

Swedenborg envisioned an afterlife that consisted of three heavens, three hells, and an interim place—the world of the spirits—where everyone went directly upon dying. Those who had accepted God's love on earth were drawn to other like-minded souls and eventually graduated as angels to one of the three heavens. Those who had loved only themselves or worldly things in mortal life discovered compatible companions in one of the three hells.

Swedenborg's reports of his communion with supernatural beings and his picture of paradise were long-winded but vivid. For those who inhabited the heavens, there were cities with broad avenues and handsome buildings, glittering palaces of gold and jewels, parks with flowering arbors, fruit trees, and pleasant walkways. Like mortals, spirits and most angels wore clothes, ate food, fell in love, and married. Children, innocent and good by nature, never went to hell.

· The nineteenth-century seer Andrew Jackson Davis of New York State claimed to experience visions of Swedenborg while in a mesmeric trance, thereby linking his two predecessors in a manner that might have surprised them both in their lifetimes. A largely self-educated, handsome young man with a bushy beard and penetrating eyes, Davis reportedly had a clairvoyant gift for diagnosing disease, but in a trance state he also elaborated on and modified Swedenborg's ideas about the afterlife.

Davis's early lectures were published in the mid-1840s, and he became known as the Poughkeepsie Seer, for the upstate New York town where he had grown up. Of course, it could be difficult for listeners to judge whether the spirits who conversed with such mystics and prophets had substance in reality or simply reflected the visionary's fertile imagination or aptitude for fraud.

A few miles from Poughkeepsie, the religious group popularly called the Shakers, for its members' physical bursts of piety, experienced an astonishing episode of spiritual frenzy in the late 1830s. The Shaker Society had been established in America about sixty years earlier by Mother Ann Lee, whose followers believed her to embody the feminine side of a dual-natured God, as Jesus had embodied his masculine aspects, and it was notably the community's girls and young women who were swept up in the excitement. Claiming to be seized by spirits, they danced wildly, sang, spoke in tongues, swayed, and swooned. These manifestations subsided in the mid-1840s, but community elders later viewed them as harbingers of the days when two other young women, the Fox sisters, would speak of strange raps.

Magicians and conjurers also weighed in on the question of raps, apparitions, and other alleged spiritual manifestations, at once playing on and distancing themselves from such beliefs. As early as 1810, a magician named John Rannie announced a campaign against those who pretended to raise the dead. He promised optical illusions that would "enable the attentive observer to form a just idea of the artifices by which they impose on the CREDULOUS and SUPERSTITIOUS in this and former ages. . . ."[17]

Nineteenth-century magicians skilled in ventriloquism, sleight of hand, and conjuring often described their work as scientific and analytical in nature, demonstrations of their proficiency in illusion, optics, acoustics, chemistry, pneumatics, and electricity. But magic, which had begun to develop a popular audience, wasn't always so complex. Books such as *Hocus Pocus; or, The Whole Art of Conjuring Made Easy for Young Persons*, published in 1846, taught parlor tricks. Nor were even rudimentary manuals required for a child to enjoy playing pranks.

"I was much interested in [magic] in early childhood," a college student wrote in 1834, "and had discovered before my tenth year, that it was an easy matter to frighten my friends by doing what they considered

wonderful." His first chance came, the young man recalled, when he terrified his cousin by producing strange raps.[18]

E. E. Lewis, who industriously collected depositions from approximately
twenty residents of Hydesville, was an attorney turned reporter from
Canandaigua, a town in a neighboring county. Disavowing any intention
to exploit the superstitious merely to make a profit on a good story, he
insisted that he only hoped to discover the truth about the rumors of
hauntings.

The bizarre events taking place were a product, he marveled, not of
the dark ages, but of the enlightened nineteenth century. Distinguishing
his interviewees from both the wily urban frauds who were said to stalk
city streets and the humble bumpkins on whom such mountebanks were
supposed to prey, Lewis described his witnesses as part of a "large, intelligent and candid community" of respectable American citizens. These
men and women, Lewis pronounced, were not easily duped.

"Hundreds have been there," he wrote, skeptics who assumed they
would quickly discover a ruse. These doubters "have first carefully examined the premises; have gone into the ghostly presence, still incredulous
and disposed to treat the affair with levity; have held converse with the
unknown one, until the cold sweat oozing from every pore has coursed
down their limbs, and they have been compelled to acknowledge that
they felt themselves in the presence of one from the spirit-country."

After denying any prior belief in the supernatural, the witnesses
whose statements Lewis printed all told a similar story, describing
spine-tingling raps that had plagued the Fox household. Most expressed
bafflement over the source of the sounds, swearing that they had looked
high and low.

Lewis not only listened to their stories but also added his own slant on
what was happening. "If the spirit of Swedenborg could . . . reveal the
coming of future events," he commented, "why cannot the spirits of the
dead come back and reveal to us that which would otherwise be
unknown?"

At the end of his pamphlet he included a petition signed by more
than forty of Bell's supporters, who proclaimed the alleged murderer a

man of honest character. Many of the signers also had witnessed the raps. While they couldn't account for the noises, they refused to accept a piece of information—Bell's guilt—that ran directly contrary to their own common sense.

Lewis's pamphlet and contemporary newspaper articles constitute the earliest known accounts of the events at Hydesville. As thorough as he was, however, Lewis made one mistake that would frustrate the skeptical, the faithful, and the curious of future generations: he failed to gather statements from Kate and Maggie. Perhaps the girls shied away from the chance, or their parents discouraged their participation. Perhaps no one thought to interview anyone so young.

Amid the clamor of voices, noises, and surging crowds, Kate and Maggie are silent.

TWO

"SOME FAMILY ANTECEDENTS"

O N JANUARY 4, 1851, Horace Greeley, editor of the *New York Tribune*, marveled at the literal and symbolic distance that the nation had traveled since the beginning of the nineteenth century.

"Fifty years ago," Greeley intoned in his column, "George Washington had just gone to his grave. . . . Thomas Jefferson had just been designated for next President. . . . The population of our Country was over 5,300,000 or considerably less than one-fourth the present number. . . . Our own State had scarcely a white inhabitant west of the sources of the Mohawk and Susquehanna. Buffalo and Rochester were forests. . . . The Erie Canal had hardly been dreamed of by the wildest castle-builder."

Kate and Maggie's father, John David Fox, was born in the late 1780s, when the American Revolution still lived in recent memory and white settlers had not yet streamed across the mountains that divided the east coast from the continent's interior.[1] A descendant of Palatine Germans who had anglicized the name Voss to Fox, he grew up in Rockland County, New York, a rural triangle of narrow valleys and rocky cliffs in the southeast corner of the state.

His father was David Fox, a blacksmith by trade. David wrote his will in March 1800 when he was forty-five years old and John still a boy, then died that April, leaving his estate to his wife, Catherine, with the proviso that each of their children receive a share on marriage.[2] She gave birth to their youngest child in May, only a month after her husband's death.

John presumably received his inheritance a dozen years later when he married a sixteen-year-old Rockland County girl, Margaret Smith, on March 7, 1812. She had been born in October 1796 to Jacob I. Smith and Maria Rutan, who fondly nicknamed their new daughter Peggy.[3]

On her father's side, Margaret's ancestry is easy to trace. Her paternal grandfather, John C. Smith, was a well-to-do farmer and civic leader; he and his wife, the former Elizabeth Blauvelt, both came from industrious Dutch families long established in the area.[4] The background of Margaret's maternal grandfather, on the other hand, is more mysterious. Perhaps it was kept so intentionally, especially if his last name—Rutan—was a variant of Ruttan. Descendants of French Huguenots, some members of this influential local family had switched their allegiance from Patriot to Loyalist midstream in the American Revolution. Afterward, having forfeited their land in the United States, they had settled on the Canadian side of Lake Ontario, where they'd been rewarded by the crown with new land in their adopted country.[5]

If Margaret Fox's maternal grandfather Rutan was an elusive figure, stories about his wife, Margaret, were family staples. Grandmother Rutan was one of a long line of relatives reputed to be blessed, or burdened, with second sight. According to family lore, she would rise dreamily in a trance between midnight and two in the morning to track phantom funerals to the nearby graveyard, her distraught husband following to ensure her safety. At breakfast the next morning, Grandmother Rutan would relate the vivid details of her adventure: whose funeral it had been, what mourners had attended, which friend's or neighbor's horses had drawn the coffin and led the procession—events quite invisible to her husband's eye. Everyone at the breakfast table would be "sadly depressed" by her tale, for the sad scenes Grandmother Rutan witnessed allegedly always took place, just as she had envisioned them, within the next few weeks.

Margaret Fox's sister, Elizabeth Smith, also reportedly evidenced the gift called second sight or clairvoyance, the ability to see what the eye can't at a distance in time or space, even foreseeing her own death. At age nineteen—or so it was later said—Elizabeth told her parents, "I dreamed I was in a new country, walking alone, when suddenly I came to a small cemetery, and, walking up to one of the most prominent head-stones, read the inscription. . . ."

Elizabeth confided that she had seen her own name on the head-stone, the first initial of her husband's last name, *H,* and the information that she had died at twenty-seven years old.[6]

Whatever mournful, clairvoyant strain may have marked the Rutan-Smith branch of her family, there's no indication that Margaret Fox predicted problems in her life. Although there may have been one child who died in infancy, she and John had four healthy children in relatively quick succession. Leah was baptized Ann Leah on April 8, 1813, in the Kakiat Reformed Church in West New Hempstead, Rockland County. Maria and Elizabeth followed. The couple's one son, David, was born in 1820.[7]

Sometime after Leah's birth, John and Margaret moved to New York City, but they retained close ties to Rockland County. John and his father-in-law, Jacob, jointly purchased a plot of land there in 1816 for five hundred dollars, selling it in 1820 for double the price.

After 1820 John and Margaret become difficult to trace through public records. Their story for the next twenty years must be pieced together largely from hints found in *The Missing Link in Modern Spiritualism,* a memoir written in the 1880s by the oldest of the Fox children, Leah, in which she explores "some family antecedents."[8] Her anecdotes suggest that in the early 1820s the Fox family relocated to the western part of New York State, joined by Margaret's parents, Jacob and Maria Smith, and by her three siblings: John J., Catherine, and Elizabeth, who had seen her own sad future.

The Fox family's decision, like that of thousands of other Americans, was undoubtedly inspired by an abundance of western land and the promise of the Erie Canal. Championed by New York governor DeWitt Clinton and initially derided as "the Great Ditch," the canal was started in 1817 and took eight years to complete. At its official opening in 1825, cannons fired and crowds cheered: a continuous inland waterway at last linked the eastern seaboard with the Great Lakes.

Traveling less than four miles per hour, crammed with passengers inside the cabin and on deck, the humble mule-drawn packet boat boosted the population from Albany to Buffalo by shortening the journey from two weeks by overland routes to only a few days. Freight could also be transported more efficiently by canal. Barges carried farmers' produce and locally manufactured goods such as flour eastward to New York and returned with textiles and other products that eased life on the farm. Shipping costs dropped, and toll revenues rose. As the shift from a subsistence to a market economy accelerated, businesses and businessmen along the route grew rich.

Towns near the canal flourished, but others did less well. When plans called for the Erie Canal to pass parallel to Hydesville's main road, for example, legend has it that the locals objected vehemently. Some declared that they would rather die than see canal boats float through their farms. Others worried that the Great Ditch would stink of garbage and stagnant water.[9] Eventually the Erie Canal was dug through the Wayne County village of Newark, several miles away. Newark boomed, and Hydesville began a long, slow process of decline.

Thirty miles to the west, the already prosperous village of Rochester—built near the falls of the Genessee River, a thundering source of water power to run mills—grew into "the Young Lion of the West." A manufacturing center best known for its flour, it was a canal town that roared with commercial vitality and that feasted as well on what some called riotous or ungodly activity. Dock workers and travelers, farmers and shopkeepers, transients and residents jammed the docks, packed the boardinghouses, and overflowed the taverns. Circuses, grogshops, and theaters attracted crowds whose nightly revels spilled into the streets until dawn.

When they first moved west, Margaret's parents, her brother, and her sister Elizabeth gravitated to the area officially designated Wayne County in 1823. According to Leah in *The Missing Link,* soon after settling there and marrying a man with the last initial *H,* Charles Higgins, Elizabeth indeed died at twenty-seven, the age predicted in her prophetic dream.

In the early 1820s John and Margaret Fox, the parents of four young children, separated. He had turned out to be what an acquaintance later called "a sporting gentleman," with a taste for liquor, gambling, cards, and horse races.[10] Whether or not John had indulged his appetites before the move, in the hard-drinking, rowdy canal towns of the day, he was far from the only man to end an afternoon, or begin a morning, with the demon rum in one hand and a fan of cards in the other. The fact that others shared his habits did little to console Margaret.

She probably survived on money inherited from her paternal grand-father, John C. Smith, who expressed his loathing for her husband in his will. Smith left a share of his estate to each of his grandchildren, but he ordered that his executors manage "Peggy's" one-eighth portion "for and during the time my said [grand] Daughter Peggy remains under Cover-ture of her present Husband John Fox the said John Fox never to have any Management Controle or profits thereof. . . ." Smith's executors were instructed further to provide whatever his "grand Daughter Peggy may need . . . and after the Death or lawful separation from the said John Fox to her heirs forever Except what is otherwise decreed." These were unusual provisions at the time and perhaps not even enforceable without John Fox's cooperation. By law, married women in most states were required to cede control of all their property to their husbands.[11]

Leah was about ten years old when John C. Smith, her great-grandfather, died in 1823. She later called him "the very noblest and grandest man I have ever known." She fondly remembered her visits to her great-grandparents' comfortable farm in Rockland County, perhaps recalling a world that offered a little girl a greater sense of security than could be found in the boomtowns of the 1820s. The trials of her grow-ing-up years were to leave Leah with a high tolerance for risk taking even as she yearned for stability.

Margaret Fox now lived with her unmarried sister, Catherine Smith, in Rochester, boarding in a house on Clinton Street, one of the neat, two-story frame structures that had sprouted everywhere to accommo-date the city's burgeoning population. As Leah later noted, her father was "absent from home much of the time."[12] A euphemism for her parents' separation, the phrase also suggests that he hadn't vanished altogether from his children's lives.

Around 1827, at the age of fourteen and a half, Leah left her mother's home and cast her lot with a man named Bowman Fish. Hardly a wise move, at the time it wasn't as scandalous a thing to do as comparable acts would become by midcentury. The median age of marriage for women was between eighteen and twenty, and on farms and in rough-and-tumble canal towns like Newark or Rochester, girls often married even younger.[13] Still, Leah's behavior must have devastated Margaret, who at sixteen had entered into her own unstable, unhappy relationship.

Leah's account of her life with Fish was brief. Her husband, she wrote, "discovered when too late that he had married a child. . . . He left Rochester under a pretense of going on business to the West." Whenever her last contact with Fish actually took place, she dismissed the occasion with a wave.

"The next I heard of him," she snapped, "was that he had married a rich widow in the State of Illinois."[14]

Leah made no mention of a legal divorce, possibly because her breakup lacked legal sanction. In the 1820s, particularly in newer towns and frontier areas, a community often accepted a de facto marriage as legitimate, so long as the man and woman viewed themselves as married by mutual consent. And even in the context of a legal marriage, desertion was frequently regarded as a pragmatic, if far from ideal, method of divorce.[15]

Leah and Fish were together long enough to have a daughter, Lizzie, who was born sometime between 1827 and 1830. Whether they had other children is unclear, since Leah would later refer to some of her nieces and nephews as if they were her own, boasting that they even called her "mama." Taking charge of other people's children in fact became one of Leah's lifelong habits; she may have hoped to save her protégés from some of the hardships she herself had suffered as a young girl.

In the early 1830s John Fox transformed himself from the "sporting gentleman" he had been in the 1820s into a sober, serious man. He became an observant Methodist who eventually served as a class leader in his church, his metamorphosis most likely influenced by the great religious and reform movements of his day.[16] In western New York, the fires of religious enthusiasm burned so brilliantly that the area had come to be known as the Burned-over District.

The region had periodically erupted in evangelical revivals from the early 1800s on. Men and women who headed west, abandoning the settled communities of their youth, craved a faith that matched their fervor and offered solace against the hardships and diseases they faced. The fierce predestination of orthodox Calvinism, which denied the individual any role in achieving personal salvation, no longer satisfied the needs of people so actively engaged in the pursuit of happiness and other worldly goals. Similarly, the rationalist ideas embodied in deism, with its suggestion that a divine being successfully set the world in motion and then retired, hardly served as a bulwark in times of trouble.

In Methodist camp meetings, however, preachers promised that human beings could shape their own destiny. The responsibility for achieving salvation came to rest squarely on the shoulders, and in the heart, of the individual. Freewill Baptists, Methodists, and Presbyterians alike urged the faithful not only to accept God but also to demonstrate their conversion by the godly ways in which they lived their lives.

Enthusiastic expressions of conversion abounded in the Burned-over District and, depending on the denomination, were encouraged and expected. Revival meetings, at which ministers exhorted sinners to convert and change their ways, became the scene of shouts and whispers, shakings and quakings, hand clapping and singing, speaking in tongues and falling down in trances. Women joined men in exuberant prayer.

Smaller religious groups, including the Shakers and the Community of the Publick Universal Friend, also established sites for their members in western New York. Jemima Wilkinson, a woman known as the Publick Universal Friend, like Mother Ann Lee of the Shakers was believed by her followers to embody a divine spirit.

Of more enduring significance than the Friend, in the 1820s an entirely new religion was born in Palmyra, New York, a town only ten miles from Hydesville, when the young visionary Joseph Smith claimed to discover two golden tablets on a hilltop near his home. The angel Moroni, Smith reported, had sent the tablets, which contained new revelations. Although no one except Smith ever saw the tablets, his assertions and teachings led to the formation of the Church of Jesus Christ of Latter-day Saints, the members of which are popularly known today as Mormons.

Revivalism and millennialism—the belief that the judgment day approached—in time helped transform the political and social landscape. The temperance movement was one of the earliest and most influential offshoots of revivalism. From camp meetings to temperance halls, speakers denounced the evils of strong drink. Conversion didn't always prevent backsliding, but the message of abstinence spread.

Some revivalist preachers, such as the charismatic Presbyterian minister Charles Grandison Finney, while often provoking ecstatic conversions, emphasized above all the life of good deeds. What better way to demonstrate godliness than by improving, not only oneself, but also one's neighbors and the rest of society? In 1830 a zealous church deacon and prosperous businessman named Josiah Bissell invited the Reverend Finney to Rochester to instill godly virtues in its citizens. A six-month revival took place during the winter of 1830–31 that created thousands of new converts. By that time, temperance reform had also become a crusade.

Bringing to an end an estrangement that had lasted more than a decade, Margaret Fox reunited with her now devout and sober husband, and the middle-aged couple went on to have what amounted to a second family. Their two youngest daughters, Margaretta and Catherine, were born in Canada, just across Lake Ontario from western New York.

The girls might have emerged from the ether, like spirits, for all that's definitively known about their childhood. Controversy exists even about their years of birth. But one of Maggie's late-in-life friends, a bookseller named Titus Merritt, maintained that she had been born on October 7, 1833, and that Kate had followed three and a half years later, on March 27, 1837.[17]

Kate and Maggie were raised in or near Consecon, a tiny village in Prince Edward County, Ontario, where John was said to have owned a farm. As late as the 1870s the village's population consisted only of about four hundred people, but Consecon lay just across the beautiful Bay of Quinte from the more populous town of Belleville, where some members of the Ruttan family had settled. It's possible that John and Margaret moved to Canada at the urging of the Ruttans, who by now were members of the United Empire Loyalists, an unofficial aristocracy comprised of early settlers who had left America to fight for the British during the Revolution.[18]

By the 1830s many more Americans were heading for Canada, both in search of new opportunities and to escape economic depression in their own country. But the life of a farmer in Canada was hard, perhaps even more so than in western New York. Someone unaccustomed to daunting physical labor, warned Susanna Moodie, a British settler who wrote about Canadian life in the 1830s, faced formidable obstacles. "The task is new to him . . ." Moodie said, describing the ordeals of ill-prepared sons of English aristocrats in a comment that certainly bore relevance to reformed alcoholic blacksmiths: "Difficulties increase, debts grow upon him, he struggles in vain to extricate himself, and finally sees his family sink into hopeless ruin."[19]

For children, isolation must have been the norm. Education was intermittent, depending on the proximity of a schoolhouse and the ferocity of the weather. Moodie's husband wrote a humorous ditty describing their own family's first cold winter night, ending with the line "It's at zero without, and we're freezing within."

Perhaps the farm failed, or family ties and new opportunities called John and Margaret back to the United States, for in the 1840s they returned to Rochester, leaving one daughter behind in her adopted homeland: Elizabeth, who married a Canadian named Osterhout.

The Fox family's name reappears in the public records in 1841, when John and his father-in-law, Jacob, jointly purchased a large plot in Rochester's beautiful new cemetery, Mount Hope, paying five dollars to secure a spot in one of the more picturesque sections. In 1842 Margaret's brother, John J. Smith, deeded land in Wayne County, New York, to his nephew David Fox.[20]

The family remained in transit and upheaval. In 1844 John's name was listed in Rochester's street directory as a blacksmith and as a resident of "South Sophia Street near Clarissa." That year Maria Smith, Margaret's mother, died and was buried in the plot that John and Jacob had purchased in Mount Hope.[21]

The next year, 1845, John's name vanished from the directory, but David's replaced it at the same address. A young confectioner named Calvin Brown, who had been adopted informally as a second son by the Fox family after the death of his own parents, lived with David. Jacob Smith most likely resided there as well until his death in 1846; then he was buried with his wife.

In the 1840s Rochester was a very different place from the free-wheeling canal town of Leah's childhood. Regular doses of piety, a legacy from the revivals held in the early 1830s by the Reverend Finney, had chastened it, and the fruits of commerce and industry had enriched it. With the success of the canal and the rise of the railroad, so many new residents had arrived that builders were struggling to keep up, replacing older homes with a new generation of Rochester's standard two-story frame houses and constructing a formidable abundance of churches.[22]

Modest homes, moreover, now stood in the company of elegant brick mansions and fashionable cottages, for the well-to-do were enjoying what their money could buy. Skilled craftsmen carved ornate tables and settees for the parlor. Stores advertised expensive goods imported from the East Coast and Europe: hats, furs, mantillas, lace, gloves, wigs, and luxurious fabrics. Factory owners, shopkeepers, artisans, and professionals prospered.[23]

Particularly among the well-to-do, changes had also taken place in the patterns of family life. As elsewhere around the nation, there was a growing divide between the sexes. In the past, with farmers' fields and artisans' shops adjacent to the home, husbands and wives had spent their days in close proximity to one another. But with the rise of a market economy, men increasingly went out to a place of business, while women—if their husbands and fathers could afford the luxury—remained behind, symbols of feminine purity and guardians of the domestic sphere, with its attendant religious and moral values.

The middle-class family, with its separate spheres for women and men, had emerged as an influential ideal, a model for the practice of genteel conduct and the nurturing of sentimental attachments and personal feelings. Even the focus of courtship and marriage, in the wake of the Romantic movement, had shifted from economic bonds to emotional ties. Children too were being viewed less as an economic asset—or liability—than as a treasure to be cherished. In families with money, young people were marrying later and were protected longer from the vicissitudes of the world.

Of course, not everyone shared equally in the city's bounty or nestled in the bosom of a middle-class home. Industrialization in Rochester, as elsewhere, was creating social divisions. The town that had first attracted farmers, merchants, artisans, and shopkeepers now had its share of mills, tanneries, foundries, breweries, and furniture and clothing factories. Immigrant women, as well as daughters uprooted from their fathers' farms, often found work either as domestics or in the clothing and shoe industries, sometimes toiling in the factories but usually doing piecework at home for long hours and at low pay. In 1851 Horace Greeley estimated in the *New York Tribune* that a family of five in an urban area needed a weekly income of $10.37 to cover food, rent, clothing, and fuel. With women textile workers making about $3.00 a week, and men double that, often whole families, children included, worked just to afford the necessities for survival.[24] Laborers, male and female, found themselves increasingly segregated in overcrowded neighborhoods where unsanitary conditions exacerbated health hazards and the risk of rapidly spreading epidemics such as cholera.

If Rochester, at least among some segments of society, had become a more polite town, the Burned-over District, the region that surrounded it and that had been the scene of earlier revivals, continued to smolder with enthusiasms both religious and political. A Vermont preacher, William Miller, prophesying that Christ would come sometime between March 1843 and March 1844, enthralled disciples among western New Yorkers, until the dates came and went with the world unchanged.

Enclaves called *phalanxes,* experiments in communal living based on the ideas of the French social philosopher Charles Fourier, caught fire and burned brightly, if in most cases briefly. The religious community of Oneida, founded on the principles of a former theology student named John Humphrey Noyes, supported "complex marriage," a system in which all community members were married to one another. In western New York, the time was always right for a new philosophy, theory, controversy, or utopia.

Rochester itself crackled with intellectual energy. The nationwide emphasis on self-improvement, in part a secular offshoot of earlier revivals, motivated young and old alike to attend lectures and programs on art, music, history, and literature. In a technological age that seemed to produce new scientific wonders every day, crowds swamped demonstrations of newfangled inventions, the telegraph among them.

Newspapers and lecturers carried word of promising new theories such as phrenology, which preached that an individual's personality could be ascertained by the shape of his or her head. Each area of the brain, phrenologists asserted, not only produced a distinctive lump on the skull but also corresponded to a specific character trait. Experts in the field drew segmented diagrams to illustrate their points and probed for revelatory lumps on the heads of volunteers.

In the midst of the ferment of ideas, Rochester had also become a vital hub of political and social reform, home to an informal network of men and women avidly devoted to abolition and woman suffrage. Frederick Douglass, the former slave who had become a noted author and abolitionist lecturer, established his newspaper in Rochester. He named it the *North Star* for the celestial beacon that helped guide enslaved African Americans north to freedom. As elsewhere in the North, stations on the Underground Railroad were proliferating. The zeal that had infused religious revivals, that aimed to perfect self and society, easily translated to impassioned politics.

Kate and Maggie were exposed to the excitement, for the girls and their parents lived for a while at the home of an activist Quaker couple, Amy and Isaac Post, in the Cornhill section of Rochester. Whether or not the Fox family boarded with the Posts or simply rented the house from them, Amy and Isaac knew the girls well enough to enjoy what he called "good understanding" with them.

The Posts were about five years younger than John and Margaret. Amy's face was serious and her body lean; she was altogether as angular in appearance as Margaret Fox was round. Isaac, the proprietor of a drugstore, had a craggy face softened by an almost beatifically sweet expression.[25]

Amy and Isaac must have been compelling figures to Kate and Maggie. The Posts were among the city's—and the nation's—most dedicated and intrepid reformers. Quakers held that each individual possessed an inner light or spark of the divine. The Posts, in a radical version of this faith, supported political and social activism in accordance with the dictates of personal conscience. Their home—the Cornhill house, as well as the address to which they moved after 1846—served as a magnet for abolitionists, woman's suffrage advocates, religious radicals, and utopian visionaries.

By the time Kate and Maggie met the spirits in March 1848, the girls were already familiar with what it meant to encompass and mediate between different worlds. They were Canadian, and they were American. Some of their old friends across Lake Ontario in Prince Edward County probably thought the American Revolution should never have been fought.

The girls had lived on a farm, then in a city, and then returned to rural life. They were deeply attached to both John and Margaret, but they surely felt the tensions between their parents, perhaps even becoming go-betweens or conciliators.

The children had relatives, such as their uncle John J. Smith, who had achieved a secure middle-class niche amid the flux of the times, but their own immediate family's financial and social status remained unstable and shifting. Their father's aspirations had come to nothing. Success had eluded him, as both a farmer and blacksmith.

Kate and Maggie knew strong and outgoing women: Leah, for example, had managed as a single mother to raise a child under unorthodox circumstances, and the astonishing Amy Post was transforming society.

But the girls were also growing up at a time when proper people, genteel ones, valued passivity and domestic grace in their daughters.

They had already been exposed to a strange and thrilling potpourri of ideas. At their mother's knee, they had heard shivery tales of second sight. They were witnesses to the intensity of their father's Methodist faith and his daily prayers. And when they lived in Rochester, every newspaper, parlor, and street corner buzzed with talk about mesmerism and phrenology, abolition and suffrage.

If the outside world sometimes seemed composed of multiple realities, so too did the sisters' own inner worlds. Lively though the girls were, they also suffered from severe headaches, pain that—as many migraine sufferers know—can create a sense of standing outside oneself, of being not oneself but another person altogether.

At eleven and fourteen, Kate and Maggie were also at the age when childhood merges into adulthood, a period that the Romantics had painted as a borderline between innocence and experience and a time when childish fears and fantasies coexist with the reality of menstruation and sexual feelings. Maggie was almost as old as Leah had been on becoming pregnant with Lizzie, but she was also growing up in a different environment. Genteel society of the mid-nineteenth century encouraged girls to remain children far longer than in the past and at least on the surface was more prudish on the subject of sex.

Although many critics have dismissed the two sisters as clever mischief makers, naughty and imaginative little girls who trapped themselves in a lifetime of fraud, it's unlikely that the truth is so simple. Kate and Maggie, containing worlds within themselves and experiencing many worlds without, were undoubtedly subject to powerful and conflicting impulses. As later events would demonstrate, they were also endowed with unusual openness and sensitivity, whether to the messages of the spirits or to the spoken and unspoken wishes of other mortals.

THREE

"VISIBLE AND INVISIBLE WORLDS"

T HE SPRING OF the peddler's return, thirty-five-year-old Leah Fox Fish was living at 11 Mechanics Square in Rochester, and she seems not to have heard about her family's troubles for close to a month. As she had been doing for some time, she was supporting herself and her daughter, Lizzie, by teaching piano. She was a robust, attractive woman with a square jaw and broad, capable hands, and her sociable personality complemented her considerable musical talent. Her husbandless status, however, now almost twenty years in duration, undoubtedly stirred at least polite disapproval among the members of Rochester's affluent and established circles. Leah probably drew her students from families with more open minds and more moderate incomes.

Her choice of work reflected her sharp eye for business as well as her good ear for music. A few decades earlier a piano had been a rare status symbol, but the upright variety had rapidly become a necessity in every middle-class parlor. Playing a musical instrument was a requisite skill for young ladies and teaching an acceptably genteel occupation for a woman.

Leah's occupation was also considered a challenging one; manuals of the day cautioned that music teachers shouldered important responsibilities. Acclaimed as "one of the sciences," music was extolled also as "a medium of sacred sentiment and reverential praise . . . the handmaid of Religion, the teacher of Truth, and the inspirer of Devotion." Teachers such as Leah were counseled to recognize the emotional impact of sound and melody in order to better exercise utmost care: given its unique powers, music could be used by the devil to incite carnal excitement as well as by angels to invite heavenly thoughts.[1]

Not surprisingly, heavenly thoughts often turned to the individual's mortality. A standard repertoire of the day, a mirror of shared values and concerns, included patriotic songs such as "Hail Columbia!"; classical pieces generically called "Symphonies"; Alpine tunes, believed to bolster good health; and an abundance of songs about death. Even young children weren't spared the constant presence of the grim reaper. The *American School Songbook* opened with a tune entitled "The Child of Heaven," and young songsters dutifully warbled its uplifting and gloomy lyrics: "How many a rose of beauty, Will bloom to fade away / And many a child of pity, Will die e'er yet 'tis day."[2]

It seems to have been the mother of one of Leah's piano students who, in late April, first heard about the Fox family's Hydesville adventures and then reported the news. Leah later insisted that she had known nothing until then, since her parents hadn't wanted to worry her with letters.

Anxious for her family's welfare and curious to find out what was going on, Leah rapidly enlisted two friends, Mrs. Lyman Granger and Mrs. Elihu Grover, for moral support, and the three women boarded a night boat headed east on the Erie Canal for Wayne County. Leah's daughter, Lizzie, may have traveled with them, or she may have been in Hydesville already, a figure little noticed there in the swirling confusion of previous weeks.[3]

In Newark the women hired a carriage to take them to Hydesville; they found the "spook house," as reporters had dubbed it, completely deserted. The carriage traveled on to David's farm, where Leah discovered her parents, Kate, and Maggie barricaded with her brother and his family. Margaret looked aged and drawn from the strain of the previous few weeks; her gray hair seemed to Leah to have turned white. Equally sunk in depression, John was stolidly working with a carpenter to complete the new house next to David's.

The move had done little to foil the crowds. The curious, while fewer in number, parked their wagons on the road, trampled through the muddy peppermint fields, and peered in the farmhouse windows. The move also had failed to deter the persistent spirit, who refused to leave and about whom further discoveries had been made. By calling out the alphabet and asking the spirit to rap on specific letters, David had determined the peddler's full name: Charles B. Rosna or Rosma.

Margaret, meanwhile, had reached a chilling conclusion, one shared by friends and neighbors. The raps weren't random; they trailed her two youngest daughters, Kate in particular.

After mulling over Margaret's theory, Leah formed a plan. She decided to take Kate with her when she returned home to Rochester to see whether "by separating the two children (Maggie and Katie) . . . we could put a stop to the disturbance."

But the effort to silence the peddler's spirit by separating Kate and Maggie proved as futile as the earlier move to David's. "We had not gone many miles on the canal . . . when we became aware," Leah wrote, "that the rapping had accompanied us."

Back at David's farm, other spirits chimed in where the peddler had left off—thumping, cracking, snapping, and knocking—apparently undaunted by Kate's absence and just as eager to communicate through Maggie. Separating the girls had demonstrated only that there were many spirits waiting to be heard and that they, unlike the suffering ghosts of the old world, weren't about to remain for eternity in a dreary haunted house. These invisibles liked to follow and visit their mortal American friends.[4]

There's no independent testimony to corroborate Leah's description of what happened next, but it's clear that Kate's first weeks in Rochester were chaotic. The spirits were overexcited and out of control. On the one hand, their behavior resembled that of a poltergeist like "Old Jeffrey," the Wesley family's resident ghost. On the other hand, the high jinks equally resembled those of high-strung and overstimulated youngsters.

On their first night together at the house on Mechanics Square, Leah, Kate, and Lizzie went to bed early.

"No sooner had I extinguished the light," Leah remembered, "than the children screamed, and Lizzie said she felt a cold hand passing over her face, and another over her shoulder down her back. She screamed fearfully, and I feared she would go into spasms. Katie was also much frightened."[5]

Disturbances continued almost until dawn, when the girls and Leah finally fell asleep. But the next night brought renewed turmoil.

"Tables and everything in the room below us were being moved about. Doors were opened and shut, making the greatest possible noises. *Then they walked upstairs,*" Leah wrote, "and into the room next to us (our bedroom was an open recess off from this room). There seemed to be many actors engaged in the performance, and a large audience in attendance. . . . One Spirit was heard to dance *as if with clogs* which continued fully ten minutes."

Leah instantly decided to abandon the house, an older residence that she maintained might be haunted, like the one in Hydesville. She may well have had another reason for the move: after two nights and a performance as entertaining as any theater troupe could mount, she may have recognized that these indomitable spirits weren't about to go away, that they were enormously clever, and that they would attract interested visitors.

Within a few weeks Leah had rented another home, one of an identical pair on a single foundation situated on Prospect Street. The house had a fresh, welcoming facade, a kitchen and pantry on the ground floor, a parlor and dining room on the second floor, and a single large room on the third floor. Leah partitioned this room with curtains, placing three beds in the more spacious area and keeping a corner for a storeroom.

The first night in the new house on Prospect Street was quiet, and Margaret and Maggie arrived as planned the day after the move for a long visit. The spirits apparently enjoyed the new quarters as much as the old. With the family reunited, they returned full force.

"All was quiet until about midnight, when we distinctly heard footsteps coming up the stairs, walking into the little room I had partitioned off with curtains," Leah remembered. "We could hear them shuffling, giggling, and whispering. . . . Occasionally they would come and give our bed a tremendous shaking, lifting it (and us) entirely from the floor, almost to the ceiling, and then let us down with a bang; then pat us with hands."

The next morning Margaret asked Calvin Brown, the young man whom she had taken under her wing, for assistance. He was invited to move into the Prospect Street house in the dual role of boarder and protector; his bed was placed in the second-floor parlor.

With the merry candor that distinguishes parts of Leah's memoir from the generally more earnest works by other advocates of spirit communication, she wrote in *The Missing Link* that in the night, everything "seemed to be in commotion" but that she herself felt more confident with Calvin there. When she heard a spirit walking around in the third-floor alcove, she began to question the invisible being, which answered by stamping its disembodied feet.

"I was amused," she admitted, "—although afraid. He seemed so willing to do my bidding that I could not resist the temptation of speaking to him as he marched around my bed. I said, '*Flat-Foot,* can you dance the Highland fling?' This seemed to delight him. I sang the music for him, and he danced most admirably."

Horrified, Margaret chastised her oldest daughter for encouraging the fiend. And the spirits indeed soon capitalized on Leah's easy familiarity with them. They made such a fearful fuss, giggling, scuffling, groaning, enacting murder scenes, and in many ways behaving like rambunctious adolescents, that Margaret cried out to Calvin to come upstairs. When he stomped into the room with a vow to end the deviltry, the spirits responded to his fighting words in kind, hurling bedroom slippers, a brass candlestick, and balls of carpet rags at him.

The poltergeists' hostility continued the next night. In the dark, the spirits took to slapping their human victims: Calvin, Margaret, Leah, Kate, Maggie, and Lizzie all felt the sting of the spirit's hand.

Suddenly, Kate cried, "O, look!"

"We all saw what seemed to be the form of a large man," Leah wrote, "lying across the foot of our bed, breathing irregularly and apparently in great distress. (The sheet was wrapped around him, muffled closely about his neck.)"

At that moment Kate was slapped a second time, and she fell "to all appearances lifeless," instantly becoming the focus of everyone's terror and alarm.

Margaret was at the point of calling in someone else for help when Kate groaned deeply, a sign that she was, if just barely, still alive. "We held her hands, but could not perceive the slightest pulsation," Leah stressed. "After remaining in this unconscious state for some time, she again moaned piteously and raised her hand, pointing at something she saw, and explained to us afterward. We asked many questions which she answered by pressing our hands."

As she regained consciousness, Kate communicated that she had witnessed the terrible events at Hydesville, and she sobbed inconsolably. Afterward, according to Leah, the eleven-year-old girl recited "twenty or thirty" verses of poetry, ending with the line: "To be with Christ is better far."

In the dark, the scene just before Kate's swoon must have played out like a game of blindman's bluff, except that everyone was at once the stalker and the stalked, and the talk of demons must have heightened the teasing to breathless terror. Kate may have been stunned half senseless by a worldly or otherworldly slap, fainted from the orgy of excitement, or gone into a trance, overcome like someone at an evangelical revival by the thrilling events of the night. Or she simply may have been a splendid dramatic actress, as young girls can be. Or she may have been possessed by spirits determined to demonstrate their power to disrespectful mortals such as Calvin.

One of the first independent accounts of the spirits' activities in Rochester was written by Lemuel Clark, a Congregational minister from Westford, New York. Traveling on business in June 1848, the Reverend Clark stopped in Rochester to visit two of his closest friends, Mr. and Mrs. Lyman Granger. The Grangers, a Methodist couple, were also acquaintances of the

Fox family; she had been one of the two women who accompanied Leah to Hydesville in early May.[6]

Clark found his hosts cordial but surprisingly tense. After supper Granger invited Clark to sleep with him that night, a not uncommon platonic practice and a signal, Clark realized, that his friend wanted to talk in private.

The two men were settled comfortably under the sheets before Granger hesitantly revealed his news: his older daughter, Harriet, had contacted her family. As the dumbfounded Clark well knew, Harriet had been murdered—poisoned—several years before. Her husband, a physician, had been tried for the crime but acquitted by an allegedly fixed jury.

Harriet's spirit, Granger continued, had been communicating with them by uncanny sounds that could be heard in the presence of a particular young girl, whose family had been troubled by similar sounds—"like persons rapping with knuckles"—since March, and who had recently moved to Rochester to live with her older sister. The child Granger was referring to, of course, was Kate.

The Fox family, as Granger told the story, had wished profoundly to keep the whole noisy affair quiet. But discretion proved impossible. "As a woman's secret will out," Granger observed, "it soon leaked out into the ears of some confidential friends who would help them keep the secret. . . ."

Outraged by what he considered blatant fraud, Clark instantly resolved to investigate the raps himself. He hoped to deliver his friend Lyman from "the snare of the devil"—a demon, the minister had no doubt, who would turn out to be very human.

At five o'clock on a sunny June afternoon—Clark reported several months later in a letter to his brother—his first chance to sleuth presented itself when nine people joined him in the Grangers' parlor: Granger and his wife, Adelaide, along with Elizabeth, their fourteen-year-old daughter; Kate and Margaret Fox; Leah and Lizzie Fish, whom Granger judged to be about fifteen although she was probably closer to twenty; Calvin Brown; and Mrs. Elihu H. Grover, the other woman who had gone to Hydesville with Leah. Maggie wasn't listed as present, although presumably she was in Rochester at the time.

The parlor, a spacious twenty-foot-square room, was furnished modestly, with simple blinds rather than the usual, fashionably heavy draperies on its four large windows and a coarse rag rug on the floor. Worldly as well as spiritual matters drew the company together. They sat around a six-legged cherrywood table, which the Grangers had set for tea.

Raps began almost immediately, interrupting Clark's brief blessing over the gathering and the food. "I felt myself insulted," he wrote, "by what I considered the perpetrator of the trick, and concluded that he or she, as it might be, had vastly underrated my powers of scrutiny."

After grace, the company posed questions, some to the spirit of the Grangers' daughter, Harriet, and others to the murdered peddler of Hydesville, Charles B. Rosna. "Is this the spirit of Harriet?" someone asked. "Is it Charles? . . . Was [sic] you murdered in anger or malice?"

Gentle taps. Harriet. Thumps. Charles. Raps even as all mortal hands busily juggled knives, cakes, and teacups.

A barrage of additional questions followed, including those of the Reverend Clark, who had some queries of a philosophical nature about the spirit world. When he asked whether God had sent the spirits and whether he had an important purpose to accomplish in doing so, the good minister was gratified to be answered with raps that were very "loud and rappid [sic] as if with two hands. . . ."

Would the Reverend Clark like to see the table move? one member of the group inquired.

He would indeed, he admitted.

He ordered the participants to draw their chairs back about a foot, to place their feet on the chair rungs, and to raise their hands high in the air, clearly visible to all. Everyone complied. Without human effort, as far as Clark could tell from studying the serene faces of the others in the room, the table slid toward him across the knobby rug as though "impelled by the Strength of a man." In a second experiment, Clark pulled the heavy table close to him; on his command, it skated back to its original position.

Clark failed to say whether the parlor's blinds were closed during most of the afternoon, but he carefully examined the table in the waning sunlight. Finding no rollers, machinery, or hidden wires, and unable to explain the events, Clark readily agreed to attend a second gathering the next day.

This second session, held with the same group but this time after tea at Leah's house, began under an unsettling pall of silence.

"What can be the matter?" someone in the room asked.

"I know," Leah replied grimly. Then, much to Clark's surprise, she erupted in a fury at her daughter. In a letter to his brother, Clark recalled Leah's harsh words, Lizzie's woeful protests, and the spirits' role in the quarrel.

"You are the cause of this silence," Leah accused Lizzie. "You have been a very wicked girl. . . .You have grieved the Spirit."

There was a confirming rap.

"That's it!" two or three people shouted at once. "Spirit, has Elizabeth done wrong?"

Another rap.

"I can't help it," Lizzie sobbed. "I said just what I thought, and if I am to blame, I can't help it."

"You can help it," Leah insisted. "You must repent and ask forgiveness."

A third rap echoed through the room.

"Must she repent, Spirit, and ask forgiveness . . . Will you give us answers freely if she will?"

Shaking with tears, Lizzie interrupted her mother: "I can't repent, I don't know but I did wrong, but I was sincere, I don't know how to repent."

Appalled at Leah's cruelty, Clark demanded to know Lizzie's awful offense. In response, Leah related yet another episode of dangerous play with the spirits, one as frightening as the earlier slapping incident had been, and one that ended as before with Kate falling into a fit, her face twisted in a frightful grimace and her lips moving in silent speech. On waking, Kate had murmured something about being in contact with the spirits but had refused to say more. Afterward, Leah explained to Clark, Lizzie had fervently announced that she wanted the spirits to go away, for she was afraid someone might be injured or her mother and child-aunts labeled frauds. And Lizzie had stated in no uncertain terms that she hoped never to pass through a scene like Kate's.

Leah concluded by telling Clark that Lizzie's attitude had offended not only the spirits but also the entire Fox family. And to the minister's dismay, further attacks on Lizzie immediately resumed. The spirits once again rapped their disapproval of the girl, and the mortals at the table continued to hound her to repent her words. At last, after a miserable inner struggle, Lizzie fell to her knees and wept a heartfelt apology.

But the spirits weren't ready to say goodnight, and the minister witnessed further manifestations that summer evening. "It was considered by the company . . ." he said, "something of a gratification to *feel* the raps as well as to hear them." When he put his hands on the table, "the blow was distinctly felt . . . on the underside of the leaf."

Clark also heard construction noise—not usually surprising in a house still under construction—but this seemed to him otherworldly, a sound "exactly like the sawing of a board." Clark noted ominously: "Someone said 'It is making a coffin.'" And the invisible spirit touched several people, tugging at their clothes and feet.

The next night, the last evening of his visit, Clark asked Leah to play the piano for him, something that he had been given to understand she did remarkably well. Skilled in making music and trained to identify the emotions it evoked—with, as she said, the help of the spirits—she played and sang, her voice "sweet as melody itself," accompanied by soft raps. Then, as the first verse ended, she invited the spirits to continue on their own.

"A gentle touch sufficient to jar the table commenced the Symphony," Clark wrote, "and carried it through with super exquisite skill. The sound of the instrument and voice again arose, and with them my spirit went up in an ecstacy, nor did I awake from the seeming trance, until the conclusion of the piece, when I found that, dissolved by the sweetness of the music, I had yielded my mind to the supposition that the visible and invisible worlds had met together. . . ."

Later that night, the Reverend Clark and Lyman Granger knelt in the latter's parlor and prayed together. All the while gentle raps, apparently on the outside of the parlor's four large windows, beat time to their solemn words, although the two men prayed so quietly that Clark could not imagine "how any person living could have known what we were doing."

After the Fox family's first few weeks in Rochester, spirits and mortals alike seemed to recognize that their encounters too often turned rowdy, even dangerous. The spirits calmed down—unless someone tried to "go contrary to their wishes." Calvin was a continuing target of their animosity.

"Once," Leah wrote, "he arose from his chair and reached across the table for a heavy pitcher of water, when the chair was instantly removed and he sat down on the floor, spilling the water all over himself."

Several people found their lives changed. The Grangers' fourteen-year-old daughter, Elizabeth, discovered that the spirits sometimes visited her even in the absence of her friends Kate and Maggie. Lizzie was banished and sent to live with other relatives, most likely joining her father in Illinois.

The gatherings or sessions that soon became known as *spirit circles, seances,* or *sittings* were already assuming a recognizable shape. The meetings attended by the Reverend Clark were held in a domestic setting, the parlor, with a limited number of people who had been drawn there by similar but not identical motives: the Grangers to contact the spirits, Clark to detect possible fraud in the manifestations. The mysterious raps and table tiltings, like a provocative puzzle, had stimulated everyone's excitement and curiosity; the process of questioning had been participatory; and the music had inspired a sense of religious awe.

With the exception of the prayerful moment shared by Granger and Clark, Kate was present as the medium, the exquisitely sensitive individual through whom the spirits were said to communicate. This was a role that, whether or not enabled by the spirits, Kate and Maggie were to fulfill memorably and with singular originality over the next few years, attracting an international audience, inspiring others to explore their own mediumship, and satisfying the hunger of many nineteenth-century Americans for guidance in their tumultuous daily lives and for knowledge of their own and their loved ones' immortal destinies.

In mid-nineteenth-century America, concern about death was rooted in reality: in the sheer numbers of men, women, and children who were struck down at a young age by accident or disease, without medicines to cure them and often after great suffering. The fear of death, however, was also entrenched in the imagination, the product of uncertainty about the nature of an afterlife.[7]

One hundred years earlier, the Protestant theologian Jonathan Edwards had dramatically evoked the stark horrors of hell in his sermon "Sinners in the Hands of an Angry God," and for many churchgoers, eternal damnation remained a very real and terrifying prospect. Evangelical ministers who, unlike Edwards, rejected the notion of predestination nevertheless still used the threat of fire and brimstone to convince sinners to convert; having the power to shape one's own destiny, it was assumed, didn't necessarily guarantee one would make the right choices to gain entry into heaven. Moreover, as liberal theologians shifted emphasis from God's anger to his benevolence, new questions arose to cloud the issue of what lay beyond. Did hell await even the most well intentioned of backsliders, or was God more forgiving than that? What fate awaited little children, so innocent despite the long-presumed burden of original sin? Uncertainty haunted even the growing numbers among the faithful who believed in a benevolent deity.

Others, disillusioned with religion and the debates it engendered, turned to science for answers. They found little help there, however, for science called immortality itself into question. In the absence of any evidence that could be verified by the senses—material proof—it was argued by some that the only basis for faith in an afterlife was faith itself. And faith, as many people knew, could falter.

In the past as well, men and women had been anchored in cohesive communities through ties such as church membership and extended kinship. But as nineteenth-century men and women found themselves increasingly on the move, seeking new lives in strange cities or unfamiliar territories, they also found themselves more isolated when confronted with the deaths of their loved ones. With death omnipresent, and neither religion nor science nor community of much comfort, the bereaved took solace in their immediate families, in sentimental rites and remembrances, and in other expressions of personal feeling.

The genteel middle class, which valued each family member in life, equally cherished the departed and demonstrated its devotion in new ways. Funerals and mourners' finery grew more elaborate, traditions imported from England, where the wealthier middle classes imitated the ostentation practiced by their royal betters. Memorial portraits of the dead—either in their last days or in their coffins—were placed prominently in the home, and friends sent outpourings of poems and letters to console the bereaved. A curl of hair from the departed, tied with a ribbon, was often kept in a locket worn on a necklace or watch chain, and sometimes a small shrine of favorite artifacts and memorabilia would be arranged in a corner of the parlor or bedroom.

Christianity had long encouraged an acceptance of death and had promised a heavenly afterlife to some if not to all. Now, however, the increased focus on each person's specialness seemed to make it that much more difficult to let someone go. The rise of magnificent rural cemeteries in the 1830s was one of the most striking examples of a shift in attitude. The word *cemetery*, derived from the Greek, was just coming into use and literally meant "sleeping place." Burial grounds, formerly modest plots behind churches, expanded into parks with vistas and gardens, not unlike the vision of heaven described by the philosopher Emanuel Swedenborg. In dedicating one of these cemeteries, a Supreme Court justice noted that its lush surroundings existed "as it were, upon the borders of two worlds." Families strolled through these scenic graveyards not only to visit the departed but also for melancholy pleasure, and it's hardly surprising that one of John Fox's first acts in returning to Rochester was to buy a plot for his family in Mount Hope.

Encouraged by the culture to dwell on their feelings, individuals poured their grief and their hope for immortality into their poems, prose, art, and architecture. These works abounded in consoling images of loved ones in heaven but also had a paradoxical effect: they turned mourning into a way of life that pervaded everything, from Sunday strolls among cemetery tombs to the songs sung by children at their music lessons.

Soon after the Reverend Clark's visit to Rochester in July 1848, the Grangers and a few other friends accompanied Kate, Maggie, and Leah back to Hydesville with the goal of finding Charles Rosna's bones. The peddler's spirit had predicted that his mortal remains would be uncovered that month.

Joined by David Fox and Maria's husband, Stephen Smith, the men descended into the basement of the now-abandoned house. Once again they dug until rising water forced them to quit, but this time they met with greater success than in April. They turned up smashed bits of pottery, strands of hair, and bone fragments.

To those inclined to believe in the spirits, the discovery confirmed that the raps indeed were spiritual in origin. The Hydesville rapper, according to this line of reasoning, not only had described a set of obscure events but also had led searchers exactly to the material evidence, the bones and pots, which proved its sad story to be true. The fact that no mortal had been caught making the sounds seemed to further support the rapper's otherworldliness.

The implications of such an assumption were enormous, for if the raps emanated from a spirit, potentially they could provide what had long been hoped for: evidence of immortality and knowledge of what the other world held in store.

Skeptics, unmoved by the significance of the buried artifacts, scoffed at the diggers and claimed that the bones belonged to a farm animal—a pig or a horse. Others—whether friends of the accused murderer, John Bell, or religious enthusiasts who feared that the devil had been raised from the cellar's dirt floor—had a more hostile response. About a week after the bones had been found, an angry mob of agitators, some carrying shotguns, assembled outside David's farm.[8]

The potential for violence was real. Joseph Smith, the Mormon prophet, had been murdered by just such a mob in Illinois in 1844 for the radical beliefs he propounded and practiced. Although Kate and Maggie hadn't yet posed a comparable threat to mainstream religion and morals, the possibility that they talked to the dead was incendiary. In the not-so-distant past—the Salem trials of the 1690s were among the most famous examples—women had been labeled witches and condemned to death for much less. Although the nineteenth century abjured such superstition, fear had an insidious way of persisting.

Kate and Maggie's brother, gentle David, diffused the danger by showing his usual common sense and courage. Rather than resorting to guns for protection, he invited the crowd to come in and search the house. On recognizing David, one man reportedly cried out, "My God, Dave Fox, is it YOU they have said so much about? No, we won't come in. We'll go home and come back another time, properly, as we should." And the mob dispersed.

The following week Leah, Maggie, and Kate all returned to Rochester, only to find themselves rushing back to Wayne County in early September to mourn the unexpected death of David and Eliza-beth's two-year-old daughter, Ella.[9] Kate and Maggie, like the rest of their family and community, suffered loss and grief at first hand, and the girls undoubtedly wondered what it felt like to die and whether there was such a thing as immortality.

FOUR

"IT SEEMS TO SPREAD FAST"

ISAAC POST, the Fox family's Quaker neighbor in Rochester, wasn't superstitious, and when he first heard about the Hydesville rapper he "paid no more heed" to the news than he did to stories of the old Salem witch trials. Like most nineteenth-century Americans, he consigned that stain on the nation's soul to dark days, before science and reason shone so brightly. It was easy for a sensible man to dismiss the whole subject of spirits.[1]

Then Isaac learned the identity of the haunted children, either from Leah or from a mutual acquaintance, and he realized that he knew them well. The bond that he had formed with the Fox family when they lived in his old house in Cornhill, his belief in their honesty and integrity, prevailed over Isaac's initial disinterest.

Soon after joining Leah in Rochester, Kate and Maggie visited the Posts at the couple's new home on North Sophia Street. The girls hardly conveyed the sense—or at least not to Isaac—that the raps were a potentially earthshaking matter. Instead, Kate and Maggie seemed eager to please their adult friends, "very anxious," Isaac said, "that we should enjoy what they did."

But the Posts didn't hear the raps until several days later, when Kate returned alone for a second visit. After dinner she invited Amy and the couple's friends, Abigail and Henry Bush, into another room. A few minutes later she asked Isaac to join them.

"I went with as much unbelief as Thomas felt when he was introduced to Jesus after he had ascended," Isaac admitted. But his attitude shifted instantly when he peered in the door with his "countenance so doubting" and saw the Bushes "looking as tho they stood before the Judgment seat. . . ." And he felt "rebuked" for his initial skepticism.

From then on Isaac's entire household became absorbed in the effort to communicate with the other world. He and Amy, as well as their two oldest sons, Jacob and Joseph, often spoke with the spirits. Eighteen-month-old Willie loved to "put his ear down" to hear the raps. Even the Posts' Dutch serving girl liked asking questions of her own.

Not that spirit communication came easily. Isaac acknowledged that his family never received answers to questions "without one of the Sisters are present and not always then for I have been in quite large companies and all would be still. It is natural to suppose that it is very difficult to converse where there is nothing said but thumps."

It was Isaac who reinstated a method of communication previously attempted by both David Fox and the Foxes' neighbor, William Duesler. If someone called out the alphabet, Isaac suggested, the spirits could spell their messages by rapping on particular letters, thereby conveying more meaningful responses than yes or no.

Once the invisible beings could make themselves better understood, Isaac hoped they would behave less restlessly and be less provoked by mortal obtuseness. The first time he and the Fox sisters tried this tactic, they were rewarded with the name Jacob Smith—the girls' grandfather.

Slowly through the summer of 1848, methods of communication between mortals and spirits were refined and codified, although most would be modified again in time. Three raps indicated yes and five signaled a demand for the alphabet. Silence or a single knock meant no.

These methods received their first great test when the Posts' cousin George Willets visited Rochester that summer on business. He was there to meet with a local resident who owned a plot of land for sale in Michigan, property that Willets had recently seen and was interested in buying. But the contemplated move meant uprooting his family from their home in Waterloo, New York, and planting them down in what he called "the wilds of the West," untamed territory as rife with danger as it was rich in opportunity.

The Posts, of course, were bursting with news about the mysterious raps, which they believed "displayed intelligence, and purported to be made by 'spirits' or persons invisible."[2] Skeptical but curious, as Lemuel Clark had been, Willets attended a gathering to converse with the invisible beings and was astonished by what transpired.

The raps answered several other participants' questions, then communicated the request "that three persons be magnetized, two of whom were present. . . ." The third person whom the raps wanted magnetized—a word often used interchangeably with *mesmerized*—was sent for, Willets testified in a statement later written for publication, "from a neighboring family." Willets mentioned no names, but the threesome presumably included Kate and Maggie, who were central to efforts to talk with the spirits, and Leah, who seems to have been in the process of exploring her own clairvoyant capabilities, a legendary legacy on her mother's side of the family.

Although Willets insisted that no one in the room knew him except Isaac, the "clairvoyants," as he called the trio, demonstrated uncanny knowledge of his dilemma and plans. They spoke as if with one voice: "We have got to go to Michigan." And they proceeded to describe in detail the places and things he had seen on his recent western trip, until, he wrote, they "came to a piece of land which they said was the place they came to look at. They then described the land so accurately, which I had stopped in Rochester to buy, that I began to wonder who had told them."

The message he received was not encouraging. "They all with one accord then said, 'But he must not go there. His father says that he had better not go.' "

A host of raps, each with a different timbre, seemed to him to signal the presence of his father, his mother, and his sister, all in resounding agreement that he shouldn't purchase the land. Sweating with anxiety, Willets ventured a step further.

"As you assume to know my father, and what his mind is concerning me, perhaps you can tell me his name," he asked.

Loud deliberate raps tolled under George Willets's feet, and the clairvoyants·spelled William Willets, the correct name.

Later George Willets and the Posts met alone with Kate for three hours. During this second meeting William continued to tap his paternal advice, while the child helped convey the spirit's meaning: George should remain east. He wouldn't enjoy himself in new country such as Michigan and also might jeopardize his health.

Then what should he do? Willets asked.

Move to Rochester instead of Michigan.

Without a job?

He would have a job if he moved.

Where would he live?

The spirit advised him about a lot for sale, then specified a time and place to meet with the owner as well as the exact price he could expect to pay for the land.

George Willets tried to contact the owner a few hours earlier than advised but was unsuccessful. From the hour of the assignation—ten in the morning—to the land's price, everything seemed to him to turn out exactly as the spirit had predicted.

Although he wrote only reluctantly for publication, Willets's private letters also reveal his state of puzzled indecision. Home again in Waterloo, he worried. The idea of moving to Rochester appealed to him, but he had no job prospects there, and he hesitated to follow blindly the spirits' instructions.

"All that hinders our going immediately," he confided to Isaac, concerned that others would treat the move as a fools' errand, "is to see some employment which if I should move there and not obtain would render me unhappy and give the ridiculers more reason to say that it was an Ignis Fatuus that we had followed."[3]

Despite their doubts, by Christmas 1848 Willets and his wife, Ann, had settled in Rochester. He still had no employment, although Isaac had been on the lookout for possibilities since the summer.

The couple had been living in their new home only a few days when Kate visited, bringing two spirit messages: in four days' time Willets would know what his work was to be.

"In the mean time," Kate advised on the spirits' behalf, "the anti-slavery folks are going to hold their fair; would it not be well for thee to help them?"[4]

Several days later she visited again, with word that the spirits wanted him to apply for a job with the Auburn and Rochester Railroad. Willets did so, only to be disappointed. William Wiley, the railroad's superintendent, assured him that all positions were full and that there were no prospects. Downhearted, Willets again went in search of Kate. Steadfast as an oracle, the raps consoled him: *"Thee will have a place on the cars, and will know it before the week is out."*

That week, as predicted, Wiley reversed his decision and hired Willets.

"One month after I had been running on the cars," Willets marveled in his statement, "I learned that the person whose place I took had done things worthy of a dismissal, *previous* to my being directed to make application, and which did not come to Mr. Wiley's notice till *the day on which I received the appointment.*"

It was a triumphant moment for the spirits. Whether they had obtained their information through mortal or immortal means, they had demonstrated what seemed to be stunning foreknowledge of events, and they had exercised an exhilarating influence over Willets. In doing so, they had shown that they had reformed their ways; they had abandoned their habit of provoking people in favor of helping them.

By assisting Willets, the spirits had also evinced a certain bias. They had kept him close by, in New York, near the Posts and other friends who cared about him. Their advice to him suggests that they valued warm family ties, bonds like those enjoyed by Kate and Maggie, and that they discouraged the kind of transience the Fox children had endured in moving from one home to another.

July of 1848 witnessed an event that helped shape the future of the United States: the Seneca Falls Convention, the first women's rights assembly organized in America. The meeting took place in the Burned-over District, on a site about forty miles from Rochester and less than twenty from Hydesville.

The twin struggles for the abolition of slavery and women's rights were closely allied in the 1840s and 1850s, although conflict eventually erupted over differing priorities. Many abolitionists were also feminists. The plight of women, whatever their race, was compared in kind if not in severity to the bondage imposed on enslaved African Americans: women too were considered inferior and treated as subordinate by the dominant white male culture; they too were denied the vote and opportunities to work and be educated and, if married, the right to control their own wages and property, to sign contracts, and to protect their bodies from their husbands' unwanted advances. Enslaved African American women, of course, endured far worse, some of it at the hands of their white sisters, and free black women in the North also remained subject to specific injustices produced by racist prejudice and discrimination against them. Nevertheless, the Seneca Falls Convention represented the beginning of a remarkable revolution in women's lives.

Amy Post and her good friend Abigail Bush were both present, as were a number of their other friends. Many of those in attendance, such as Frederick Douglass, the famed abolitionist and author, and Elizabeth Cady Stanton, an emerging leader of the women's rights movement, had already heard about the possibility of spirit communication through their Rochester acquaintances, and others soon learned of it. Raps were reported to have struck the very table at which Stanton and her colleague, Lucretia Mott, had drafted the convention's resolutions.[5]

A few people began to feel as if they too might become the mediums—transmitters—for the spirits to converse with mortals. George Willets, for one, frequently began to hear gentle taps in the area of his neck and coat collar, but to his regret he wasn't yet able to converse with the spirits or to interpret their messages for others.

"So what it is or whether I shall ever be able to talk with it," he wrote to Isaac, "I do not know but hope I shall. Thomas McClintock's folks are . . . sure that they have heard the same. Also Elisabeth Stanton—Gerrit Smith's daughter—was on a visit to E. Stanton and heard about it.

She went home and told her mother who had full faith in it and the daughter wrote to E. Stanton a day or two since that her mother had heard it several times so if it is Humbug it seems to spread fast."[6]

As interest and curiosity grew among those who had attended the convention, the Hydesville peddler, his horrific accusations muffled, retreated into the background. The spirits of relatives and friends swarmed into the sittings to bring loving advice and consolation. Amy and Isaac were no exception; like many other early believers in spirit communication, they had experienced their share of personal tragedy. Only a few years earlier, in the mid-1840s, their little daughter, Matilda, had died. If concern about the afterlife nurtured interest in spirit communication, so too did a yearning to connect with the departed.

"I believe [the spirits] always speak of seeing Matilda," Isaac wrote with some poignancy. "[They] say she is happy [and] is around us." Kate interpreted other raps as messages from his late sisters, Phebe and Lydia.[7]

Radical reformers of society on earth, the Posts were as willing to scrutinize conventional religious wisdom as they were to question state and federal laws. Although Christianity generally taught that alleged spirit visitations in the present day were either human delusions or demonic manifestations, Amy, Isaac, and members of their circle refused to dismiss the possibility that the spirits were who and what the raps claimed.

After meeting with one of the Fox sisters, the Posts' friend and fellow activist, Sarah Fish, regretted not hearing "that little girl out instead of interrupting her." She vowed that she would be more patient in the future. That night, as Fish lay in her bed thinking about "the mysterious workings of Providence," she decided that she had "resisted the divine spirit in my own heart by making light of what that child said and turning it away. . . ." At that moment she heard soft knocks emanate from underneath her pillow, a sign that she took to affirm "the truth that our departed friends are with us striving for our good. . . ." The recognition calmed her, easing her dread of death.[8]

The spirits were equally reassuring to Isaac, for when he asked whether enjoyment in the afterlife would "be in accordance with our lives hear [sic]," he received "a very loud response."[9] Well-intentioned men and women, it seemed, could feel confident of their immortal future.

Quakers such as Amy and Isaac, however, were inclined toward sympathy with spirit communication as much by the nature of their faith as by their rejection of orthodoxy. The couple had twice resigned from Quaker organizations after disputing the extent of the institution's authority over the individual; in the 1840s they and other like-minded Quakers had founded a new branch of the faith known as the Congregational Friends. Its members' unstinting devotion to the concept of an inner light—something deeper than but akin to individual conscience—not only supported their political activism but also underscored the notion that ordinary men and women could forge a profound connection with a transcendent spiritual realm. Faith in an inner light endowed even young girls like Kate and Maggie with radiant potential, making otherworldly inspiration seem a less heretical possibility.

Not that what the spirits had to say always seemed inspiring. One day, for instance, Kate attended a family tea with the Posts and other friends, an ordinary enough event until one of the adults objected to the lavish amount of molasses that Joseph Post, a boy no older than Maggie, was pouring happily on his pudding. An urgent shower of raps called for the alphabet, and the mortals laboriously decoded a message dear to any youngster's heart.

"Put on as much molasses as he likes," the indulgent spirit advised.[10]

Isaac recorded many aspects of the spirit sessions. Sometimes, he wrote, Kate and Maggie were magnetized when the raps occurred. He noted as well that the girls frequently spoke simultaneously with the sounds and that on occasion the raps raised subjects that no one in the room had asked or thought about. Such independent thinking had significance, for it implied that the girls weren't simply mind readers—an amazing enough feat in itself—but spoke instead on behalf of the spirits.

By the late autumn of 1848 the mysterious noises had been investigated, wrote Isaac, "by many" without trickery being discovered, so that he believed "every candid person admits that the girls do not make it."[11]

But not every "candid person" agreed with him. Others who heard the raps continued to grapple with doubts. Who really made the sounds? Whose intelligence informed them? Were the Fox girls responsible or the spirits or some third force such as electricity or mesmerism?

Arriving at any definitive answers seemed, to the skeptical as well as to the hopeful of heart, to depend on investigations designed to prove the presence or absence of fraud. The challenge of the detective work undoubtedly excited some of the curious as much as did the notion of spirit communication itself.

Along with physical searches for mechanical devices and careful scrutiny of the girls, *test questions,* as they were called, became an essential investigative tool. No question was too trivial, for the specificity of information tested a spirit's authenticity. Whose spirit was speaking? What had been its occupation? Favorite color? Place of birth? The cause—accident, murder, disease, old age—that had carried it off to the spirit world?

One early investigator, Eliab W. Capron, like the Posts was a Congregational Friend dedicated to radical causes. Although Capron and his wife, Rebecca, lived in Auburn, New York, he was a native of Rhode Island where his relative, Dr. George Capron, was known for his research on mesmerism. Interested in such subjects himself, and an ambitious young journalist too, Eliab Capron traveled to Rochester in November 1848 to meet Kate, Maggie, and the increasingly newsworthy spirits.

On his first visit he found himself astonished by the spirits, who answered correctly not only questions he asked aloud, but also ones he either wrote down or asked mentally. On his second visit he challenged the sisters with what was literally a shell game.

"I tried the experiment of counting in the following manner," he wrote. "I took several shells from a card-basket on the table (small lake shells), closed my hand and placed it entirely out of sight, and requested as many raps as there were shells. It was done correctly. As I knew how many shells there were in my hand, I resolved to test it another way, to see if there was a possibility of my *mind* having any influence in the matter. I took a handful of shells, without knowing how many I took myself. Still the answers were correct."[12]

Sometimes raps answered correctly, identifying a spirit to the investigators' satisfaction. Occasionally, however, answers were way off the mark. Weary or bored spirits didn't hesitate to announce "done" when they wished to retire.

Once, Leah recalled, "the word 'done' was spelled."[13]

Not to be discouraged, the questioners continued to press for answers until a series of exasperated raps spelled out, "Why the devil do you ask questions after you have been told done?"

This, Leah noted, "was a terrible damper to us all."

She explained that these instances of rudeness, along with misleading answers, confused the mediums as much as the investigators but that such troubling episodes only demonstrated the flawed nature of certain spirits.

"When manifestations and communications were consistent," she said, "we believed them to come from good Spirits; but when they were to the contrary, we condemned them all as evil."

The Christian establishment, not surprisingly, regarded the Fox family's otherworldly visitors as emissaries of the devil or the delusions of the sisters' fevered imaginations or the product of mischief and fraud. One young Methodist clergyman who visited Margaret offered to conduct an exorcism of the house. She permitted him to do so, but as he walked through the rooms, raps dogged his every step. Failing to rid the house of spirits, the clergyman departed with harsh things to say about the Fox family, an experience that effectively ended Margaret's churchgoing days.

Within a year after the peddler's first visit to Hydesville, Leah herself was delivering spirit messages, although only to a few close friends. The invisible beings didn't rap in her presence, as they did with her two younger sisters, but appeared to her instead while she was in a magnetic sleep. Like her sisters, she suffered from severe headaches, and Isaac, in his amateur role as a mesmerist—and perhaps also in his professional one as a druggist—was often on hand to help her.

"I went up to see Leah last evening, having heard of her being unwell," Isaac wrote to Amy in the spring of 1849, when she was out of town. "I asked if I should put her asleep and perhaps I could cause relief. She was quite willing. . . ."[14]

In the usual way of mesmerists, Isaac gently passed his hand over the most painful side of Leah's head, and as he did so she began to speak.

Leah's range—or the spirit's—was large. She first offered soothing words of consolation, comforting Isaac with her vision of his deceased first wife and little Matilda, all now spirits in a better land. Then she moved on to the practical suggestion that Amy visit William Fishbough. Both

Fishbough and Samuel B. Brittan, his colleague, were early associates of the mystic Andrew Jackson Davis as well as editors of a short-lived but influential journal called *The Univercoelum and Spiritual Philosopher.* Former Universalist ministers on a quest for an "interior and spiritual philosophy," the two men believed in spirit communication; however, their philosophical focus had drawn little popular attention, particularly in contrast with the excitement generated by the theatrical raps. The magnetized Leah, or a politic spirit, was gently suggesting that the esteemed Amy Post could help forge an alliance between these formidable men and the Fox girls.[15]

After predicting that Frederick Douglass's struggling newspaper, the abolitionist *North Star,* stood a good chance for survival, she concluded with a juicy bit of clairvoyant gossip. She confided that Dr. John Hardenbrook, a man accused of a murder splashed across all the newspapers, had actually tried to poison his victim, the husband of his lover, twice before succeeding. And there was more: the good doctor's lover had been his accomplice, Leah revealed, and the means had been arsenic rather than strychnine. As it turned out, this information was either so secret or so inaccurate that it never came out at Doctor Hardenbrook's trial.[16]

In July 1849 Isaac's friend John S. Clackner wrote to him from Ohio to ask whether the spirits, as rumored, had expressed the wish to dictate a book to Leah, who would record it with the assistance of another friend from Rochester, Mrs. John Kedzie.

How do "Leah and the Spirit get along with the manuscript in Contemplation?" Clackner asked. Kate and Maggie's oldest sister had now laid her own claim to the spirits.[17]

The spirit world that summer seemed filled with a promise reflecting the changes in the material world. At the conclusion of the Mexican War in 1848, Mexico had ceded land to the United States, territories that would become the states of California, Nevada, Utah, Arizona, and parts of Colorado and New Mexico. Earlier that year prospectors had discovered gold in California. By the summer of 1849 news of the windfall had spread across the continent, and more people were heading west than in all of the nation's brief history. The term *manifest destiny,* coined by a journalist, justified expansion as something divinely ordained.

Expansion, however, exacerbated sectional conflict. With the balance of power between the agrarian South and the industrializing North dependent in part on whether new states were admitted to the union slave or free, the organizing of each new territory and the admitting of each new state became a battle. In 1820 the Missouri Compromise had established a boundary north of which slavery was to be banned, but Southerners argued that the settlers of each prospective state should have the right to make up their own minds. California was admitted as a free state, but the decision about the other territories acquired in the Mexican War was postponed.

If manifest destiny found an echo in the expansive world of the spirits, and if slavery's abolition was a common bond among many believers, cholera helped create the circumstances in which a movement that promised immortality could grow. In 1849 an epidemic broke out in Europe, and newspapers tracked the disease's advance as it moved across Canada and the United States. Although its impact in Rochester was less severe than expected, there were fifty deaths a week that summer in Albany, and in Cincinnati so many died that carts piled high with scores of bodies rumbled through the streets daily.[18]

Whether in search of safe harbor from the plague or simply for a family visit, Kate, Maggie, and Leah returned to Wayne County that August, most likely staying at their father's house on the grounds of David's farm. It's also possible that the sisters temporarily lacked a home in Rochester, for Leah's kindly neighbor on Prospect Street, who had tolerated poltergeists with equanimity, had passed away. The new tenant blamed ventriloquists rather than the spirits for the turmoil next door, and he had insisted on Leah's eviction.

The three-week stay in Wayne County, Maggie wrote to Amy Post, felt more like three months.

"I promised to write to you and I should have written before if my health had been better," she apologized. "My health has been very poor for the last few days." The doctor had given her some medicine, as he suspected that she had an intermittent fever.[19]

It had been raining all morning, turning the fields into rivers of mud and drowning Maggie in gloom. Apparently she was alone in the house, at least for a few hours, for the hush of her surroundings disturbed her.

"Oh how still and silent it is here today," she mourned.

It's possible that she was remembering Ella, her two-year-old niece who had died the summer before. Without question, she was feeling "lonesome" for her mother, even though, as she told Amy, she understood that Margaret couldn't always be with her. Maggie didn't say where Margaret was, nor did she mention her father.

Complaints aside, Maggie went on to describe a surprisingly sociable time. For entertainment just the day before, she and Leah had visited Newark. "We had a fine time," she wrote, confiding that they "stayed until nearly ten o'clock." And as soon as the rain slowed down, Maggie continued, she would join friends in Palmyra.

But Newark and Palmyra paled when she thought of Rochester, which she called her "much loved home."

"I am anxious to get back to Rochester again . . ." she confessed, and a few sentences later, she explained why: "I love the noise and Confusion of the city. . . ."

To stress her point, or perhaps to alert her older, more mature friend to what felt like a dangerous passion, fifteen-year-old Maggie went on to tell a story: she compared herself to a woman who had become so used to her husband's snoring that she couldn't sleep without it.

"At length," Maggie wrote, "he was required to attend Court some hundred miles distant. The first night after his departure she never slept a wink. The second night passed in the same way without sleep. She was getting in a very bad way and probably would have died had it not been for the ingenious Servant girl." The servant girl, Maggie continued, cleverly took a coffee mill into her mistress's bedchamber and "ground her to sleep at once."

"That's the way with me," Maggie admitted.

"I have become so accustomed to the rattling of Carriages and ringing of bells that I am afraid I shall have to have the Coffee Mill as something to lull me to sleep."

For Maggie, sound seems to have been linked with comfort, companionship, and excitement. Noise surely signified pleasure, but it may also have served as a distraction from boredom and depression, from thoughts that—absent city bells and coffee mills—lingered too long on separation and loneliness.

FIVE

"A GREAT VARIETY OF SUPERNATURAL SOUNDS"

TEDIOUS SUMMER DAYS in the country ended soon enough. After returning from Wayne County in September 1849 Leah moved her family to a new home on the corner of Troup Street, in a location on the edge of Rochester's fashionable Third Ward. The house was modest, but the area nearby was resplendent with fine homes and mansions, some built in the classical Greek Revival or the stately Queen Anne style, others adorned with the gables and gingerbread of the Gothic Revival. The move, Leah's second in a little more than a year, continued her ascent into ever more desirable housing.

Her sisters' reputation as spirit messengers by now had started to spread to nearby counties, with visitors to Leah's household ranging from evangelicals to radical reformers, from grief-stricken parents to suspicious skeptics. Interest in the noises, however, still remained largely local to western New York. Those who came consisted primarily of friends or the friends of friends, those who had learned about the raps through hearsay.

Kate remained only briefly in Rochester. At the invitation of the journalist Eliab Capron and his wife, Rebecca, she visited Auburn, New York, staying at the same comfortable boardinghouse where they were living. Capron, who regarded Kate as the most impressive medium in the Fox family, wanted to test her powers in a setting apart from her family.

The visit must have been an ordeal at times for the twelve-year-old girl, even as it was undoubtedly an adventure for the family of Capron's landlord. "The medium was tested in every conceivable way," Capron observed. "She slept with the ladies in the house—different ones—and was tested by them, as well without a dress as with."[1]

The spirit manifestations that followed Kate to Auburn, Capron testified, astonished his acquaintances. He later published an account of her visit, a record he claimed to have drawn largely from journal entries he made during her stay in 1849.

Sounds ricocheted through the boardinghouse, he wrote, and through other homes where curious investigators met. Spirits had characteristic raps, and attuned listeners became able to identify each spirit by its sound—hollow or ringing, heavy or light.

Every variety of test, he insisted, was set to challenge the spirits. In different hosts' parlors, with the gas turned down or candles extinguished, tables tipped over and flipped back. Small chairs pinioned themselves to the floor and could not be budged. Combs flew out of ladies' upswept hair and fastened themselves to other women's topknots.

The dead sprang to life through sound and touch, raps and tugs. Eternity's silence, it seems, was turning out to be quite noisy, vanquished as much by the sensory excitement of the gatherings as by the content of any specific message.

Music continued to hold a pivotal place. Unseen fingers played the guitar, Capron said, "so exquisitely . . . that it seemed more like far-distant music to one just aroused from midnight slumbers, than the music of an instrument a few feet from us."

In the dark an invisible hand might tap a sitter's arm, charging the spot with a feeling of electricity. A spirit's hand felt like that "of a person who is in a magnetic sleep, being colder . . . and having a moisture like a cold perspiration upon it. . . ."

Yet on request such a hand could change both its temperature and texture. "It will in one instant feel as cold as ice," Capron wrote, "and as warm as a common hand of flesh." One sitter asked to see a spirit's hand. A moment later, silhouetted, it drifted across the moonlit window.

The local newspapers called the meetings tomfoolery. A reporter for the *Auburn Daily Advertiser* revived the story that Kate and Maggie's father, John, had first instigated the craze, creating "a great variety of supernatural sounds" and wonderful sights such as "the locomotion of chairs, tables, books, and other household fixtures." But as soon as the so-called spirit of Hydesville was unmasked, the reporter joked, "it departed in disgust, and has remained in retirement until its present visit to Auburn."[2]

The newspaper, of course, was wrong. The spirits had been continuously active for a year and a half in Rochester. And for most of that time, prayerful John Fox, long past his days as a gambler and troublemaker, had stayed in his new house in Arcadia, his hopes of reuniting his family waning as the fortunes of the spirits waxed.

By the fall of 1849 the invisible beings themselves had grown insistent in pressing certain demands, lobbying believers to proclaim the truth of immortality to the wider world. But the Fox family seemed ambivalent about taking this next step. Maggie and Leah expressed concern not only about subjecting themselves to ridicule for their beliefs, but also about making a public appearance outside the home, an act considered improper for respectable women of the day. Even men such as Isaac Post and George Willets, who boldly stood up for causes such as abolition and women's rights, urged discretion in the matter of the spirits. Isaac had his drugstore to run and Willets a job to keep, and neither was anxious to invite further controversy.

But with Kate in Auburn that autumn and with Margaret on a visit to John in Arcadia, the situation in Rochester abruptly changed. Apparently grown impatient with mortal cowardice, one afternoon at a small gathering that included Isaac Post, George Willets, Maggie, Leah, and several other friends, the raps abruptly spelled a startling message: "We will now bid you all farewell."

The medium and author Emma Hardinge later evoked the impact of that statement in her milestone history of the movement, *Modern American Spiritualism,* a book for which she conducted interviews with those who had experienced the sudden hush.

"A mournful silence filled the apartment which had but a few minutes before been tenanted with angels, sounding out their dear messages of undying affection, tender counsel, wise instruction, and prescient warning," Hardinge wrote. "*The spirits indeed were gone. . . .* There was a mighty blank in space, and a shadow everywhere, but spirit light came no more to illuminate the thick darkness."[3]

Maggie and Leah at first seemed relieved by the spirits' departure, but the Posts and others felt desolate over the loss—for a second time as it seemed—of contact with their deceased friends and relatives. The sisters soon joined in these expressions of grief. Still, there were no reassuring raps. Silence.

When George Willets and Eliab Capron, a frequent visitor to Rochester, stopped by almost two weeks later, Maggie and Leah greeted the two men with the sad news of the spirits' continued absence. "We answered," Capron ventured, "that perhaps [the spirits] would rap for us, if not for them." His influence in the other world must have been strong, for as the foursome stepped into the front hall, raps suddenly thundered a welcome on the walls, ceiling, and floor.

"Had a long-lost friend suddenly returned, the two sisters could not have been more rejoiced," Capron recalled.

Whether the spirits, or the mediums, had genuinely wished to retire or merely to test their powers of persuasion, now the future course was set. "You all have a duty to perform," the raps reiterated. "We want you to make this matter more public." This time the mortals listened and took action.

The spirits gave highly specific instructions, placing Willets in charge of business affairs and giving Capron the responsibility for drafting a lecture on spirit communication. A great deal of preparation was necessary, the spirits stressed, before anyone appeared in public.

Over the next month practice sessions were held at different homes in Rochester, each with about twenty invited guests. Test questions were banned. The meetings' main purpose was to determine if the sounds were loud enough to be heard in different places and among a large crowd. However, R. D. Jones, a newspaper editor and a believer in spirit communication, offered an additional reason for the gatherings. There had been "inquiry as to the object of the meetings and why these strangers to the manifestations were invited," he explained at a later date.[4]

"The answer was: 'We wanted prominent persons to hear the sounds who should know they were not the result of trick or deception, for the influence they may exert on the public meeting; and more than all, to give friends confidence in our ability to make the sounds in a public meeting.'"

After a number of successful rehearsals, the spirits ordered Capron and Willets to rent Rochester's largest theater, Corinthian Hall, for the night of November 14, 1849.[5] Built only a few months earlier, Corinthian Hall symbolized the town's burgeoning appetite for information, culture, self-improvement, and performances of all kinds, sometimes presented in a bewildering mix. Pugilists and humorists, gymnastic demonstrations and Shakespearean readings, and lectures on mesmerism, phrenology, and the marvels of the telegraph—secular entertainments of the sort previously frowned upon by the religious town fathers—vied for the public's attention. Circuses, banned for years, visited Rochester, among them P. T. Barnum's extravaganzas. Promising to deliver exactly what the public craved, Barnum's advertisements touted shows "combining both instruction and amusement."[6]

Centrally located behind the popular shops of Rochester's most important commercial building, the Reynolds Arcade, Corinthian Hall could seat eleven to twelve hundred people in its theater and also housed a law library, public reading rooms, and offices on its top floor. So impressive was the new theater that Horace Greeley in the *New York Tribune* complimented its "lofty ceiling, admirable lighting, air ventilation and thorough adaptation to speaking and hearing."[7] Only its entryway disappointed him; he thought it too narrow to accommodate the potential crowds.

On Tuesday, November 13, 1849, the *Daily Advertiser* printed a paid notice announcing the Fox sisters' public debut: "Doors open at 7 o'clock.

Lecture to commence at 7 1/2. Admittance 25 cents; 50 cents will admit a gentleman and two ladies."[8] The next day—Wednesday, November 14—the paper added a word of its own: "Corinthian Hall is this evening to be the theatre of very new and startling developments, or the exposure of one of the most cunningly devised and long-continued impositions ever practiced in this or any other community."[9]

SIX

"THREE DAYS OF THE STRICTEST SCRUTINY"

THAT NIGHT four hundred people crowded through Corinthian Hall's single doorway, spilled into a corridor that spanned the length of the building, then turned left or right to climb the steps to the theater on the next landing. They entered through one of the two doors that framed the stage, facing as they did so a large, level seating area, with six raised tiers of additional seats behind it. After settling in their places, audience members gazed ahead at a platform stage, an alcove at the back of it formed by the two Corinthian columns that had given the building its name.[1]

A few of the Fox sisters' supporters—among them, Amy Post and Lyman Granger—sat onstage, there both as silent observers, lending moral weight to the proceedings, and also as gentle protectors, ready to intercede on the sisters' behalf if the lively crowd turned angry. Audiences of the day were known to be rambunctious; given the controversial nature of the event, this group may have been even rowdier than usual.

Some in the audience came primed to expose chicanery—and a few to unveil witchcraft. A milder sentiment, curiosity, motivated others. The evening promised to be all the things audiences of the day enjoyed, whether in circuses or dramas: a spectacle at once exciting, instructive, and entertaining.

Some of those who attended that evening undoubtedly hoped to hear news of the departed. They may have been looking to shore up their faith or for a specific sign from someone they had loved. They may have welcomed relief from the burden of sorrow their age imposed on mourners, for spirit communication as transmitted through the Fox sisters was the opposite of lugubrious, sentimental mourning. It was lively—and alive.

Dark-haired Maggie was said to have worn a soft blue dress onstage that night, and the image is evocative. She surely seemed, even to hostile members of the audience, to be an appealing but otherwise unimposing figure. She was neither a philosopher of the divine as Emanuel Swedenborg had been nor a mystic like Andrew Jackson Davis, who spoke from his own private visions. Instead, as everyone in attendance well knew, the sounds that followed her—puzzling and stimulating—were as accessible in their way as she was approachable in hers. If there were raps to be heard, the curious men and women in the audience expected to hear them, and to judge their meaning, for themselves.[2]

Kate was absent, said to have remained in Auburn with friends. Surprisingly, since to this point she still publicly disavowed her powers, Leah joined Maggie onstage, took part in each public appearance at Corinthian Hall, and submitted to all the examinations that followed.

That night Capron delivered a lecture on the "full history of the rise and progress of these strange manifestations," while raps—some said muffled—were heard throughout the room. A reporter for the *Auburn Daily Advertiser* expressed droll ambivalence about the lecture itself, commenting dryly that the audience "listened to a long address from E. W. Capron, Esq. of Auburn, which contained much abstract truth and but little that related to the business that had called the audience together." On the other hand, the writer expressed reluctant admiration for Maggie, Leah, and the spirits.[3]

"The 'ghost,' however," he remarked, "a good deal more observing than his spokesman commenced his manifestations immediately after the young ladies, whom he always attends, had entered the hall. Yes, the 'knocking' commenced forthwith, and continued during the entire evening, to the great astonishment of those who had gone thither, with gaping ears, to catch the mysterious sounds."

If in fact everyone with "gaping ears" heard the raps, the evening must have been an engrossing one indeed, engaging listeners' attention and involving them, not just as observers of an event, but as participants in it. Prodded by disembodied sounds, audience members had three choices: they could share in an active and lively sense of bewilderment, imagine themselves as someone whom the spirits wished to contact, or project themselves into the role of triumphant investigator. At least in the moment, the twin acts of listening and deciphering turned the audience into a company of equals in the presence of the mystery, a dramatic side effect of an evening already sizzling with the hint of supernatural visitation.[4]

At the conclusion of the first night's lecture and demonstration, the audience delegated, probably by a process of nominations and catcalls, a committee of five men to inquire further into the matter of spirit communication. The *Rochester Daily Democrat* had prepared in advance a scathing review of the evening but scuttled it when events went smoothly for the spirits.

Without giving Leah and Maggie any warning, the committee decided early on Thursday, November 15, to hold its investigations that morning at the Sons of Temperance Hall and that afternoon at the Posts' home. That night an even larger audience than on the previous evening came to Corinthian Hall to learn the results.

Eliab Capron and George Willets wrote the most detailed and influential—if not entirely accurate—account of the events at Corinthian Hall. Their version, published on December 8, 1849, in Horace Greeley's *New York Tribune,* reached a readership that relished news spiced on occasion with more sensational fare.

According to their article, the first committee announced "in substance" the following: During their morning hours at the Temperance Hall, members had heard raps on the walls and floor and had asked questions that were answered "not altogether right nor altogether wrong." After moving to the Posts' home in the afternoon, they had heard more raps, and they had also conducted a variety of experiments with Leah and Maggie.

"One of the Committee," Capron and Willets wrote, "placed one of his hands upon the feet of the ladies and the other on the floor, and though the feet were not moved, there was a distinct jar on the floor."

The committee members had noticed a characteristic sound: "On the *pavement* and on the *ground* the same sound was heard,—a kind of double rap, as if a stroke and a rebound, were distinguishable. When the ladies were separated at a distance no sound was heard; but when a third person was interposed between them the sounds were heard."

In sum, Capron and Willets reported, "all agreed that the sounds were heard, *but they entirely failed to discover any means by which it could be done.*"

With the exception of believers, the audience registered shock when the first committee delivered its report at Corinthian Hall. How was it possible that five respectable men, after an entire day's worth of examinations, had failed to expose two presumably fraudulent females and to discover the means of their deception?

To double-check the findings, the crowd insisted on choosing another committee of five men, an impressive group that included the vice chancellor of New York State, Frederick Whittlesey, who was appointed chairman. His committee met with Leah and Maggie in his office on Friday, November 16, but disagreement and a whiff of scandal almost immediately soured the proceedings when Whittlesey stood accused of going "over to the enemy." On the very night of his appointment as chief investigator, he had been seen accompanying the Fox sisters to Corinthian Hall. Under a cloud, the chancellor resigned from the committee, Leah later admitting that he indeed had sworn friendship.

"He said to me," she remembered, "'Now don't be alarmed. . . . I have read [Andrew Jackson] Davis's Revelations, and I believe fully that Spirits can communicate. You shall have a fair investigation.'" The chancellor's words seemed especially comforting to her after another committee member, a physician named H. H. Langworthy, behaved in a way she found "very insulting and even violent."[5]

The investigation was thorough and may well have been intended to be humiliating and rough. The sisters were placed on a table to permit the male committee members all the better to touch, hold, and closely observe their subjects' feet. The gentlemen also tied cords around the sisters' dresses at a point that corresponded, according to Langworthy's oblique reference, to "gentlemen's inexpressibles." He later modified this phrase to "ankles"—still a body part little discussed in polite company at the time. Langworthy further insisted that the committee heard no knocks whatsoever during these particular tests, although he admitted to hearing them at other times during the examination.

Capron and Willets glossed over the discord in their article for the Tribune. They instead implied that Langworthy had lent his seal of approval to Maggie and Leah, and they specifically noted that the doctor "made observations with a stethoscope to ascertain whether there was any movement of the lungs, and found not the least difference when the sounds were made; and that there was no kind of probability or possibility of their being made by ventriloquism as some had supposed—and they could not have been made by machinery."

Whatever the squabbling second committee actually reported to the audience on the night of Friday, November 16, its members wound up as stymied as the first committee by the mysterious sounds. The restless and increasingly disgruntled crowd at Corinthian Hall proceeded to appoint a third committee, this one even more skeptical and determined than the previous two. One man swore that he would destroy his favorite beaver hat if he couldn't outwit the sisters; another announced that he would throw himself over the Genesee Falls.[6]

The spirits must have anticipated an excited audience and a good financial return, for George Willets had already booked Corinthian Hall for a fourth consecutive night. The third committee promised to conduct its investigations and deliver its findings on Saturday, November 17.

For the sake of the spirits, Maggie and Leah allowed themselves the next day to be held, bound, manipulated, and maneuvered as before, but they also suffered a new indignity. With the sisters' reluctant consent, a subsidiary Committee of Ladies took them into a separate room, then stripped and searched them, examining both "their persons and clothing" in search of noisy devices such as leaden balls. Mortified, both sisters wept through much of their ordeal, until their sobs reached such a pitch that Amy Post burst into the room and brought the investigation to a halt.

And in the end, the good women of Rochester failed to find evidence of duplicity. A certificate issued by the Committee of Ladies sidestepped the more delicate parts of the examination, focusing instead on tests designed to prove that the raps weren't caused by electricity. When the sisters "were standing on pillows," the certificate noted, "with a handkerchief tied around the bottom of their dresses, tight to the ankles, we all heard the rapping on the wall and floor distinctly." Maggie and Leah were also made to stand on glass, another nonconductor of electricity.[7]

By that Saturday afternoon, however, rumors of serious trouble were already circulating. Some of Rochester's leading citizens, outraged by the events, asserted that the three committees hadn't been objective at all but had been packed with spirit sympathizers. Head of the cadre was Josiah Bissel, son of the fervently religious businessman who had invited the Reverend Charles Finney to hold revivals in Rochester in the 1830s. Bissel's father had been not only devout but industrious, leaving behind an earthly fortune. Josiah Bissel the younger came from one of Rochester's wealthiest and most established families.

Bissel may have been incensed during the Corinthian Hall investigations by what he considered blasphemy and outraged by women who were willing to flout conventional morality. In an era that valued middle-class privacy and feminine purity and that damned public expressions of sexuality, the Fox sisters not only had offended morality by daring to appear onstage but had allowed themselves to be physically handled in a way that was considered highly unseemly—and the procedures to be discussed in a very open forum. Undoubtedly, Bissel also had decided in advance that the sisters were frauds and that Rochester would become known as a place haunted not by ghosts but by credulous fools duped by two attractive young women.

Maggie and Leah, well aware of the threats against them, retreated to the Posts' home for their own protection. Frightened by the rumors and exhausted from the grueling investigations, Maggie refused to go to the hall that last night. Amy planned to attend anyway and sit onstage in a symbolic gesture of support for her friends and the spirits. Leah, who had been wavering, resolved: "Amy, if you will go, I will go with you, if I go to the stake." And just as the two women were leaving, Maggie relented, saying, "I cannot have you go without me. I must go, though I expect to be killed."[8]

That evening, Capron and Willets wrote, the final committee—the third—made its report, stating that despite all its precautions the sounds had been heard and that various questions asked of the spirits had been answered generally correctly. The man who had sworn to destroy his hat and his friend who had promised to hurl himself over the falls chose not to deliver on their vows.

So it was, Capron and Willets concluded, that after "three days of the strictest scrutiny by means of intelligence, candor and science, were the persons in whose presence these sounds are heard, acquitted of any fraud."[9]

The two men had shaded the facts about the unanimity of the second committee, and it was optimistic at best to say that the investigators had acquitted Maggie and Leah of deliberate deception. It was absolutely true, however, that no one had proved beyond a shadow of a doubt whether—or how—the sisters made the raps. After "three days of the strictest scrutiny," they had won a remarkable victory.

But it was a victory that left Josiah Bissel and his cronies unimpressed, and they behaved in anything but a genteel fashion themselves: they lit firecrackers and bombarded the room. In her history of Spiritualism, Emma Hardinge underscored the sexual nature of the attacks, stating, "Josiah Bissel, writing himself 'Esq.' and 'gentleman,' proceeded to distribute torpedoes amongst 'the boys,' and on every side the explosion of these noisy tormentors distracted the ears and stimulated the ribald jokes of the mob against 'the rappers.'"[10]

Bissel and others who considered themselves "leaders of public opinion" then mounted the stage, Hardinge continued, "and invited up the 'rowdies' for 'investigation,' until the police, perceiving the disgraceful turn the proceedings were taking, urged the ladies and their friends to retire. . . ." Ashen and terrified for their safety, Leah and Maggie were escorted out of Corinthian Hall under the police chief's protection.

As it turned out, Bissel's efforts backfired. The cause that "the *elite* of

Rochester citizenship" had tried to disgrace, Emma Hardinge wrote, "rose triumphantly out of the ruins they strove to create. The aim of wide-spread publicity was attained."

The events at Corinthian Hall—and the article by Capron and Willets in the *Tribune*—stimulated an interest in spirit communication that transcended the confines of western New York. But Maggie and Leah had paid a steep price for their success by submitting to humiliation and abuse. If their faith in the spirits was genuine, they had done so for an important cause. Whatever their motives, it's certain that an event that they had tried to shape, by holding rehearsals and soliciting allies, had spiraled beyond their control.

Fame was theirs but at the cost of notoriety. And the criticism didn't stop. H. H. Langworthy went on from the committee to mount a serious attack on the Fox sisters, one published in the *New York Tribune* and other newspapers. He insisted in print that "by placing the girls on a table and putting our hands on their feet, the knocking stopped. By tying their dresses around their ancles [sic] with cords, it also ceased. . . . When there was a knocking on the doors and tables . . . these girls were in every case, touching these articles with the back of their dresses. . . ." Langworthy concluded that "this 'mysterious rapping' was so connected with the persons of these girls, that were they thoroughly examined *sans* culottes, they would stand out in base relief. But we were *men* and as the girls were cornered and very much frightened, we let them go at this. . . ."[11]

Eliab Capron angrily responded that Maggie and Leah had in fact been examined "sans culottes" or very close to it by the diligent "Committee of Ladies." His assertion may not have kept Dr. Langworthy and other male investigators from entertaining—and enjoying—the notion that had *they* stripped the sisters, the outcome might have been different.

The Corinthian Hall demonstrations sparked confusion even among those who supported the sisters. In a letter to relatives, a member of the Post family—possibly Isaac himself—pondered the contradictions that puzzled him. "If the spirits of our departed Friends are watching over us for good and are willing to communicate with us," he commented, "it seems strange to us, it should be nessary [sic] to go to two or three girls to have the raps explained."[12]

Others stood firmly by the sisters yet worried about what would happen next. The abolitionist William Cooper Nell, a former associate of Frederick Douglass on the *North Star*, often visited the Town and Country Club in Boston, a place frequented by luminaries such as Ralph Waldo Emerson and A. Bronson Alcott.

"We all meet here and discuss about the many things *Celestial* and *Terrestrial*," Nell wrote to Amy Post.[13]

Nell devoted much of his letter to matters celestial: "spiritual matters which have thus far excited many circles aside from Western New York." William Lloyd Garrison, Nell said, planned to publish parts of Capron's *Tribune* article in the *Liberator*. Garrison was not altogether sure what he felt about the "mysterious Knockings," Nell confided, but was nonetheless a seeker of light. As for the *Tribune*, Nell continued, another article on the mysterious knocking had already appeared, accounting for it "as of a similar fact with those . . . in the history of Swedenborg and A. Jackson Davis."

Nell reminded Amy that he considered Kate, Maggie, and Leah "as entirely honest in the business and on those premises the *wonder* and *mystery* is augmented. I can appreciate the trials to which you and they were exposed during the investigation. . . . Your motives are Godlike and your satisfaction will be ample," he assured his friend but added with obvious concern, "even though the result may be different so far as the Girls are concerned from what you and other friends expect. . . ."

Nell was right to be worried. However radical in her political and religious actions and opinions, Amy Post was a mature, middle-class married woman, well known and respected in the circles in which she moved. Kate, Maggie, and Leah, relative newcomers in the public arena, had no such long-established reputation for wisdom and integrity. Moreover, the girls were young and single, and Leah had no husband in evidence to provide a veneer of conventional respectability. John Fox had absented himself from his children's lives, and Margaret rarely objected to what her children did. Apart from a small group of friends, the sisters had no one to protect them from the demands of the spirits or their own desires or the probing hands, curious eyes, and mocking words of their contemporaries.

PART II

THE PROGRESS OF MODERN SPIRITUALISM
1849–1852

PART II

THE PROGRESS OF MODERN SPIRITUALISM
1849–1852

TALKING TO THE DEAD

SEVEN

"GOD'S TELEGRAPH HAS OUTDONE MORSE'S ALTOGETHER"

ONSTAGE AT Corinthian Hall in November 1849, Maggie and Leah had briefly joined the legions of Americans who broadcast new scientific, social, political, religious, and medical theories from platforms across the country: phrenologists who displayed their marked charts of skulls; mesmerists who magnetized audience members; inspirational speakers like Andrew Jackson Davis, who expounded on his visions of the afterlife; social and political reformers; healers, doctors, and quacks hawking their cures.

Some of these lecturers and demonstrators believed in what they preached; others didn't. But in the cause of commercial enterprise, with rare exceptions the sincere and insincere alike hoped to spread their ideas while making money from their performances and books.

Amid the exuberant clash of theories, who could know for certain what was real and what wasn't? Scientific and technological advances had helped create the question. Rational, scientific inquiry seemed capable of providing answers.

In the 1840s the word *scientist* itself was just coming into popular use, as scientific study fragmented into discrete professional fields such as chemistry and physics. What helped unite these separate disciplines, it was argued, was method: the scientist's process of developing general truths from carefully observed facts.[1]

Throughout the nineteenth century new discoveries challenged old ideas and riveted the public's attention. The unimaginable turned out to be possible; mysteries proved penetrable. Nor were scientists shy about trumpeting their achievements in museums, exhibitions, and magnificently illustrated books. In the 1830s the English scientist Michael Faraday experimented with electromagnetism and hosted Friday evening lectures to describe his own and other scientists' work. His discovery of electromagnetic induction, important both theoretically and practically, also stimulated widespread fascination with the elusive force of electricity.

From observing rocks and fossils, geologists postulated that the earth and its varied species had evolved over millions of years. In the early 1800s the fossilized bones of enormous creatures resembling mythological dragons began to be collected for systematic study. In 1841 the English anatomist and zoologist Richard Owen gave these prehistoric reptiles a name: *dinosaur,* meaning "terrible lizard."[2]

Amazing events could seem theatrical, contrived, or even terrifying. In 1854 the first life-size reconstructions of dinosaurs were displayed outside London on the grounds of the Crystal Palace. Women and children screamed and fainted on catching sight of the nightmarish beasts.

Naturalists traveling far and wide reported on equally astonishing, living species of flora and fauna: in the Amazon, one intrepid explorer observed a bird-eating spider so large that children tied a cord around its middle and walked it like a dog.[3]

Who could doubt that the skies held wonders rivaling the earth's? Andrew Jackson Davis, the American mystic known as the "Poughkeepsie Seer," confidently expressed his belief in extraterrestrial beings, suggesting that contact with spirits, when it became commonplace, would resemble that "now being enjoyed by the inhabitants of Mars, Jupiter, and

Saturn, because of their superior refinement."[4] Although apparently uninhabited by extraterrestrials, Neptune was discovered in 1846, the first major planet to be identified on the basis of mathematical calculations rather than from being observed directly with the human eye and telescope.

Anything seemed possible, but some things were just hoaxes. In the 1840s Barnum exhibited a Mermaid, a preserved monkey's head attached to a fish tail, at his American Museum. His practical, nineteenth-century audiences were open to everything but convinced of nothing until they had their empirical, material proof.[5]

Advances in the so-called pure sciences were matched by technological leaps. The proliferation of steam-powered machines enhanced productivity. A revolution in transportation had produced the steamboat, the Erie Canal, and the railroads. The telegraph, still a novelty in the mid-1840s, seemed a marvel in its own right, capable of communicating messages almost instantaneously across great distances. Improved printing methods, along with the telegraph, had created a lively and querulous press.

Of course, not everyone unconditionally applauded each forward stride. "Things are in the saddle, / And ride mankind," Ralph Waldo Emerson warned in 1847.[6] In "The Celestial Railroad," a short story by Nathaniel Hawthorne, passengers rode straight to hell in a roaring, belching locomotive. Critics worried that the material evidence demanded by science, coupled with the material prosperity promised by technology, would diminish or obscure the spiritual dimension of life.

The plethora of discoveries often seemed to contradict orthodox religion, a quandary that was difficult to resolve then as it is now. With the authority of the Bible undermined, weakened by historical explanations, geological explorations, and liberal theologians who stressed human goodness rather than sinfulness, churchgoers sometimes felt their faith rested on shaky ground. Still, science and liberal theology alike promised that humankind would progress ever upward and onward, advancing in knowledge and marching toward perfection.

In February 1850 Eliab Capron, in collaboration with a friend from Auburn, Henry D. Barron, issued a pamphlet that presented the surprising argument that spirit communication should be viewed, not as a *supernatural* phenomenon, but as a *natural* one produced by natural causes. The pamphlet, the first substantive one since E. E. Lewis had published his in 1848, was titled *Singular Revelations: Explanation and History of the Mysterious Communion with Spirits, Comprehending the Rise and Progress of the Mysterious Noises in Western New-York Generally Received as Spiritual Communications*. It was intended specifically to remove the spirits from the shadowy realm of superstition and place them squarely within the sunny domain of scientific reason.

"By natural causes," Capron and Barron explained, "we do not mean that the cause is known to man at the present time; or that it is produced by collusion or machinery of any kind. We *know this is not the case*." Instead, the communication between "superior and inferior intelligences" was part of a grand scheme, the underlying laws of which had yet to be discovered. Once scientists better understood its principles, it would rightfully be viewed as one more scientific wonder in their wondrous scientific age.[7]

"The why of its appearance just at this time," Capron and Barron wrote, "or the reason why it has not become more extensively known before, we are as unable to tell as we should be to tell why all the great discoveries in science were not made known to man at once."

The authors' emphasis—an extension of their own and the nation's fascination with science and empirical investigation—had more in common with Enlightenment rationalism than it did with religious enthusiasm, and it was an approach that potentially held appeal for a wide audience. Capron and Barron hoped to appeal to seekers who wanted to reconcile faith with science as well as to men and women who might otherwise have spurned the spirits as supernatural bosh.

The material and the spiritual, they argued, were intimately connected, although the connection wasn't fully understood. Theoretically, they mused, "It is no more proof that [spirits] are not thus about us because not seen, than electricity or the numerous animalculae which we are constantly eating, drinking, and breathing, although unseen, do not exist for the same reason."

On a practical level, skeptics—like scientists—could devise experiments to investigate the raps under strict test conditions, then arrive at conclusions on the basis of empirical proof.

Singular Revelations, though small in size, was ambitious in scope. The authors established not only a scientific rationale for the spirits but a historical pedigree as well, describing the intrusion of "Old Jeffrey," the fractious poltergeist, into the household of John Wesley's family. *Singular Revelations,* like a manual or reference book, synthesized for a bemused and curious public many of the theories about spirit communication that had been circulating since Hydesville.

The authors praised the Fox sisters' honesty and courage but also stressed that spirit visitations were by no means exclusive to the Fox family. A former church deacon from the nearby town of Greece had experienced raps long before hearing of Kate and Maggie. The loudest noises to date followed twelve-year-old John Beaver, another resident of New York State. Marvelous spirit feats could be experienced daily, the authors asserted, in the presence of Auburn's homegrown medium, Sarah Tamill, who had become active after meeting Kate.

The pamphlet's focus on the growing amount of spirit activity argued for Kate and Maggie's historic instrumentality: when Kate assumed the Hydesville rapper was sentient and snapped her fingers . . . when Maggie asked it to count to four . . . at that moment, Capron and Barron intimated, the close connection between worlds had been disclosed. With other demonstrations occurring around the state, Kate and Maggie surely could be absolved of mischief and deception.

To explain the presence of such communicative and humanlike spirits, Capron and Barron drew primarily on the ideas of their contemporary Andrew Jackson Davis, who in turn derived them from the eighteenth-century philosopher Emanuel Swedenborg—or from conversations, as Davis claimed, with Swedenborg's spirit. Davis had already produced an astonishing body of lectures and books developing what he came to call a "harmonial philosophy" in which like attracted like. So great were the similarities and affinities between beings of both worlds, Davis had written, that the recently deceased often failed even to recognize that they had died. Naturally, they felt a profound attachment to the mortals they had left behind.[8]

Capron and Barron also relied on Davis's work to help them explain the existence of mischievous or evil spirits, the sort who pulled hair or deliberately lied on test questions. The authors of *Singular Revelations* dealt with this persistent problem by adapting Davis's theories on the structure of the other world.

There were seven spheres through which spirits passed, Capron and Barron wrote, proposing that the term "higher and lower spheres" substitute altogether for heaven and hell. Although immortal spirits at first closely resembled their mortal selves, flaws and all, everyone passed to a superior condition immediately upon dying. The longer a spirit inhabited the heavens, the farther it progressed through the seven spheres, advancing in ethereal virtue.[9]

The authors had effectively sidestepped the whole issue of hell and eternal damnation that had so troubled the Posts and others. Immortal souls, like ambitious nineteenth-century Americans, had hope for self-improvement.

What if a mortal was contacted by the resident of a lower sphere? Capron and Barron counseled their readers to trust themselves and their instincts. Good spirits spoke the truth. Spirits that had not yet progressed teased or told lies. Sensible men and women, they argued, would discern the difference.

Horace Greeley's review of *Singular Revelations* for the *New York Tribune* managed to balance serious interest in the subject matter with tongue-in-cheek skepticism about some of the authors' assertions. He noted, "No theory of collusion or juggle or ventriloquism or hallucination suffices to account to our mind for the concussions, sounds or 'knockings' which have been heard by hundreds of the most respectable and sedate citizens of Western New York."[10]

Still, he found parts of the book irresistibly amusing. "According to this," Greeley commented, "a man wishing to get out of Hell has only to cut his throat, which most people would consider a far more likely way to get *into* that interesting predicament."

He ended his review with a sensible caveat: "We have not meant to imply that any statement in this book is *necessarily* false or incredible, but only that they are of such a nature as to require a very large amount of unimpeachable evidence to sustain them."

Letters about the spirits were now appearing almost daily in the *Tribune*, irate denunciations alternating with impassioned defenses, and other pamphlets on the subject swiftly followed *Singular Revelations*. With a title that outdid Capron's for sheer length, *History of the Strange Sounds or Rappings, Heard in Rochester and Western New York, and Usually Called the Mysterious Noises! Which Are Supposed by Many to Be Communications from the Spirit World, Together with All the Explanation That Can Yet Be Given of the Matter*, appeared in March 1850. It was written and published by a Rochester printer named D. M. Dewey, who, like Capron and Barron, reprinted letters, testimonials, and newspaper columns and who also expressed sympathy for the notion of spirit communication. He emphasized, however, that it was up to "every man to decide for himself. . . . No man should believe without evidence."

With the publication of Dewey's pamphlet and the hundreds of others that followed, Kate and Maggie's story evolved into a multiauthored tale. Conflicting opinions about the spirits influenced different versions; factual errors, deliberate distortions, and conscious or unconscious omissions and embellishments added a level of further confusion through the years. Dewey, for example, wrongly stated that Maggie, not Kate, had originally accompanied Leah to Rochester, an assertion that was often repeated. Reports of a famous comment attributed to Kate in her first encounter with the peddler—"Here, Mr. Splitfoot, do as I do!"—may have been accurate, but they didn't appear in print until years after the event. By the end of the girls' lives too, their purported ages at the time of the Hydesville raps would vary from account to account, some authors averring that Kate and Maggie had been only six and eight when the murdered peddler first knocked.

In the winter of 1849–50 the Fox sisters retreated from the public arena of the stage—it had proved a dangerous forum—to a private arena where women of the day typically exercised power and wielded spiritual authority, the parlor. There they pursued the more typically masculine activity of earning an income and making a living.[11]

When Kate returned from Auburn, the three sisters began holding large gatherings for the general public at Leah's cottage on Troup

Street. In response to the recent publicity, visitors packed every room upstairs and down, sitting on the stairs when necessary. Although the word itself wasn't used widely until the Civil War, the *seance* as we know it had been born.

The Fox sisters now presented themselves as a public threesome. Although accounts differ, at this point Leah apparently neither was attended by raps nor called herself a medium but instead guided the communications with gentle but leading questions. "Spirit, do you know this person?" she frequently asked as a way of introducing a new visitor.

In the course of the winter the sisters also began accepting payment on an informal basis for their seances, possibly at Amy Post's worried suggestion. They had never needed financial support before, Leah wrote, managing on food David sent from the farm and her savings from teaching. But with her nest egg gone and no time for piano students, she was grateful for monetary gifts "offered in kindness and good faith."[12]

A wealth of anecdotes and reminiscences provide a picture of what the early months of 1850 were like for the Fox sisters and those who visited them. While this material offers little insight into what Kate, Maggie, and Leah were thinking and feeling, it illustrates how they and the spirits behaved with their public and what strangers and friends alike experienced in the sisters' presence. The passage of time, an individual writer's inclination to believe or disbelieve, and a tendency to exaggerate events for the sake of publication surely colored what was said. Nonetheless, the witnesses' accumulated observations help create a vivid portrait.

The spirits, at least those on the lower spheres, couldn't always be counted on for reliability. The author and abolitionist Frederick Douglass was so incensed at one gathering by the spirits' failure to respond that he later apologized to Amy Post for his behavior.

"You misunderstood me in supposing that I applied the term *atrocious* to the company," he earnestly explained. "That term was applied to the *rapping* when it refused to *answer* the question . . . when that question was the only one put which would *test* the intelligence of the agent by which the rapping was made."[13]

As Augustus H. Strong realized, participants at the same seance could experience very different things and so emerge with opposite opinions about what had taken place. Strong, the son of a Baptist deacon named Alvah Strong, had met the spirits when he was a boy of fourteen in 1850. As an adult he reminisced about the encounter, which was initiated by two of his father's out-of-town guests. The couple, "a tall and stately man, a Presbyterian Elder," and his wife, had asked to be introduced to the Fox family, a request that the disapproving Deacon Strong was too polite to ignore.[14]

When the deacon and his guests visited the Troup Street house, Margaret informed them there was no more room that day. Would the sisters be willing to schedule a future appointment? Margaret bustled down the front steps to the brick walk, followed by Kate, and posed the question to the spirits. The visitors were promptly showered with affirmative raps in a spontaneous outdoor demonstration, which surely surprised them.

When and where could the meeting take place? The raps announced, much to Deacon Strong's shock, that they would meet him at his own house that very evening. Deacon Strong again allowed etiquette to get the better of him and agreed to the date.

The evening was a memorable one for young Augustus Strong. "It began very solemnly, with the wheeling out of a heavy mahogany center table into the middle of the parlor," he recalled. "Then the company gathered tremblingly around it and formed a closed circle by clasping hands about its edge. Then we waited in silence. Katy Fox was opposite me. I thought I observed a slight smile on her face," Strong wrote. "I was less observant of the proprieties at that time than I have been since, and I ventured, alas, to wink at Katy Fox. And I thought that Katy did something like winking in return. She was a pretty girl, and why shouldn't she? But she soon composed her countenance. The seance proceeded solemnly to the end. But for me there was no more solemnity or mystery. All the rest of the performance seemed a farce."

Although Strong heard loud, clear raps, he felt the answers to his questions were "ambiguous or commonplace." His father's guests, however, disagreed, and the courtly Presbyterian sank to his hands and knees to examine the underside of the table. On rising, he pronounced himself satisfied that the mediums were above reproach. He and his wife soon converted to a belief in the spirits, while Deacon Strong, according to his son, "never forgave himself for leading those two innocents into temptation."

Augustus Strong also reported on a gathering attended by Miss Mary B. Allen, the preceptress "of the best Rochester school for young ladies," and possibly one of Kate's former teachers. On hearing raps, purportedly from her grandmother, Miss Allen promptly asked her invisible relative to spell *scissors*.

"*S-i-s-s-e-r-s*," rapped the obliging spirit.

"Oh"—and the teacher seems to have pounced with glee—"that is just the way Katy Fox spelled 'scissors' when she was a scholar in my school."

Whether or not Kate actually attended Miss Allen's school, which opened only in 1847, the spirits' spelling mistakes troubled others. A defender of the Fox sisters, a man simply called "P-," commented on the spirits' failing grades: "I had at several times received communications in which the words were misspelled," P- wrote, "and persons sitting at the table made the remark: 'Well I don't believe in spirits that can't spell right.' These remarks would cause some merriment," P- continued, "and at one time the alphabet was called by the usual signal and the sentence spelled out: 'You need not laugh at him. He never learned how to spell.' "[15]

Other witnesses mentioned spats between mortals and spirits. One evening the invisible beings refused to answer questions for a friend of Isaac Post who had tested the sisters a number of times. Finally Leah overruled the spirits, who fervently wanted the visitor banished for some unexplained reason, and invited him to stay. The spirits, according to the gentleman, "immediately called out for the alphabet and spelled: 'Leah has done wrong—he must go.' "[16]

Moments of levity, rare squabbles, spelling mistakes, wrong answers, confused milling here and there between different rooms, and a habit of asking strangers to go away and return on another day: these are part of the pattern of the early, hectic seances held by the Fox sisters. So too, however, are moments that levelheaded men and women found inexplicable, emotional, and miraculous, instances that seemed to them to defy human capability.

William McDonald, one of the editors of a publication called the

Excelsior, swore to having exercised his utmost ingenuity to solve the mystery, only to fail. Although he continued to withhold final judgment, McDonald admitted, "We have seen and heard things to us wonderful and unaccountable. . . ."

Charles Hammond, a Universalist minister, attended a gathering of about twenty people at the Troup Street house in January 1850. He reported that the three sisters struck him as more cheerful than he had expected; he had anticipated solemnity, given that they engaged in hourly conversation with "the spirits of the revered dead."[17]

The spirits rapped answers to some participants' questions but to his disappointment refused to answer his. They promised to do so, however, if he returned the next day. And when he did, the spirits seemed so familiar with every detail of his life that Hammond dismissed any idea of fraud. The possibility that the sisters had used the extra time to research his background seems not to have occurred to him. He was inclined instead to credit the answers he received, not to the spirits, but to the sisters' clairvoyant powers or to the heightened sensibilities he attributed to mesmerism. The immortal beings promised further demonstrations to erase his doubts.

On his third visit he sat alone with "the 'three sisters' and their aged mother" at a table with a lighted candle on it. Margaret and Kate were on his right, Leah and Maggie on his left. After a cacophony of loud and violent raps, the table seemed to him to float up and then to pass "out of the reach of us all—full six feet from me, and at least four from the nearest person to it." He swore that "not even a thread" connected the sisters to the buoyant piece of furniture and that when the sitters summoned the table to come back, "back it came, as though it were carried on the head of some one, who had not suited his position to a perfect equipoise, the balance being sometimes in favor of one side, and then the other."

Other manifestations followed, some part of a now-familiar repertoire. While the family sang, the spirits marked time on the table; a transparent hand wafted across Hammond's face; fingers pulled the hair on the left side of his head; his right leg was tugged underneath the table.

Then, most unnerving of all, the room sprang to life, as in a haunted house nightmare: a window curtain rolled up and down, a lounge shook

violently, bureau drawers slammed open and shut, and "a common spinning wheel seemed to be in motion, making a very natural buzz of the
spindle—a reel articulated each knot wound upon it, while the sound of
a rocking cradle indicated maternal care for the infant's slumbers."

Many of the Fox family's visitors over the next few years would echo
Hammond's conclusion: "That any of the company could have performed these things, under the circumstances in which we were situated,
would require a greater stretch of credulity on my part, than it would to
believe it was the work of spirits."

Though the spirits could be playful, they could also be sensitive and
astute. John E. Robinson, a Rochester clerk and bookkeeper, recalled an
evening when a mother received a message from her child's spirit. "That
mother left the room in tears," Robinson wrote, "but they were not the
outburst of sorrow. Gladness was in her heart, (as she said,) for the first
time since she laid her darling child—her first born—down to sleep on
the bosom of its elder mother, earth."[18]

A bachelor in his thirties who became a close friend of the Fox family, Robinson fiercely defended the sisters' honor and respectability. So
too did many of the other witnesses who visited. Leah's hand was at
work in some cases, gently sculpting an irreproachable image for herself.

"The elder sister, Mrs. Fish, is a widow lady," William McDonald of
the Excelsior commented.[19] In fact it's not clear that the husband who had
deserted her, Bowman Fish, had traveled by that point beyond Illinois to
the spirit world. But for Leah to claim widowhood certainly sounded
better than to admit to desertion or divorce.

In an effort to position the sisters within a genteel context, Robinson
stressed that they had never behaved in an inappropriate fashion by pursuing the spirits or "set up the false claim that they, as individuals . . . have
a mission from the Deity to this world.

"They are merely the passive media through whom these communications are made to us from the world of spirits." His emphasis on the
words passive media may have been intended to protect the sisters from
the imputation that they were far too assertive for respectable women.

Other visitors, while accepting in principle the theory of passive
mediumship, recognized that Kate and Maggie seemed to exercise

greater control over their circumstances than did mesmeric subjects. In fact, Kate and Maggie were beginning to rival the spirits for attention. One visitor, an editor of the *Merchant's Day Book,* discussed the two separately rather than simply referring to them, as many people did, as "the girls" or "one of the girls" or "the youngest" or "the older." To him, they weren't just mediums for the spirits but individuals in their own right.

"One of them is only 12 years of age, and evidently has no more conception of the rapping than a canary bird," he remarked, painting a picture of Kate as a naive child. Like subsequent observers, he added a year or two to Maggie's age, commenting on her poise and frank demeanor: "The other is a young lady, apparently 17 or 18 years old; her manners are rather prepossessing, and although not decidedly a beauty, she has a mild and gentle expression of countenance, a face indicative of no superior cunning or shrewdness, but on the contrary one that any person at all acquainted with human nature would pronounce artless and innocent."[20]

With an astute eye for detail, the editor related an anecdote about Kate that highlighted certain lifelong traits: her childlike, breathy verbal expression, her wish to please others, her distress when she failed to do so. "The youngest one in fact appeared innocent of even a suspicion that she had any agency in it," he observed, "and with that earnest simplicity peculiar to children, expressed a wish that it *would do* something just to let me see how strange it acted sometimes, and went on to relate in a hurried manner—when we were leaving—how it sometimes took the books off the table and piled them up in her lap, how it drew out the piano and played tunes, &."

At twelve, Kate was pretty and flirtatious, if the tale of her winking at young Augustus Strong can be believed, and she behaved as though wholly engaged with the spirits—whether fabricated or real—whose feats she assured visitors were remarkable and whose failures she took personally. Maggie, already sixteen, seemed on the surface more poised; others would comment in years to come on her air of gentle reserve in public. Her demeanor suggests formidable willpower for, given her love of "the rattling of Carriages and the ringing of bells," her composure most likely concealed an excited response to the tumultuous events of which she was part.

Both girls, like Leah, continued to suffer from severe headaches. One or all of the sisters, like others of their time, may have sought occasional relief for pain not only in mesmerism but also in medications legally made with alcohol or morphine, substances that have been known to blur the line between the real and imagined.

The desire to establish proof of spirit communication found a hopeful symbol in a great technological achievement of the age, the telegraph. One of the first individuals to draw the analogy, the Reverend Ashahel H. Jervis, was a machinist and Methodist minister who had joined the Fox sisters onstage during their demonstrations at Corinthian Hall. One afternoon Jervis's out-of-town houseguest, a man named Pickard, was visiting other local friends; they were trying to initiate spirit contact when raps delivered tragic news: Pickard's son had died suddenly a few hours before. The distraught father rushed to catch the next stagecoach home.

That night a telegram for Pickard arrived at the Jervis household. When Jervis opened it, he read the same sad news reported earlier in the day by the spirits. Drawing a parallel between the revolutionary advance in human communication and the little-understood phenomenon of spirit contact, Jervis announced to his wife: "God's telegraph has outdone Morse's altogether."[21]

Another incident underscored the analogy. In a letter to the *Rochester Daily Magnet* in February 1850 Nathaniel Draper, a farmer and Rochester pioneer, described what happened when he magnetized his wife, the purportedly clairvoyant Rachel. To the couple's surprise, she was contacted by neither friends nor family but by the spirit of Benjamin Franklin, who appeared to her in a vision.[22]

Asked why he had come, the founding father told Rachel that he was establishing a new line of communication, the term *line* a reference to the telegraph. Franklin then urged the Drapers to invite Kate, Maggie, and a few others for an experiment to determine the feasibility of establishing "communications between two distant points by means of these rappings."

Understandably dubious, Nathaniel Draper asked Franklin to give him a signal to confirm his identity. Franklin, an early promoter of electricity, promptly administered an electric shock to wake up the magnetized Rachel, who assured her worried husband that the jolt had only helped clear her head.

The Drapers obediently assembled a group of about ten people, including Kate and Maggie. Franklin appeared to Rachel Draper soon after she'd entered the magnetic state and through her ordered the group to be divided in two, with half of the participants sent to a room at the opposite end of the house. In both places, the participants were startled to hear taps like those of an unusually loud telegraph. Franklin was "trying the batteries," Rachel Draper commented. But the spirit, apparently disappointed with the outcome, scheduled another session for the next day, this time inviting Leah too.

At this second session Franklin again divided the group, assigning Maggie and the Drapers to remain with those in the parlor and Kate and Leah to join the others at the far end of the house. The mysterious telegraph resumed its loud taps, a sound so strange that Maggie apparently became alarmed and wondered aloud, "What does all this mean?" Rachel Draper, her face radiant in her magnetic state, explained that Franklin, as before, was testing the batteries. At that moment, raps called for the alphabet, and Franklin's spirit slowly spelled a message, letter by letter: "'Now I am ready, my friends,' he rapped. 'There will be great changes in the nineteenth century. Things that now look dark and mysterious to you will be laid plain before your sight. Mysteries are going to be revealed. The world will be enlightened. I sign my name Benjamin Franklin.'" The spirit concluded a bit more prosaically, "Do not go into the other room."

After waiting a respectful few minutes, the Drapers' awed guests reassembled in the parlor to compare notes. What greater reassurance could mortals puzzled by the raps possibly hope for? The two groups agreed that each had heard the same auspicious message, given via the tap-tap of the ineffable telegraph in two different places at once.

EIGHT

"THE KNOCKING SPIRITS ARE ACTUALLY IN TOWN"

ELIAB CAPRON may have been sincere in his beliefs, but he was also a newspaperman with his eye on the main chance. Soon after *Singular Revelations* came out in 1850, he tried to pressure Margaret into allowing her daughters to go to New York City, and he criticized her for hesitating. Delay, he warned, might offend persons who "stand among the first in the nation for science and influence."[1] He assured her that powerful supporters could put to rest rumors that the girls were frauds. Sensitive, eager little Kate, the sister he had taken to Auburn with him, "might convince some of the best minds in the nation," he enthused.

He resorted to wheedling: "Now I want you to answer and do say that Cathy may go.... Why you would hardly realize her absence, we could go to New York and back *so quick*." He also threw in an appeal to the girl herself. "You want to go, don't you Cathy? It would be a delightful trip."

Recognizing that strong-willed Leah was key to any family decision, he asked Margaret to broker his case with her oldest daughter. "I think she will say [yes] for me," he prompted. With a wry aside hardly appropriate for a supporter of women's rights, he added, "Try her. If she says no it will be the first lady that ever said so to me—*on serious matters!*"

Ending on a practical note, he admitted that eminent men of science offered no pay other than expenses, but he reminded Margaret that some people were always willing to give presents to girls. "Besides," Capron observed, "money is not always the *greatest* advantage to be made by a good deal."

Margaret Fox held her ground for a few months, keeping her daughters closer to home. By April 1850 a sufficient interval had passed for the sisters to dare to return to Corinthian Hall, this time under the protection of a former Universalist minister named R. P. Ambler, who took Capron's place as lecturer. "Public opinion had changed since the first lectures on the subject," Leah wrote. If some members of the audience remained hostile, the sisters' many new friends rushed to the stage afterward to congratulate them on a successful appearance.[2]

The Fox sisters now launched their first professional tour to spread word of the spirits. While John, as always, remained in Wayne County, Calvin Brown accompanied Margaret and her daughters to their next engagement, scheduled in Albany, New York, with Ambler once again delivering the lecture. The sisters found themselves in demand not only for large public events at Albany's Van Vechten Hall but also for seances held at their hotel. Their expenses amounted to about one hundred fifty dollars per week, but by charging a dollar per person for a group session and five dollars for a private one, the Fox sisters easily covered their budget. The Albany appearance, Leah wrote, was the "first stage of the fulfillment of our mission."[3]

They moved on to Troy, New York. "The 'knocking' spirits are actually in town," the *Troy Daily Whig* announced on May 1, 1850, "and 'knock' at Apollo Hall for a night or two more. The Professor's lectures may be all well enough but the 'spirits' will draw the quarters."

The sisters were besieged by the converted and curious, but new problems surfaced. "A murmur arose among the 'women' whose conduct toward us in Troy was cruel and unchristianlike," Leah wrote. "They insinuated that if the mediums were men their husbands would not become so deeply enlisted in this unpopular, and, seemingly, weird subject. . . . One lady especially distinguished herself by her intellectual antics in her line of procedure. (Her husband was much younger than herself, handsome and prosperous.)"

Despite the slurs of jealous wives and the scorn of the press, crowds of well-wishers saluted the sisters on their departure from Troy. Fortified by their triumphs in smaller cities, Margaret and her daughters made another stop in Albany then took the night boat south on the Hudson River for New York City.

By the first week of June 1850, the Fox sisters had settled into a suite at Barnum's Hotel, an establishment on the corner of Broadway and Maiden Lane owned by a cousin of the famed impresario.[4] As she walked along Broadway, Maggie, who thrived on Rochester's noise and confusion, must have reveled in New York City's sensory assault: rumbling carriages and clanging fire bells; choruses of voices in different accents and languages; slogans splashed across brick walls and banners hanging from windows and lampposts; muddy streets and marble buildings; odors of garbage and manure, whiffs of ocean breeze and ladies' fancy perfume. "Faces and coats of all patterns, bright eyes, whiskers, spectacles, hats, bonnets, caps, all hurrying along in the most apparently inextricable confusion. One would think it a grand Gala Day," wrote one awed observer.[5]

Exploding in population, area, and wealth, New York had emerged as the nation's major metropolis. Imitating the banker and conspicuous trendsetter August Belmont, the wealthy were moving north of the city's business district to Fifth Avenue and Union Square, building marble mansions, and driving about town in gilded carriages, some drawn by as many as four sleek horses. Deluxe hotels—nineteen would be constructed between 1850 and 1854—featured ornate lobbies with overstuffed divans, red-flocked wallpaper, and glistening chandeliers. The A. T. Stewart department store, designed like an Italian palace, lured customers not just with its luxurious goods but with its fifteen plate-glass display windows, walls festooned with paintings, and full-length Parisian mirrors in which customers could view the ultimate product: themselves.

The age of public display had been born: it was splendid to look, see, admire, and be seen. New Yorkers—rich and working-class alike—aimed to be fashionable, a goal that rivaled older aspirations such as respectability and gentility.

In the nation's commercial and manufacturing capital, newly arrived immigrants joined the native born in search of a livelihood or, better yet, a fortune. Sometimes the city's population seemed comprised entirely of isolated individuals with no friends or family, no past or community. Without reference points, who could tell if people were what they said?

One widely reported incident highlighted the dangers—real and imagined—of being duped in such an environment. In 1849 a charlatan named William Thompson greeted a stranger like an old acquaintance, asking the gullible gentleman if he had the "confidence" to lend him his watch. Watch in hand, Thompson disappeared. A journalist called him "a confidence man," and the apt phrase entered the lexicon.[6]

As some entrepreneurs grew rich, extremes of wealth and poverty emerged, but the majority of New Yorkers fell within the mutable bounds of the great middle class, some members comfortably entrenched there, others rising or falling in status, depending on their enterprise and luck that week or that year. While the poorest endured crowded, filthy tenements, even their lot in life wasn't static, and New Yorkers with a little money in their pockets had more choices. Some boarded in rows of brick houses. The well-to-do might buy one of the newly constructed brownstones that lined side streets.

Professionals and wage earners alike, whatever their tastes and finances, enjoyed going out on the town, whether to restaurants, oyster saloons, theaters, dance halls, summer gardens, concerts, lectures, or operas. New York allegedly had more theaters than any other city of its size in the world, although the presence of prostitutes in the balconies often deterred respectable women from attending.

Men of all classes visited houses of prostitution. They did so, respectable husbands protested, to save their virtuous wives from the onerous burdens of sex.

New York was also the newspaper capital of the nation. With literacy approaching 90 percent among white adults, access to printed information was a common denominator among New Yorkers.[7] Innovations in printing meant that more newspapers could be sold, and sold cheaply, than ever before. Publishers raced to scoop their competitors, and the man and woman on the street were deluged daily with lurid gossip, sentimental anecdotes, and vital news about the city, the nation, and the world.

Horace Greeley, the iconoclastic editor of the *New York Tribune,* was one of the nation's most influential voices and tireless crusaders. Under his guidance the *Tribune* covered literature as well as news; championed the working class, women's rights, and abolition; and lent moral support to many of the utopian movements of the age.

Greeley's interest in spirit communication wasn't entirely objective; his curiosity, like that of many other investigators, was emotional as well as intellectual in origin. He and his wife, Mary, had lost four of their five children, the last boy less than a year before the Fox sisters' visit to New York. In 1849 the couple's golden-haired, five-year-old son, Pickie—his parents' favorite child, the light of their lives—had died suddenly of cholera.

"The one sunburst of joy that has gladdened my rugged pathway has departed . . ." Greeley mourned to his close friend, the author Margaret Fuller. After Pickie's death, Mary Greeley urged her husband to learn more about spirit communication.[8]

Even so, he wasn't the first visitor to the Fox sisters' suite. "They have already been visited by a number of persons," Greeley reported on June 5, 1850, "all of whom have been astonished at the developments made to them, and some more or less convinced of their supernatural origin." He described Leah as a lady of about twenty-five, an unwitting compliment that must have thrilled her, for she not only radiated a youthful vivacity but also suffered a reputation in her family for vanity. He also noted her "pleasing and intelligent countenance." To him, all the sisters seemed refined and their behavior proper. Their skin was almost transparently pale, he observed, like that of subjects susceptible to mesmeric influence.

Greeley heard the raps, felt the vibrations, and received correct answers to his questions, but he left the Fox sisters' rooms as baffled and curious as he was when he entered. He had gone there with a friend who received only one correct answer to his six different questions. The whole "curious and puzzling affair," Greeley concluded, could be "stripped of all supernatural interest" and still merit further investigation.

Usually joined by Margaret, a gray-haired bastion against insolent liberties, Kate, Maggie, and Leah conducted their sessions in one of the hotel parlors, gathering their guests around a large table that sat up to thirty people. They held sessions at 10 AM, 5 PM, and 8 PM, fitting private meetings between the group sessions. The sisters went to bed each night exhausted but during their long working hours found the crowds generally courteous.

Journalists, politicians, businessmen, doctors, lawyers, and ministers—those who could afford to pay—jammed the sessions. A significant sampling of Americans showed up at the door: "from sunbrowned Hoosier of the West to the Jewelled aristocracy of New York," the *Tribune* reported.[9] So popular were the seances that a well-known singer incorporated a new song, "The Rochester Knockings at Barnum's Hotel," into her Broadway act.[10]

Many investigators emerged from the hotel sharing Greeley's mystification. "The production of the sounds is hard to explain, and still stranger," mused the lawyer George Templeton Strong, "is the accuracy with which the ghosts guess of whom one is thinking—his age, his residence, vocation, and the like." After carefully weighing different possibilities, such as the sisters' ability to use sleight of hand or to read clues from facial expressions, he eliminated the notion of trickery and "deliberate legerdemain." He was inclined to believe that a mysterious but natural cause was at work, "some magnetic or electrical or mesmeric agency" that propelled the young mediums, a power that they themselves couldn't explain.[11]

Strong may have dismissed legerdemain not only because he saw no evidence of it but also because he doubted the sisters' capabilities. Nineteenth-century professional stage magicians often compared their performances to scientific exhibitions, masculine work that involved experiments in optics and chemistry and that was analytical and rational in nature. In contrast, women—long credited with wielding supernatural or spiritual powers as saints, sorceresses, and witches—were perceived as spiritual beings even in their domestic role. It may have been easier for some visitors to view the Fox sisters as mediums or sway to mesmerism than to accept the possibility of their being innately talented, largely self-taught conjurers.

The most famous seance the Fox sisters conducted in New York, held at the home of the prominent author and minister Rufus Griswold, was attended by members of the nation's intellectual elite. Among others, Griswold hosted James Fenimore Cooper, author of the *Leatherstocking Tales;* George Ripley, the *Tribune*'s literary critic and a founder of Brook Farm, the recently defunct experiment in communal living; George Bancroft, former secretary of the navy, historian, and statesman; the poet William Cullen Bryant; and N. P. Willis, editor of the *Home Journal,* a magazine that kept the fashionable apprised of what was "new, charming, or instructive in the brilliant circle of city life."[12]

The Fox party consisted of Margaret, whom Ripley called "an elderly lady, the mother of the ghost-seers"; Leah, whom he referred to as "a married lady" rather than "a widowed lady," as she presumably had resurrected Bowman Fish for the occasion, having killed him off but a few months before; Kate and Maggie; and "a couple of gentlemen from Rochester whose names we did not learn."

Calvin, now the Fox sisters' constant companion, was certainly one of the unnamed; the other gentleman remains a mystery. Ripley's failure to ascertain such basic facts is intriguing. It suggests that the literati didn't care to be bothered with those whom they considered beneath them in class or intellect except as they were a curiosity or provided entertainment. And it raises the possibility that the investigators weren't quite the eagle-eyed detectives they assumed themselves to be.

"For some time," Ripley wrote in the June 8 issue of the *Tribune,* "perhaps a little over half an hour after the arrival of the ladies no sounds were heard, and the company gave obvious symptoms of impatience. They were then requested to draw nearer the table, which was in front of the ladies, and form themselves into a compact circle. Soon after faint sounds began to be heard from under the floor, around the table, and in different parts of the room. They increased in loudness and frequency, becoming so clear and distinct that no one could deny their presence, nor trace them to any visible causes."

James Fenimore Cooper was one of the individuals invited "to enter the supra-mundane sphere." He proceeded to interrogate the spirits, Ripley wrote, "with the most imperturbable self-possession and deliberation.

"After several desultory questions from which no satisfactory answers were obtained, Mr. C. commenced a new series of inquiries. 'Is the person I inquire about a relative?' 'Yes,' was at once indicated by the knocks."

Cooper, it turned out, was thinking of his sister. How many years ago had she died?

For a few moments a clatter of rapid raps confounded the sitters, "some counting forty-five, others forty-nine, fifty-four, etc." Finally the spirit agreed to rap slowly enough for a consensus to be reached at the number fifty.

Cooper then asked about the cause of death, presenting a number of chilling options: Struck by lightning? Drowned at sea? Thrown by a horse? The raps pounded on the latter, and Cooper confirmed that fifty years ago his sister had been killed in such a fall.

In the end George Ripley remained on the fence about the raps. In concluding his article, he explained that Kate, Maggie, and Leah "have no theories to offer in explanation of the acts of their mysterious attendants, and apparently have no control of their incomings or outgoings. But if the raps are not made by their agency, are they made by the spirits of the departed?"

He provided no answer to his own question.

Visitors disagreed about the raps and their origin, but a number of skeptics emerged with a favorable opinion of the sisters, who were complimented on the good humor and ease with which they handled the visiting crowds. Several reporters noted how attractive the girls were, one calling Maggie "a very pretty, arch-looking, black-eyed, and rather modestly behaved young girl."[13] Modestly behaved, he seemed to imply, for a young woman with an arch look who happened to be engaged in such unconventional behavior.

The girls' charm had a paradoxical effect. On the one hand, it drew a scandalous number of gentlemen to their door. On the other hand, the mediums' very presence exerted its own mesmeric influence, disarming many of their most suspicious critics and giving the sisters leeway to forge ahead with their activities. The spell that they cast silenced only some of their critics, however. Others remained determined to expose the sisters as frauds and subjected them to tests that may have enhanced the spirits' reputations but surely damaged those of Kate, Maggie, and Leah.

"The only thing approaching an indignity we had to complain of among ourselves," Leah later admitted, "was the frequency with which committees of ladies would retire with us to disrobe and reclothe us, the holding of our feet, etc."[14]

William Fishbough, an early colleague of Andrew Jackson Davis, complained in the *Tribune* about one especially egregious encounter. Challenged by a man named Davies, the sisters consented to be examined by a group of mutually agreed upon women at a mutually agreed upon time. Ignoring the ground rules, however, one afternoon Davies and his wife interrupted a seance unannounced, rudely demanding that the sisters instantly submit to the proposed test. Davies further insisted on its being conducted by his wife and the three women who happened to be present for the seance. The men, of course, discreetly left the room.

After the investigation Mr. Davies delivered the committee's report, since the four gentlewomen professed themselves too modest to deliver it. The report "was to the following effect," the indignant William Fishbough wrote in his letter to the *Tribune*.

1. That the ladies [the sisters] had been disrobed with the exception of their nether garments, and that the most thorough investigation had failed to disclose any machine by which the sounds might be produced.

2. That the ladies, after being unclothed, had been placed in a variety of positions, and still the sounds were heard, while the most careful watching had failed to detect any physical movements which could account for their production.

Although Mrs. Davies had tentatively ventured a guess "that the sounds might be produced by the 'cracking of the bones of the ladies,'" the origin of the raps, Fishbough concluded triumphantly, had remained a mystery.[15]

Fishbough kindly intended to lend his support to the Fox sisters, but in effect he had produced some racy reading for the *Tribune's* audience. The public display of the nude or partially clothed human body was permissible in art, and museumgoers enthusiastically admired the female form in all its glory depicted in paintings and statues of gods and goddesses, peasants from another era, or island girls from distant lands. These images were cloaked, not with skirts, but with the romance of the long ago and far away.

Otherwise, discussion of the naked or partially clothed female body was taboo, certainly in any conversation having to do with respectable women who were neither actresses nor prostitutes. And while the Fox sisters could claim spiritual justification for their states of undress, they had ventured into dangerous territory by submitting to the invasive examinations of their contemporaries. Their behavior, in fact, was so daring that it points either to the strength of their ambition or to the courage of their convictions. Perhaps the two motivations became linked, at least for a time.

What exactly were Kate, Maggie, and Leah thinking—and doing—as they met with hosts of curious, kind, skeptical, hostile, earnest, and intrusive investigators during the summer months of 1850? Were the Fox sisters engaged in deliberate fraud? The victims of self-deception? The standard-bearers of a cause?

The spirits may have chosen them for a mission, but human motives also must have come into play to spur them on their course. Certainly the lure of fame and money played a role for Leah and excitement and adventure for Maggie. Whimsical and given to flights of fantasy, Kate may sometimes have merged her sisters' wishes with the spirits' and her own.

In August, just before the sisters left New York, they were guests for several days at the Greeleys' home, a farm in an area called Turtle Bay on the still countrified edges of Manhattan. After they departed Greeley published the most unequivocal defense of them that he had issued to date. He reminded his readers that the mediums had been subjected to every conceivable test by hundreds of citizens. Their rooms had been searched, they had been repeatedly disrobed and examined, they had been scrutinized not just in their hotel but in the homes of many discerning New Yorkers.

"Whatever may be the origin or cause of the 'rappings,'" Greeley stated, "the ladies in whose presence they occur do not make them. We tested this thoroughly, and to our entire satisfaction. Their conduct and bearing is as unlike that of deceivers as possible; and we think no one acquainted with them could believe them at all capable of engaging in so daring, impious, and shameful a juggle as this would be if they caused the sounds. And it is not possible that such a juggle should have been so long perpetuated in public."[16]

While his stance reflected careful, thoughtful investigation, it is not irrelevant that Horace Greeley had suffered another grievous loss only three weeks earlier. For many years he had found welcome companionship in Margaret Fuller, former editor of the *Dial* and author of *Woman in the Nineteenth Century*. She wrote columns for the *Tribune* and for a while had lived—as a friend and perhaps buffer between the spouses—in the Greeleys' house. But in the late 1840s Fuller had traveled abroad to report for the *Tribune* on the republican revolution in Italy; there she had met and had a child with the marchese Angelo Ossoli, whom she later married. Her long absence overseas had left an echoing silence in the lives of both Horace and Mary Greeley, who were looking forward to her return that summer of 1850.

On their way back to the United States in July, Margaret Fuller and her family died in a shipwreck off the coast of the United States, so close to land that horrified men and women on the beach watched, helpless, as the ship sank.[17]

The Greeleys were devastated, in need of solace. Both of them had been taken with Kate and genuinely moved by the girl's—or the spirits'—powers of insight. Horace was convinced that she would benefit from a first-rate education, an important tool for improving a young woman's options. With schooling, she could teach or write for women's magazines or marry a better class of man. Yearning for comfort not only from the spirits but certainly from the child too, the Greeleys invited Kate to live with them that fall, as Margaret Fuller once had. The Fox family accepted the invitation on Kate's behalf, but the opportunity meant another separation between the thirteen-year-old girl and her mother and sisters. The cost exacted by the spirits was high.

The summer the Fox sisters introduced the spirits to New York, death was on everyone's mind, intruding its grim presence alarmingly into politics when President Zachary Taylor contracted cholera and died after an illness of five days. While mourning the dead, the nation assessed the living, wondering exactly what impact Taylor's successor, Millard Fillmore, would have on the issue of slavery. He was expected by some to be a "healer," a code word selectively used to imply that he was more sympathetic to the South than his predecessor had been.[18]

That autumn Congress enacted the Compromise of 1850 with little objection from President Fillmore. Among other provisions, the compromise included the Fugitive Slave Law, which empowered federal agents to find and return escaped slaves to the South, even those who had reached free soil in the North, and which made harboring fugitives a federal offense punishable by six months in prison.

Abolitionists were stunned by the severity of the measure, however much they had anticipated its passage. Fugitives could be kidnapped from the homes, stores, and streets of Northern cities. Those who were recaptured often faced harsh reprisals and even death at the hands of white plantation owners or overseers; and men and women like the Posts who ran stations on the Underground Railroad were in danger of arrest.

Far away as she was from her Rochester friends, Kate's worries that fall were personal not political; she was predictably miserable as the Greeleys' guest at their farm, a house bitterly labeled "Castle Doleful" by Horace, who managed to be there infrequently himself. She went to school daily except Sunday, most likely as a student at one of the private academies for fashionable young ladies that were proliferating in New York. Her teachers were kind and her studies interesting, and she enjoyed her dance lessons on Mondays and Saturdays.

Enrolled under an assumed name to protect her privacy, however, she had no chance to make friends or socialize with anyone her own age. Instead, most of her time outside of school was spent at Castle Doleful. While Horace reported on the important affairs of the nation, she was left in the company of his angry, grief-stricken wife, Mary.

Lonely and sad, Kate confided her plight in a letter to "My Dear Friend," most likely John E. Robinson of Rochester, a family friend to whom she turned for sympathy and attention. Her attachment may have reflected a desire for a more involved father figure than John Fox.

"I think you have forgotten me as I am shure [sic] you would have answered my letter," she wailed. She confessed that she was powerfully homesick, then turned to another serious problem, admitting that she couldn't abide the morbid Mary Greeley.[19]

"O how I hate her," she exclaimed, adding a few sentences later, "I have cried myself almost sick. O why did I leave my mother. . . ."

She had tried writing to Leah, Kate complained, but the letters went unanswered. She had made up her mind to leave New York at the end of the fall semester of school, and she was suffering from the terrible headaches that also afflicted Maggie and Leah.

"O John if you knew how sick at heart I am you would come after me," she pleaded.

It was probably a plea she had expressed earlier to her mother and Leah. But Margaret generally complied with what Leah wanted, and Leah surely wasn't eager to remove Kate from under the wing of the influential Horace Greeley.

Despite tensions in the Greeley household, there were some interesting spirit communications, too. Immortal little Pickie recalled once disturbing Horace at work in his study and his father sternly asking him to leave the room. During a seance Mary expressed regret over the incident, but the son's spirit loyally defended the newspaper editor, rapping that sometimes his father simply had to work very hard.

"Mrs. Greeley is more and more confirmed in the communications with the spiritual world by 'Rappings,'" Horace Greeley confided in a letter to a friend, "and I am sure it cannot be accounted for by merely human agency. It is a puzzle which you will some day be interested to investigate—don't look at it till then," he counseled. "A mere fraud would not live so long and spread so widely."[20]

Greeley, along with almost every other journalist, reported extensively on Jenny Lind's first visit to the United States in September 1850, a happy distraction for the nation from the disturbing subject of politics. Known as the Swedish nightingale, the singer was sponsored by P. T. Barnum, and she was promoted not just for her beautiful voice but also for her fine morals and ladylike manners. Lind was a major celebrity, and New Yorkers of every social class packed her concerts.[21]

Like the word *scientist* and the phrase *confidence man,* the modern notion of celebrity was a nineteenth-century product. Newspapers and the telegraph were able to excite national and international interest in authors, performers, and lecturers; improved transportation allowed sponsors to create a circuit of cities for the stars to visit. Fame had become a manufactured commodity.

Jenny Lind expressed interest in meeting another celebrity, one who was emerging and more controversial: Kate Fox. In his autobiography Greeley described this seance as not entirely successful. Lind arrived with a retinue of strangers, who were seated around a large table. As soon as loud raps broke out, she fixed Greeley with an imperial stare and commanded, "Take your hands from under the table!"[22]

Much to Greeley's consternation, he realized that Lind was accusing him of creating the sounds. He clasped his hands over his head and, while raps continued around him, patiently and uncomfortably waited for the sitting to end.

Unfortunately, there's no record of how Kate experienced the seance, although other accounts suggest the meeting ended on a happier note, with Lind not only praising the young medium but kissing her sweetly in farewell. If true, the singer's kindness perhaps helped dispel for a moment Kate's depression over life at Castle Doleful.

With Kate in New York, Maggie and Leah—the latter no longer hesitant to claim her own powers of mediumship—resumed holding seances at home in Rochester. They described their work in letters to the *Spirit Messenger*, one of a growing number of newspapers and journals devoted to spirit communication.

"The ladies . . . inform us," the paper reported, "that, in the presence of a respectable circle of friends and neighbors . . . new and startling demonstrations were made. . . . The sounds were very loud upon the walls, floor, and other parts of the house. Sometimes sounds imitating heavy footsteps were heard, apparently upon the floor of the room in which the company were sitting."[23]

The spirits of Dr. John Webster, a chemistry professor at Harvard, and Dr. George Parkman, uncle to the famed historian Francis Parkman, were frequent visitors to the Fox cottage on Troup Street. Webster had been executed that year for murdering Parkman, a wealthy benefactor of the college, in a dispute over a bad debt. It must have been a nasty disagreement; the victim's dismembered body was found beneath the professor's laboratory.[24]

The two men became contrite friends in the afterlife. Webster generously acknowledged that there were "many extenuating circumstances on both sides—and all our difficulties are settled." The spirits seem to have been constantly at work, albeit after the fact, to reconcile the differences and disagreements that had troubled their mortal relationships.

What the *Spirit Messenger* on another occasion referred to as the fact "of the progress of the spirit in goodness and happiness hereafter" could sometimes confuse or frustrate people.[25] The spirit of John Calhoun, the recently deceased senator from South Carolina, returned in an effort to avert the impending national crisis over slavery. Calhoun, that stalwart champion of the South and spokesman for slavery in life, now made a case in favor of abolition. A relative of the Posts confessed that she "would much rather he had given evidence while here for his testimony now is not of much value. . . ."[26]

While startling in some respects, Calhoun's shift may have been predictable. From its inception, spirit communication had attracted reformers who rejected the established order, whether in religion, politics, or social convention. Along with proponents of abolition, the growing swell of believers included those who urged diet and health reform, who decried the current state of prisons, and who promoted communities based on socialist principles. Women's rights advocates campaigned not only for suffrage but also for changes in marriage laws. More radical yet, some men and women questioned the very concept of marital monogamy, arguing that it deprived individuals of the chance to find their true spiritual partners. Critics sometimes equated faith in the spirits with advocacy of "free love," exaggerating the relationship between the two in the interests of discrediting both.

Given the convictions of many of the mortals they visited, it's hardly surprising that most spirits supported reforms. Not unlike an individual's conscience freed from the fetters of authority, they often countenanced change when established religious institutions urged caution or noninvolvement or rejected reforms altogether. Not every spirit, however, could be expected to undergo a transformation as extreme as John Calhoun's, nor did all spirits agree with one another or progress at the same pace. Opinions varied sharply in the other world, as they did in established churches and the nation.

A gentleman in Memphis, Tennessee, while under the influence of mesmerism, asked, "Is the holding of slaves in conformity with the eternal laws of Deity?" The spirit he addressed equivocated, responding with a compromise position: "In time, but not in eternity."

Maggie stayed with Leah in Rochester for much of the fall, but in November 1850 they divided up their labors. Seventeen-year-old Maggie returned, alone, for a visit to Troy, New York. This was the city where she and Leah had experienced troubles with the married ladies the previous spring, and far more serious difficulties arose on this trip. Motivated by jealous wives, fears of witchcraft, or both, five men began following Maggie by day and spying on her at night. Her hosts, Robert Bouton and his wife, feared that the men were assassins and that "a deep plot" had been laid to destroy the medium.

"Last night Mrs. B. and Margaretta went to the door of a shed together," Bouton wrote to Leah, "and a stone was thrown at them. One man on the roof made an angry exclamation on finding that the two were together, instead of Margaretta alone."

Violence escalated. Maggie's enemies, who hid in the lumberyard next to the Boutons' property, first hurled rocks through the windows then broke into the house. Prepared for the attack, the family drove the men away. After locking Maggie in a small room for her own protection, Bouton telegraphed Leah to come immediately and in secret to escort her sister home.[27]

The panic-stricken Leah boarded the train for Troy, convinced the whole way that mysterious men were stalking her. Her fears were reinforced on her arrival, when she saw her host brandishing a pistol to hold her enemies at bay. A mob greeted them in front of the house, but the Boutons' friends shielded her by lifting her up and carrying her bodily inside. She found Maggie sobbing and vomiting from fright in the room that had been her prison for several days. Shots were fired through the windows, but the agitators eventually dispersed. With Maggie too ill to travel far, Leah took her to Albany to recuperate.

Fears were difficult to dispel. For weeks Maggie cried out in her sleep. After returning to Rochester Leah became convinced that confederates of Maggie's Troy persecutors had been prowling around the house in her absence. But no further incidents occurred, and the two of them resumed holding seances, safely among their Rochester friends.

If the Fox sisters were fast becoming modern celebrities—promoted, loved, and despised as fervently as movie stars, athletes, and others in the public eye are today—they also fell within a long-established tradition that accorded fame, not just to royalty, military heroes, and statesmen, but also to religious figures. A few women in the United States had served as religious leaders, for example Mother Ann Lee of the Shakers, but virtually all middle-class women in the nineteenth century were responsible for shaping the religious and moral atmosphere of the home. Children, moreover, had been spiritualized and sentimentalized by the Romantic movement, which painted them, as Wordsworth wrote, "trailing clouds of glory."

Kate and Maggie, country girls on the cusp of adolescence at the time of the first raps, benefited from the aura of religiosity surrounding women and children. To many of those who believed in spirit communication, it seemed that Emanuel Swedenborg and Andrew Jackson Davis had prepared the way for new revelations but that the two young mediums had ushered in a new stage of human development, the dawning of an era in which human beings would recognize that death did not exist.

Charlotte Fowler Wells, a publisher and phrenologist, was among those who, in the wake of the Fox sisters' New York visit, began to host private gatherings to commune with the spirits. Horace Greeley sometimes attended these events, occasionally bringing Kate with him. By December 1850 members of the New York Circle, as the group called itself, were meeting on a weekly basis without charging fees, and Wells's brother, Edward Fowler, had become a medium himself, passing into a trancelike state to communicate with the other world. In a process known as automatic writing, the spirits sometimes used his hand as an instrument to transmit messages; alternatively, words sometimes seemed to materialize on paper without human intervention in a process called spirit writing. Messages were often scrawled in hieroglyphics or foreign languages with which Fowler allegedly wasn't familiar, and they generally were philosophical or theological in content, elaborating, for example, on the seamless connection between matter and spirit.[28]

Similar circles were forming in other cities: Philadelphia, Providence, Cleveland, Boston, St. Louis, and elsewhere across the nation. Eliab Capron, by now working on the *Providence Morning Mirror,* claimed that there were fifty to one hundred mediums in Auburn, New York, alone.

"The ball once set rolling in New York," the historian Emma Hardinge wrote two decades later, "sped on with an impetus which soon transcended the power of the press, pulpit or public to arrest it, despite of every force that was brought to bear against it."[29]

NINE

"THE IMPUTATION OF BEING IMPOSTERS"

As the Fox sisters' influence grew, so too did the number of battles waged in the press over the spirits' authenticity. One of the mediums' most virulent antagonists, Stanley Grimes, was a well-known lecturer on mesmerism and phrenology. He was also the man who had first magnetized Andrew Jackson Davis, although he had dismissed the soon-to-be famous seer as a weak and uninteresting subject, a mistake Grimes surely regretted.

In a series of letters to the *Tribune,* Grimes adopted a scattershot approach to the sisters, accusing them of virtually every trick in the book, from ventriloquism to the use of mechanical devices to collusion. Their success depended in part on their sex, he wrote; men didn't have the luxury of voluminous skirts to conceal their feet. Worse than that, he asserted, the mediums hired confederates to research their mortal visitors' backgrounds. From a phrenological point of view, he absolved Kate and Maggie of any innate predisposition to have chosen such a course for themselves. He pointed the finger at Leah, however, whose phrenological chart apparently revealed the ominous traits of intelligence, skepticism, and masculine ambition.[1]

C. Chauncey Burr, a lawyer who became a Universalist minister then a lecturer on mesmerism and electrobiology like Stanley Grimes, had decided to make exposing the Fox sisters his fourth career. His attacks multiplied in January 1851 when he and his brother, Heman, announced that they had produced the raps "so loud that they were distinctly heard in a hall that was crowded with an audience of a thousand people."[2]

They had managed this accomplishment, the Burr duo informed readers of the *Tribune,* by cracking their toes. Heman Burr subsequently responded indignantly to those who doubted this achievement, providing them with a list of variables that he claimed could alter the raps' volume and tone, such as a particular toe's size and strength, a shoe's fit, a foot's moisture or dryness, and the substance—wood, glass, or metal—on which the medium stood.[3]

Believers in the spirits ridiculed "Toe-ology," as some papers gleefully labeled C. Chauncey Burr's theory. But his demonstrations attracted a new class of critics to test the Fox sisters: professors of medicine and medical doctors. Maggie and Leah were about to come under harsher and more expert scrutiny than any they had endured before.

Not that the medical profession could call itself an altogether objective or disinterested party, since many mediums, like mesmerists, claimed the ability to diagnose and heal disease. Mesmerists credited these powers to electromagnetic fluids in the atmosphere and body, while mediums relied on the advice and guidance of the spirits. Already losing patients to the more gentle regimens of homeopathic physicians, some medical men sensed competition from the other world and quickly dismissed all mediums as quacks.

Despite her unhappiness in the fall, Kate had agreed to stay in New York that winter, probably because Margaret finally recognized her daughter's cry for companionship and joined her there. Reunited following the Troy fiasco, Maggie and Leah set out together in February 1851, traveling west from Rochester to meet the residents of Buffalo, New York, who were invited to attend sittings at the sisters' hotel, the Phelps House.

Later that month the Buffalo *Commercial Advertiser* published a letter by three medical professors at the University of Buffalo—Austin Flint, Charles A. Lee, and C. B. Coventry—who described a visit they had recently made to the sisters' quarters. Everything about the letter struck Maggie and Leah as an insult, particularly the tone in which the doctors referred to them as "females," a term that one influential magazine editor sniffed could apply as readily to horses as to ladies.

"Reasoning by way of exclusion," the doctors wrote, they had gone into the meeting having agreed in advance that a spiritual explanation for the raps couldn't be considered until all possible physiological explanations had been eliminated. And the gentlemen had emerged from the meeting convinced, after careful observation, that Maggie's barely perceptible bodily movements produced the noises.[4]

Maggie's tired expression, they argued, gave her away, proving not only that "the sounds were due to the agency of the younger sister" but also that they involved her conscious effort, "the action of the will, through voluntary muscles, on the joints." Then the doctors dropped their bombshell: by coincidence, they had met a woman who produced the exact same raps by using, not her toes, but her knees.

"Without entering at this time into a very minute anatomical and physiological explanation," the doctors wrote, embarking on just such an explanation, "it is sufficient to state that . . . the large bone of the leg (the tibia) is moved laterally upon the lower surface of the thigh bone (the femur) giving rise, in fact, to partial lateral dislocation . . . occasioning a loud noise, and the return of the bone to its place is attended by a second sound."

The force of such a dislocation, they continued, was sufficient to jar doors and tables if the medium's offending knee was in contact with the furniture.

When a critic delivered a copy of the accusatory article to her room, Leah slammed the door on him. Then she and Maggie responded in kind by placing a challenge to the doctors in the newspapers. They resented "the imputation of being imposters," the sisters wrote, but were nevertheless willing to undergo further examinations, provided that six of their own friends could be present as witnesses. If indeed the raps were to be explained on anatomical or physiological principles, so be it. Let the doctors expose any humbug if they could.

A series of grueling investigations at the Phelps House ended in a draw. The sisters again agreed to be contorted into a variety of positions: heels on cushions, legs extended, feet elevated. During one four-hour experiment, the doctors sat directly in front of Maggie and at periodic intervals seized her knees through her dress. At the insistence of the eight or ten onlookers, the investigators reluctantly abandoned their plan to bandage Maggie's legs, cynically noting that the young medium's tears had "excited much sympathy."

Afterward, the doctors reaffirmed their conviction: Maggie made the raps; virtually no sounds were heard when her knees were held or otherwise constrained. On the rare occasion when she managed to produce a faint rap, Dr. Lee (who defined his role as "being the holder") maintained that he could feel the motion of the bone.

In a subsequent letter, to account for the way the sounds varied and seemed to ricochet around a room, the doctors turned to the laws of acoustics. "Those having a nice musical ear," wrote Dr. Lee, "can generally locate [the raps] directly in [Miss Fox's] vicinity. But if the attention is drawn to another part of the room, then, as in the case of ventriloquism, the sounds seem to proceed *thence.*"

Leah responded with her own aggressive press campaign, skewering the Buffalo doctors for deliberate obfuscation and stating that they had heard many more raps than they were willing to admit. However, she did acknowledge occasional lapses on the part of the spirits, admitting that "when our feet were placed on cushions stuffed with shavings, and resting on our heels, there were not sounds heard. . . ." But she insisted that the spirits had been well within their rights to retreat, offended as they were by the harsh behavior of their medical persecutors.

The dispute, as Leah later said, "had put all Buffalo on the boil." Slogging through deep rivers of melting snow and mud, the result of the unseasonably warm, sunny March weather, eager crowds descended on the Phelps House. Demonstrating a gift for public relations, Leah refused for a fortnight to charge a fee. So crowded were the sessions that Charles White Kellogg, a produce commission merchant, complained about being turned away twice before finally having a chance to meet with the sisters. "Mrs. K and I visited Mrs. Fish and Miss Fox, the celebrated Rochester Knockers," he wrote on the evening of March 18.

"Amongst other remarkable demonstrations," Kellogg confided to his journal, "a large Dinner Bell & a small tea bell sitting under the table rang frequently & traveled from one end to the other, the large one frequently coming up agst. the table with such force as to knock the table, as hard as a man could strike it with a heavy hammer— knocking the candlestick six inches or more clear of the table & the candles out of the sticks, & put the candles out. The small bell would change from outside to inside of the large bell, both keeping their perpendicular position. A violin under the table was played & moved from place to place, so far as could be discovered by 13 of us, without human agency—in short, all was done without our being able to discover the why or *wherefore*."[5]

When Maggie and Leah left Buffalo in April 1851, they could readily call their visit a financial success. "Not a few of the principal gentlemen of the city sent us parting gifts of congratulations on a noble scale of munificence," recalled Leah, "as tributes of sympathy for what we had had to bear, and of gratitude for the demonstrative proofs of immortality it had been ours to bring to their experimental *knowledge*."[6]

Leah may have conducted a fortnight's worth of free sessions, but she could afford to do so. The Fox sisters were now financially secure enough to dress well, to travel more comfortably, and to give generous presents to their family and friends in Rochester and Wayne County. Perhaps in part because she felt so flush, Leah changed her residence in Rochester for a third time, moving to a fine, large home ideally situated on the corner of Troup and Sophia Streets, no longer on the edge but in the heart of Rochester's wealthy Third Ward. The stress of the Buffalo investigations and the strain of moving, however, were too much for her. Ill and exhausted, Leah took to her bed to recuperate.

Spring of 1851 found Kate and her mother still living in New York, spending most of their time at Castle Doleful but occasionally visiting other investigators. A student by day, Kate continued to participate in seances at night. As the Greeleys' guest, she received no fee for her work; she was considered a subject of scientific interest.

A New Yorker named Charles Partridge, a wealthy match manufacturer, had met both Kate and Maggie previously; like the Greeleys, he and his wife were so drawn to Kate that they invited her to their home for several weeks that March. According to an account by the Fox family's friend Eliab Capron, Partridge's neighbor adamantly insisted the medium was a fake until, finally, the spirits politely inquired whether anything could change his mind.

"He replied," Capron wrote, "'To see the medium stand up in the chair so that we can see her feet, and then hear the rapping.' The spirits then spelled, 'Cathy . . . stand up in the chair.' She stood up in the chair, and the rapping was made in various places, and in great abundance. She was then requested to sit down, which she did, when the lamp on the table was moved about, without any visible means, to the entire satisfaction of the skeptic."[7]

Perhaps in reaction to having to convince so many suspicious strangers of her worth, fourteen-year-old Kate's affections for her family's tried-and-true friend, John E. Robinson of Rochester, seem to have developed into a full-blown schoolgirl's crush. A bachelor twice her age, Robinson may have been flattered at first, but his indulgence soon shifted into a serious concern for Kate's welfare. As he wrote to Leah, the little girl who captivated everyone with her compelling presence and her intuitive, or spiritual, gifts was swiftly growing up.

"I received a good letter from your witch sister, my darling little Katie, this morning," he told Leah. "She writes with much cheerfulness. Says she has commenced another quarter at her school. . . . She says also she is 'crazy' to see me! You know just about what is intended to be understood when she thus addresses me (her friend and advisor); but Cathie is fast learning to be a woman, and my prayer is that she may escape the bitter trials through which you and your mother have been called to pass."[8]

The trials to which Robinson undoubtedly referred were the consequences of a rash, precipitous, and unsuitable choice of husband, a choice Margaret had made at sixteen and Leah at younger than fifteen.

Not all of Kate's trusted allies were so protective of her, and in April 1851 the Wayne County township of Arcadia—home to her father and her brother, David—produced a traitor, or a liar. David's wife, Elizabeth, had a sister-in-law, Mrs. Norman Culver, who announced in a deposition that the previous year Kate had confessed to fraud. The deposition had been solicited by C. Chauncey Burr, who hadn't abandoned his efforts to destroy the Foxes.[9]

At the time, Culver explained, she had made up her mind to get at the truth behind the spirits. She waited until Maggie was away, then approached effusive Kate with a proposition: a cousin of hers wished to attend a seance, Culver said. How could she help Kate ensure the seance's success? Kate, Culver continued, had accepted the bait and volunteered to teach her how to be a medium.

"She said that when my cousin consulted the spirit, I must sit next to her," Culver testified, "and touch her arm when the right letter was called. I did so, and was able to answer nearly all the questions correctly. After I had helped her in this way a few times, she revealed to me the secret. The raps are produced by the toes. All the toes are used. . . . Catharine told me to warm my feet, or put them in warm water, and it would then be easier work to rap; she said that she sometimes had to warm her feet three or four times in the course of an evening. I found that heating my feet did enable me to rap a great deal easier."

According to Culver, Kate then moved on to admit to other tricks long familiar to magicians—for example, to reading facial clues and body language for answers:

"[Kate] said the reason why they asked people to write down several names on paper, and then point to them till the spirit rapped at the right one," Culver stated, "was to give them a chance to watch the countenances and motions of the persons, and that in that way they could nearly always guess right."

And to misdirecting the audience's attention:

"She told me," Culver recalled, "that . . . when I wished to make the raps sound distant on the wall, I must make them louder, and direct my own eyes earnestly where I wished them to be heard."

And to collusion:

"Catharine told me," Culver concluded, "that, when the committee held their ankles in Rochester [during the Corinthian Hall investigations], the Dutch servant-girl rapped with her knuckles under the floor from the cellar. The girl was instructed to rap whenever she heard their voices calling the spirits."

Eliab Capron derided Culver as Burr's pawn and contested her claims point by point. He asserted that, since Kate had been in Auburn during the Corinthian Hall demonstrations, she hardly could have known much about them. The investigations had been held at several different locations, he emphasized, without advance notice given to Leah and Maggie. And, he noted, the Fox family "did not have, and never had, a Dutch or other servant-girl in the family at Rochester up to the time of the investigation."

He failed to mention, however, that some of the investigations had been held at the Posts' home and that a Dutch servant had been working for the family at the time. Along with Amy, Jacob, and Joseph, the young woman whom Isaac called "our little Dutch girl" had loved to ask questions of the spirits.[10]

Even Mrs. Norman Culver's testimony failed to diminish popular interest in the sisters, although Kate no doubt felt betrayed. That spring, around the same time Culver's deposition was published and while Leah was still recuperating from her recent move, Maggie joined her mother and sister in New York City. There the mediums continued to build their own and the spirits' following. One highly influential newcomer was Judge John Worth Edmonds, chief justice of the New York State Supreme Court, who had become a serious investigator of the spirits soon after his wife's death in 1851.

Edmonds's state of mind when he met the sisters suggests the appeal of spirit communication for men and women who were grappling with changing ideas about the afterlife. "I was occupying all my leisure in reading on the subject of death, and man's existence afterward," he wrote. "I had, in the course of my life, read and heard from the pulpit so many contradictory and conflicting doctrines on the subject, that I hardly knew what to believe."[11]

He had remained dubious about the spirits, however, so much so that when he attended a seance at the home of Charles Partridge, the match manufacturer, on the night of May 21, 1851, Edmonds was still seeking proof which he hoped "should be entirely satisfactory."

To Partridge, that particular evening seemed to have been expressly "selected for the purpose of producing these proofs" to convince Edmonds. Maggie was there, as was Dr. John Gray, a respected homeopathic physician and a friend of the Fox family. Other participants included a white-haired medium named Henry Gordon, famous for his levitations, and an anonymous observer who, along with Partridge, left an account of the evening's events. Both accounts are worth quoting almost in their entirety, for the witnesses saw and heard very different things.

The session began with one member of the group playing the piano while the spirits marked time by raps. As Partridge wrote down his account, he felt the table on which he was leaning vibrate beneath his hands. Soon the spirits suggested that the room be darkened, the better to demonstrate their own otherworldly glow.

"We accordingly did so," wrote Partridge, "and the lights which had been desired, were at different times and in different places seen, sometimes resembling phosphorescent flames, occasionally forming luminous clouds moving about the room; sometimes they appeared like bright, glistening stars, and at other times, like sparkling crystals or diamonds. . . . Physical manifestations increased in variety and force, and continued for three hours during the whole of which time the Judge seemed to be in the possession of the spirits. Many things occurred to him (which he mentioned) that he alone could be conscious of; though we could perceive that something extraordinary was going on within and around him. Many things, however, occurred which all could witness and did.

"The card table before mentioned began to move with violent force from one side of our circle (which was large) to the other, rocking and raising up and coming down, and finally the leaf was shut up, the cover turned round in its place, the table was gently turned upside down and laid at our feet. . . . A chair, which stood outside of our circle and several feet from any one, was suddenly moved up to the circle and back, rocked, and finally, with great rapidity, conveyed from one end of the room to the other, winding its way among the people who sat there . . . at times passing with fearful rapidity within an inch or two of our persons.

"We were touched on different parts of our persons, simultaneously, as by a human hand, so distinctly that its size and temperature could be felt. . . . Mr. Gordon was required to go into a closet, and the door was shut by some invisible power.

"Some of the party, among whom was Judge Edmonds, were requested to go into another closet . . . where there was a guitar, bass viol and violin, all of which were played upon, separately at first, and finally all together, in marked time, which was beat out by raps, sometimes on the viols, floor, ceiling . . . the bow often touching the persons there.

"Afterward, the bass viol and violin were raised above their heads and out of the reach . . . and in this position they were played and rapped upon as by human fingers. . . .

"A dinner bell on the shelf was raised up and rung over their heads, then taken out into the parlor and carried over the heads of fifteen or twenty persons sitting in the circle there. . . . Another small bell was taken off the shelf, rung, and placed into and taken out of the hands of several persons. A pocket handkerchief was taken from the Judge's pocket, and tied into many knots, and put back again. . . .

"Such things," concluded Partridge, "went on for a period of about three hours, and it was asked: 'Why are these strange and apparently inconsiderable things done?' it was answered: 'that you may know it is super-terrestrial, and not the work of mortal hands.'"[12]

While Partridge viewed the manifestations with reverence, the observer who left an anonymous account also couldn't believe his own eyes.

"After the spirits desired the lights put out," the unidentified witness wrote, "and every vestige and gleam of light being excluded, in the most pitchy darkness, a series of proceedings took place which utterly and entirely disgusted me; of course, anything done in the dark is useless so far as convincing people goes. We sat and listened, for about one hour and a half, to a perfect pandemonium of noises, bangs on the table as loud as could be made by hand or foot, loud slaps, bells ringing loudly, the table creaking, flapping its leaves and turning quite upside down, as was announced by the exclamations of those about it, Judge Edmonds continually exclaiming, 'I'm touched—now I am tapped on the shoulder—hear that—now they are at my feet, now my head,' and then he would cry out, 'They are pulling my coat-tails—they are pulling me towards Margaretta.'. . . . Meanwhile the white-haired [medium, Henry Gordon] was going on in the most extraordinary manner, crying out, seemingly scuffling and contending with the spirits who wanted to take possession of him. At one time Dr. Gray says, 'They have lifted him up in the air,' and someone else rejoined, 'No, he is standing on his chair'; at length, amid a loud outcry, and exclamations of 'Don't, I don't want to; leave me alone,' accompanied by the noise of a struggle, he was dragged into the closet and shut up there; this we knew from Dr. Gray's exclamations. Presently Dr. Gray was also sent in there, then Judge Edmonds, finally all the mediums and some others. We were then favored with the most absurd series of noises from this closet that ever was heard: loud bangings, a chorus of Auld Lang Syne, sung by all the *closeted,* accompanied by raps on the door, and scrapings on an old violoncello, which was in the closet. . . . We left them at last at half-past eleven still in there, the noises going on as loud and meaningless as ever."[13]

What to one observer seemed miraculous, to the other seemed ridiculous. To Partridge, the manifestations that night offered proof of immortality, but to the other unidentified gentleman, they offered proof only of human credulity.

TEN

"MODERN SPIRITUALISM"

AS SOON AS Leah felt well enough after her recent illness, she began to think about expanding—and defending—the Fox sisters' work by traveling to new cities. Cleveland, Ohio, seemed a natural choice. She could anticipate a receptive audience, for the city already had a number of existing spirit circles and enthusiasts; moreover, she had been warned by friends that C. Chauncey Burr was plotting a major toe-snapping campaign there. Never one to sidestep a battle, Leah made plans to travel west in May of 1851, accompanied by Calvin, her sister Maria Smith, and Maria's toddler, Charlie. There was a certain amount of risk involved in more ways than one; Kate and Maggie were still in New York City with their mother, so for the first time outside of Rochester Leah was to meet the public on her own, without either of her more celebrated younger sisters by her side.

The editor of the *Cleveland Plain Dealer,* coincidentally named John Gray like the Fox family's New York friend, welcomed her with the hearty announcement: "There are to be rapping times in Cleveland this week." He knew the notice would sell papers, but he also was sympathetic to the idea of spirit communication and did little to hide his bias. He mocked the Burr brothers for their "jokes and grimaces" and labeled the Buffalo doctors' conclusions "lame and impotent."[1]

Leah and her entourage settled into a comfortable suite at the Dunham House, a bustling inn, tavern, and stagecoach stop. She held her own nicely, quickly impressing the influential Gray as an "intelligent lady, agreeably spoken." Her earnest manner, he commented, divested her "of all mystery which imagination has thrown about her person, and all prejudice which slander may have attached to her character."

Leah may have pleased John Gray, but the two "Misses Fox" delighted him even more when they finally joined their sister later in the month. The manifestations struck him as incrementally stronger in their presence. "They are very fine girls and with their older sister, make a very interesting group," Gray advised his readers. "By this accession the strength of the spiritual battery is largely increased, and the raps in their presence more than threefold than with Mrs. Fish alone." Leah graciously acknowledged that her little sisters were the world's most perfect mediums for spirit communication.[2]

Perhaps the strain of being once again on the road exacerbated tensions, however, for the sisters' nerves seemed frayed, and a disagreement with a Rochester friend, Lemira Kedzie, caused a flurry of quarrels. A reformer with close ties to Amy Post, Kedzie had chaperoned the girls to Cleveland and apparently expected to take them on from there to visit other western cities, a tour she hoped to launch from her hometown of Cincinnati. Kedzie's motives aren't clear; she may have counted on a share of the tour's income, envisioned herself as a good influence on the girls, or wished to be part of a mission to help spread the word.

Whatever the sisters may have agreed to beforehand, on arriving in Cleveland Kate and Maggie adamantly rejected the plan. Kedzie promptly turned to their older sister for help in bringing them into line, but by then Leah already knew she needed at least one of the girls by her side to boost "the strength of the spiritual battery." Negotiations ensued, winding up in a compromise. Maggie, who had often teamed up with Leah for arduous but successful investigations in the past, remained with her older sister and Calvin. Kate, by now used to working independently, went off to Cincinnati with Maria, little Charlie, and the disappointed Kedzie.

Some Cincinnati residents claimed to have heard strange raps long before noises were reported in Hydesville but to have kept the incidents secret. Then, after visiting the sisters in Rochester in 1850, Mrs. G. B. Bushnell had emerged as Cincinnati's first public medium—*public* a word mediums usually preferred to *professional.* By the time Kate stopped there in June 1851, the spirits already had built a loyal following. One interested investigator, an editor named William T. Coggshall, was especially impressed by the peaceful domestic setting of a seance he attended. As raps echoed through the room, he and Kate were chatting while Maria Smith was sewing and Lemira Kedzie was reading a newspaper.

"They must be remarkable women," he noted, "if they can attend to such business as this, and at the same time personate all the mysteries ascribed to them."[3]

Harmony didn't last. From Cincinnati, Kate's little group moved on to Columbus, Ohio, but here Kedzie's already compromised western tour ended abruptly when Maria's Charlie fell ill. Leah summoned everyone to return to Cleveland, where she claimed to heal the child with the help of the spirits. As soon as Charlie seemed well enough to travel, Maria returned home to Wayne County. Kedzie departed for Rochester shortly afterward, bitterly complaining that Leah was a weak and extravagant manager. Leah promptly developed a crippling headache that lasted for days, her own misery compounded by worry over Calvin, who had contracted a severe cold that had settled on his lungs. Being on tour had turned out to be an ordeal for all involved.

By late June matters were improving for everyone but Calvin, who was retching quantities of blood. Amy and Isaac Post's nineteen-year-old son, Joseph, visited Cleveland and reported news of the Fox family back to his parents. Margaret had finally made the journey to Ohio and had taken Kate back to Columbus to fulfill the medium's obligations there. Maggie and Leah were managing well. They "had one spat while I was there but soon got over it," Joseph wrote with the breezy familiarity of one who had witnessed other sisterly spats between them.[4] The terrible headaches that plagued Leah continued to come and go.

That June an abolitionist magazine began serializing a new novel by a former Ohio resident named Harriet Beecher Stowe: *Uncle Tom's Cabin*, the searing indictment of slavery that inflamed emotions North and South. In the wake of the Fugitive Slave Law of 1850, the Posts were sheltering as many as ten or twelve refugees a night in their home while also continuing their work on behalf of women's rights. Like many reformers on the front lines of the antislavery and women's rights movements, Amy Post derived strength and inspiration from her belief in the spirits. She corresponded with the Fox sisters regularly, and she believed that they deserved her gratitude for helping transform her life.

"I have often thought of thee and thy company since you left your beautiful home for an Ohio city," she wrote to Leah, "and have been much delighted to hear you have found friends who can appreciate the value and importance of this wonderful development to mankind."[5]

Amy expressed a loving debt to the mediums for helping her realize the spirit world existed, and her words provide insight into the Fox sisters' impact on their supporters' lives. "It is a wealth I had despaired of ever obtaining," Amy explained, "to be convinced that we have commenced to live a life which will never end—a life whose joys, too, are enhanced by our practices of goodness."

Although she had been drawn to such a vision in the past, Amy confessed that previously she had been unable to erase doubt, that her wish to believe had always been "accompanied with a desire for more *positive proof* of immortality."

The nature of the afterlife also had worried her. The fate to which orthodox and even some liberal denominations condemned those poor souls who failed to achieve salvation had seemed stark. "For some time before your family made me acquainted with this blessed Spirit-rapping dispensation," Amy explained, "I had become more settled in the belief . . . of there being no half-way house; but we must go either to Heaven or Hell."

How could anyone question the Fox sisters' integrity, Amy demanded, when they had accomplished so much?

"Oh! could strangers only know as I have known the trials you have endured and the sacrifices you made the first two years," she wrote, "they could not be made to believe it an invention of your own, nor pursued for mercenary purposes."

It was a powerful letter, one that Leah, ever aware of public relations, promptly arranged to have published, later asking to be forgiven for making such a warmly personal note so public.

It was to Amy that Leah unleashed her own frustrations. "My trials in this beautiful Western part of the world have been at times very great," she complained, presenting her own version of the quarrel with Lemira Kedzie. Troubles with Kedzie, Leah confided, had reached such a peak that "the whole subject of spirits was for a time completely sunk—we feared never to rise again."[6]

Since Kedzie was spreading tales among their mutual friends in Rochester that Leah was an incompetent spendthrift, Leah in turn impugned Kedzie's character and motives to Amy. "I believe it is generally allowed by all who know anything about the matter," Leah fumed, "that she is a very improper person—and has no business in the matter except to make a little Speculation out of the 'Knockings.'"

However, Leah mused, she and Kedzie might have ended up the best of friends except for the shenanigans of Kate and Maggie. "Much of my trouble is caused by the girls," Leah continued, "—who are always planing [sic] out something and then if they fail in their calculation they throw the whole thing on my shoulders."

Leah portrayed herself as the responsible one who hardly knew how to bear up under her difficulties with her willful, charming, unpredictable sisters. "Now after they have been the cause of all the trouble between Mrs. Kedzie and me," she wrote, "they write loving letters to Mr. Kedzie to try to currie [sic] favor with him. . . .

"I can tell you truly, if it had not been for them I should never differ with many—but they are always working so underhandedly that I am tired—tired of Life or in other words of so much deception—"

By *deception* Leah seems to have meant a propensity on the part of her sisters to stir up trouble, to gleefully foment disagreements, and then to behave as absolute innocents. The portrait wouldn't have surprised many of the girls' public detractors, who had long viewed the two of them as mischief makers at best.

✳   ✳   ✳

In the summer of 1851 the three Fox sisters, Margaret, and Calvin completed their tour of Ohio, then returned to Cincinnati to satisfy the crowds who had missed Kate the previous spring. The family remained there despite the sweltering heat of a merciless July. Calvin, who had never completely recovered from his cold, was too ill to travel farther, and when his lungs began to hemorrhage one night in late August, doctors who responded to the emergency offered little hope.

For hours that night Margaret and Leah watched by his bed, both of them mourning the man who had been the Fox family's steadfast friend and protector. By morning he had improved enough to speak, and in yet one more show of devotion he took Leah's hand in his and asked her to marry him. He was thinking only of her welfare, he explained.

"The best legacy I could leave you, as a protection when I am gone, is my name," Calvin said. "If we were married now, your widowhood would be a protection from the importunate intrusions to which you are so frequently subjected."[7]

He and Leah had been inseparable for years; during that time their relationship may or may not have evolved beyond affectionate friendship into a sexual one. Faced now with Calvin's impending death, Leah weighed the decision for several days before accepting his proposal. Having conquered her doubts, she married him on September 10, 1851. Calvin then surprised everyone by recovering; instead of simply bearing the protection of his name, Leah found herself with a living, breathing husband. The newlyweds returned to Rochester, where they were greeted by Leah's daughter, Lizzie, who had been banished from home in 1848 for criticizing the spirits. Welcomed back into the family fold at last, Lizzie helped nurse her new stepfather back to health.

Kate, Maggie, and Margaret remained in Cincinnati through much of the fall. The work in Ohio had been an unqualified success, Kate reported to Amy that October, and they had convinced many skeptics. "Oh Amy the Spirits do such wonderful things," Kate enthused. "They ring the bells, move the tables, all when our feet are held."[8]

As always, though, she missed Rochester and her many friends there.

With the flourish of a sentimental schoolgirl, she ended the note: "*Dear Dear Amy,* on the wings of the mind I send a kiss. . . ."

But an equally schoolgirlish, petulant postscript followed, aimed at John Robinson.

"Ask John why he does not reply to my letters. *Is he mad."*

Amy responded with one of her kind letters, for Kate wrote again with heartfelt thanks. "I wish you knew how I felt. Oh so homesick. I want to see you Amy."[9]

To offset Kate's woes, exciting activities kept her from pining unduly: private parties as well as public demonstrations. Cassius Clay, the abolitionist editor and former captain in the Mexican War, attended a sitting with Kate and Maggie, chaperoned by Margaret. Clay, whom Kate called a great man, held her feet, and the proprietor of the hotel held Maggie's. All the while, Kate reported, the spirits played the guitar, the bells, and the accordion that the mediums had placed under the table.

"Cassius Clay is one of our best friends," Kate bubbled. She also added more realistically that he was a great flatterer.

Still, she had another subject on her mind, more urgent even than the spirits. Robinson had done the unforgivable.

"You know my friend John Robinson," she cried, "or he who used to be my friend wrote me and forbid [sic] me even writing him again, for the mere reason of my writing him a little *funn* [sic]."

She felt betrayed by his unfeeling behavior: "To think how much I thought of him and he should change so soon."

And she was plotting revenge: "But if I meet him face to face, I will never speak to him, never notice him, now I am as firm as a Rock, ask the Spirits if I am not right."

It's difficult to guess what the spirits, given the chance, might have answered, since Kate had already violated her own vow to snub Robinson. She behaved exactly as he had asked her not to do. "I wrote him a long letter," she said, "asked his forgiveness . . . *but no answer, no answer.*"

Maggie too was feeling the strain of constant investigations and had grown frankly bored in Cincinnati. Whereas Kate tended to melodrama, Maggie was ironic in venting her complaints and briskly informed Amy,

"We are still in Cincinnati, leave for Louisville in two weeks, and as Byron says I shall leave it without regret. I shall return to it without pleasure."[10]

Frederick Douglass happened to be in Cincinnati during part of her stay, and his presence cheered her up considerably. "O how glad we were to see his sweet face once more," she wrote Amy; "he is liked here *very much indeed*. I wish he would give a Lecture here," Maggie continued, "it would make the people *crazy*." She made a cursory reference to the spirits, mentioning almost offhandedly how they were doing "wonderful things all the time." But her interests clearly were focused on mortal men.

"Frederic [sic] is as fine looking as ever. I think he is the finest looking gentleman I have seen since I have been in Cincinnati," she announced to Amy, adding that she had insisted on his accompanying her back to her hotel. Perhaps it's no wonder that the wives of Troy worried about Maggie's influence over their husbands. Clearly the teenage Fox sisters had an eye for the gentlemen—and didn't always take pains to disguise their admiration.

After the "Ohio Campaign," Kate and Maggie visited St. Louis, Missouri, in January 1852. As in other cities, they submitted to examinations by various investigators, one group composed of three physicians, as the previous year's Buffalo committee had been. Dr. A. J. Coons, chair of the St. Louis trio, reported that he and his colleagues had successfully exposed "the Rochester Knockings" but that despite this achievement—which he never fully explained—the mediums had converted a troubling number of his fellow citizens to a belief in spirits.

Back home in Rochester, Leah—now Mrs. Brown—was planning yet another move, a strategy that, like the Ohio tour, had the potential for widening the Fox sisters' circle of support. She took no credit for the decision to relocate but instead attributed it to pressure from others.

"Many friends to the new cause urged their advice that we should establish ourselves in one of the great centres of population and movement," Leah wrote.[11]

In the early months of 1852 Leah, Calvin, and Lizzie left Rochester for good and moved into a large brownstone at 78 West Twenty-Sixth Street in Manhattan. Leah's fourth residence in four years quickly became famous for the seances the Fox sisters held there. Kate and Maggie lived with her when they weren't traveling or staying as the houseguests of notable investigators. Margaret spent much of her time there too, providing her daughters with love and comfort and becoming almost as much a fixture at seances as they were. John remained in Arcadia, living in the house that he had built next to David's, unshakable in his Methodist faith and apparently indifferent to or disapproving of the spirits.

And the controversy continued, generating a growing body of alternative explanations for the raps and related phenomena. Some writers speculated that the manifestations were the product of the individual's fevered imagination, played upon by the medium and perhaps enhanced by hallucinogens such as opium, which were widely available in medicines of the day.

Or, it was argued, electricity created the manifestations. Like physics today, electricity at the time seemed to promise a scientific explanation for the dazzling prospect of an alternate, coexisting reality.

Or, it was suggested, a theoretical substance known as the Odic Force, said by some scientists to permeate the universe, produced the raps, table tiltings, and floating orbs of light.

Or, a deliberate combination of collusion, ventriloquism, and conjuring tricks did so.

Or, the unconscious, involuntary movement of the medium's muscles or joints . . .

Or, were certain mediums' singular powers of mind—what today we might call psychic powers—the mysterious force that enabled them to read the thoughts of others, even to move objects without touching them? If so, were such exceptional powers either attained or heightened through mesmerism?

Later in the century the burgeoning fields of psychology and neurology would begin to redirect interest in spirit communication toward the human mind itself, with hypnosis, thought transference or mental telepathy, and syndromes such as the one today called multiple personality disorder emerging as areas of study.

While the public debated the causes of alleged spirit demonstrations, critics worried about the damaging effects of belief. Those who fell sway to mediums were said to be courting sin and adultery in the intimate half light of the seance room. Sensitive souls were cautioned against the madness that might result from the feverish visions of their own overwrought minds. The Reverend H. Mattison tallied up "the number of inmates treated in different insane asylums in the country during the year 1852, who lost their reason by 'spirit-rapping,'" and he arrived at the number ninety.[12]

Neither had arguments about the Fox sisters subsided. Were the mediums, as Amy Post believed, brave pioneers, martyrs in the name of a noble cause? Or were they mountebanks who toyed with people's most cherished beliefs? Mature Leah tended to be categorized at one end of the spectrum or the other: as the saintly protector of her siblings or the mastermind behind them. But to many of those who met or read about them, Kate and Maggie seemed more difficult to place; the girls continued to pose a tantalizing mystery. How could anyone so young and apparently so guileless be adept in the arts of deception?

"[Kate] is certainly a witch, for you cannot help looking into the dreamy depths of those sweet violet eyes till you feel magnetized by them," reflected Susanna Moodie, an author who lived in Canada near the girls' sister Elizabeth. "I do not believe that the raps are produced by spirits that have been of this world, but I cannot believe that she, with her pure spiritual face, is capable of deceiving."[13] Not long after meeting Kate in the mid-1850s, Moodie converted to a belief in the spirits.

Defying taboos in so many ways, particularly for young girls of their day, Kate and Maggie had shown a capacity to stir up trouble, to get themselves into predicaments, and then to emerge unscathed. That remarkable resilience, coupled with their reputation as the "original rappers" in childhood, raised persistent questions for many of their contemporaries: under the scrutiny to which the two girls had been subjected, how could they possibly just be frauds or con artists? What if they *were* what believers claimed for them? Messengers of the divine spirits? Or agents of the devil?

Cloaked in an aura of the other world but living very much in this one, Kate and Maggie, like the trickster figures of myth and literature, seem to have eluded definition. Were they innocent or calculating? Serious or mischievous? Soulful or irreverent? Active or passive? Answers abounded, but as a twosome the girls seem to have embodied the trickster's appeal and double-sided nature.

Like tricksters as well, Kate and Maggie crossed borders. Fluent in the language of the pragmatic, materialistic, everyday world of their time, the girls were steeped as well in the poetry of the spiritual world, where people mused about second sight, prayed with the fierce enthusiasm of revivalist Methodism, and worried about heaven and hell. The two young mediums' ease and background in both worlds either may have made them ideal receptors for the spirits or exquisitely attuned them to the material and spiritual concerns of their culture.

In the 1850s so much seemed bifurcated: heaven and hell, separate spheres for men and women, North versus South, material and technological progress juxtaposed with spiritual doubt, families uprooted and divided. The impulse to create a harmonious whole, although not universal, was powerful, and those who straddled the border between worlds—children, tricksters—and who, like Kate and Maggie, seemed propelled by a wish to bring everyone, spirits and mortals, together, possessed great appeal. The Fox sisters vibrated to invisible waves of thoughts and feelings—whether from mortal or immortal beings—and they transmitted melodies and messages that pleased their listeners. Although they needed neither the spirits nor mental telepathy to do so, perhaps they were blessed with both.

Or at times, perhaps, they believed they were.

Arguments on the subject notwithstanding, by 1852 the nation's passion, both for the spirits and for the pleasures of the spirit circle, had grown. Westward migration, urbanization, immigration, and the rise of a market economy had created a society that was more anonymous and atomized than in the past. Circles of mortal investigators, holding hands, clustered around a table, felt connected: with one another and with the spirits, with the past and with the future.[14]

Visits from Benjamin Franklin and other heroic spirits, simulated or real, served a twofold purpose. The encounters seemed to provide continuity with the idealized values of the early American republic, conceived of as a simpler time, in retrospect if not in reality more unified than the present. Yet these historic, otherworldly figures simultaneously lent their imprimatur to a technologically exciting future. The raps and other manifestations also promised to dissolve the contradictions that had emerged between science and religion by supplying the evidence of immortality that science demanded and that faith desired.

Benjamin Franklin probably visited more often than any other famous spirit. Given the multiple identities he had assumed in his lifetime—inventor, trickster, magician, founding father, and diplomat—he was an ideal representative from the other world.

The spirit circles themselves were appealing as democratic, participatory, and theatrical events, with manifestations that were generally audible or visible to one and all. No longer were the thundering minister and the isolated mystic the only ones with knowledge of a transcendent reality.

The other world emerged as democratic, too. All spirits had the capacity to progress in virtue. All had the ability to communicate with the friends and relatives they had left behind and to impart to them their newfound spiritual wisdom. Since hell was essentially banished, there was little to fear from the afterlife. The other world was a great leveler.

To attend a circle was exhilarating, however, not only in the promise held forth for eternity but also in the intensity of the experience. To an individual immersed in the sustained gloom of sentimental grief, the seance provided a rush of adrenaline, emotional release, and a provocative challenge to probe for truth. No longer was it necessary to wait until death to be freed from depression or despair. A good seance stirred the blood, proving one's own vitality in the here and now. It brought the living and the dead equally to life.

In the brief four years since the peddler's Hydesville visit, the Fox sisters had forged the way in founding a popular movement based on a belief in spirit communication. Tens of thousands of men and women across the nation were said to share the faith. The influential New York Circle, formed late in 1850, expanded its membership and changed its name to the New York Conference. In 1852 the conference began holding lectures and meetings open to the public at a chapel on Broadway. Philadelphia boasted sixty or more circles of investigators. Providence,

Rhode Island, was credited with forty or fifty mediums. One newspaper editor estimated that twelve hundred mediums had emerged in Cincinnati in the wake of the Fox sisters' visit there. The trend was so popular that the *Spirit Messenger* suggested guidelines for establishing an ongoing spirit circle of one's own:

First. Let none join your circle but those who feel attracted. Invite none but those who feel a desire to search for truth, and would be congenial with you.

Second. When you have a medium present, communications are promised *conditionally*. If you come with candid minds and a desire to know the truth, the spirits will endeavor to communicate with you.

Third. Let one among you be appointed to repeat the Alphabet.

Fourth. Your meetings should be opened with singing and close with singing; and all should *pray*, cherishing an inward desire to have good spirits with you, or those who are most progressed.

Fifth. In the absence of a medium, the Circle should be formed with the same harmonious feelings; and the spirits will be with you, and impress you with truthful thoughts.

Sixth. Those who unite with the Circle must not indulge in inharmonious feelings, strife, or bitterness, but follow the example of Christ in doing good.

Seventh. All strive to live cheerful and happy, and there will be a corresponding harmony between you and the Spheres.[15]

Manifestations also were becoming more diverse. Mediums performed ever more astonishing feats of levitation: white-haired Henry Gordon was seen floating in the air across a sixty-foot space, balanced on nothing but one of Charles Partridge's fingers. Trance mediums delivered inspiring addresses to large audiences on the pressing issues of the day, such as perfecting the body through diet and exercise or rehabilitating criminals through prison reform. Some mediums danced, others spoke in tongues. The number of healing mediums multiplied.

To speed the process of spelling messages during seances, mediums began writing down the alphabet then pointing to specific letters rather than calling them out. In a room built by a man named Koons solely for the purpose of otherworldly communications, several spirits seemed to speak in their own voices, their words projected through a small trumpet.

Although many believers were feminists, as the movement expanded a division of labor nevertheless emerged that largely reflected social roles: female mediums generally ruled over uncanny manifestations in the parlor while male mediums expressed themselves in a more "philosophic" vein on paper; men tended to appear onstage as fully conscious lecturers and women as dreamy trance speakers. Even so, mediumship gave women an opportunity to speak in a public forum, albeit in a trance and with their ideas attributed to the spirits.

Believers defended not only the authenticity but also the importance of the various manifestations. One author explained that communications, whatever the type, demonstrated not simply the truth of immortality, but "the *nearness and connection* of that world with this. . . .

"Why ridicule the movements of articles of furniture by unseen power?" he demanded. "If they are spirits, they take the nearest and most convenient thing at hand, and thereby demonstrate a great fact, namely the existence of a spiritual power above all this gross materialism."[16]

Neither were the messages themselves to be derided. "Their object appears to be now," he observed, "not to startle the world with any new and wonderful revelations, but to startle it gently, as human nature requires, out of this deep sleep of materialism and unbelief."

Many of the Fox family's close friends were discovering their own gift for mediumship. Isaac Post found that if he entered a trance, he was guided by the spirits to write down their messages. In 1851, the year that *Uncle Tom's Cabin* first appeared in serial form and Hawthorne's *House of the Seven Gables* and Melville's *Moby Dick* were published, Isaac compiled messages from William Penn, George Washington, Thomas Jefferson, Emanuel Swedenborg, and others into a three-hundred-page volume called *Voices from the Spirit World; Being Communications From Many Spirits by the Hand of Isaac Post, Medium.* The messages, Isaac said, had been transcribed through automatic writing that sometimes occurred in the presence of "A.L. Fish (a rapping medium)." In 1852 Charles Hammond, the Universalist minister who had watched in awe as the furniture danced and floated in front of him at one of the sisters' early seances, produced a book called *Light from the Spirit World; The Pilgrimage of Thomas Paine, and Others, to the Seventh Circle in the Spirit World.*

Other acquaintances of the Fox family also became prominent. The Reverend R. P. Ambler, who had accompanied Leah and Maggie to Albany in 1850, wrote *The Elements of Spiritual Philosophy; Being an Exposition of Interior Principles.* And Charles Partridge, the match manufacturer, became a highly successful publisher, joining with the editor Samuel B. Brittan in 1851 to establish a magazine that explored the philosophical questions raised by spirit communication. The two men titled the new journal *Shekinah,* a Hebrew word long used to evoke the radiance of the divine.

The name also reflected the then-current romantic fascination with cultures—Jewish, Catholic, Asian, Native American—that seemed to some Protestants to be foreign and mysterious, even enchanted. Like the spirit world, these alluring "other worlds" seemed to invite investigation, at least insofar as they represented the remote in time, physical distance, or culture. Romanticized views, however, generally bore only an inverse relationship to the actual treatment of minority groups in the culture. As the Native American population disappeared under the brutal onslaught of white settlers, for example, P. T. Barnum was inspired to present scenes of "American Indians who enacted their warlike and religious ceremonies on stage" at his famous museum, and Native American spirits became equally popular attractions in visions and seances. Deemed wise representatives of a simpler, more natural way of life, Native Americans evidently appeared less threatening in immortal than in mortal guise, and like other spirits they were eager to reconcile with their enemies and forgive any trespasses committed against them.[17]

Pleased by the *Shekinah's* expanding circulation, in 1852 the firm of Partridge and Brittan introduced a weekly newspaper called the *Spiritual Telegraph.* Its name, chosen with equal care, underscored the connection the editors made between current technology and the promise of immortality.

Horace Greeley continued to reach the widest audience with news of the spirits. He was publishing less on the issue than in the past, overwhelmed by the deluge of attacks and counterattacks, but in the spring of 1852, in a review of the *Spiritual Telegraph,* he called attention to the remarkable rise of the new movement, and he gave it a name: "*modern Spiritualism.*"

Its believers he called *Spiritualists.*[18]

New technology for mass-producing images turned famous names into familiar faces, and in 1852 Nathaniel Currier issued a print of the three spirit-rapping Fox sisters. The portrait was copied from a daguerreotype made by a Rochester photographer in 1851.

Daguerreotypes themselves were the product of a relatively new process developed in France and first introduced into the United States in the 1840s by Samuel Morse, inventor of the telegraph. Like the telegraph, the daguerreotype was an innovation with resonance for the Spiritualist movement, for the images created by the process eerily evoked ghostly second selves. Later in the century, when new technology made negatives possible, photographers would produce pictures that purported to show actual spirits—pale, transparent apparitions—hovering next to mortal subjects.

The Currier print of the Fox sisters, while it makes no otherworldly claims, is memorable. Maggie and Leah, each with her hair piled in an austere topknot, both draped in shawls as enveloping as religious robes, sit on either side of the luminously beautiful Kate. Standing a step behind her sisters, Kate wears a demure high-necked dress, and her hair falls almost to her waist in two long braids. The image is reminiscent of an icon: a youthful saint with her watchful ministers at her right hand and her left.

While the Currier print has a quality of genteel religiosity, there is nothing remotely saintly about the daguerreotype of Kate and Maggie taken by Thomas Easterly when the girls visited St. Louis, Missouri, in 1852. This portrait reveals two lovely flesh-and-blood young women, dressed in fashionable gowns with square-cut necklines and tight-fitting bodices. The fabrics look rich even in black and white. Each sister wears her glossy hair pulled back softly in the style of the day. Their sensuality—Maggie's earthiness and Kate's delicacy—is dignified, natural, and visible. The two youngest Fox sisters, as John E. Robinson of Rochester had noticed, were growing up, and the impact of their mediumship on their personal lives, and vice versa, would become increasingly complex.

PART III

DARLING LITTLE SPIRIT
1852–1857

ELEVEN

"DOCTOR KANE OF THE ARCTIC SEAS"

IN THE FALL of 1852 Kate was fifteen and Maggie nineteen. They were financially secure, able to afford luxuries for themselves and their loved ones, but freedom from gossip and innuendo was not so easily purchased. Kate and Maggie—like many working-class girls—mixed constantly and informally with strangers, men other than their own relatives. However well chaperoned by Margaret or Leah, the two young mediums greeted their public in rooms where the lights were often dim, where intimate feelings were exchanged, and where hand-holding was an integral part of the moment—scandalous behavior at the time. The beliefs and practices that gave Kate and Maggie the means to live like the respectable middle class in effect excluded them from a comfortable niche within it.

Not that they necessarily craved stuffy respectability. Kate may have longed for the protective veneer of a conventional middle-class home, but Maggie openly thrived on the excitement and challenge of her mediumship and on the attention it brought her from men and women of all social ranks. Snubbed by some, the Fox sisters were the darlings of others, and many of their wealthy and fashionable clients pampered them with gifts of jewelry and the best French champagne.

The sisters' developing sexuality, however, began to create a new problem, one that hadn't existed in the early years of their mediumship. Although the word *demon* had been hurled at them occasionally, and they even had been hounded once or twice by jealous wives, in the past they had generally been perceived as country children. Youth had helped protect them from unwanted advances and accusations of improprieties.

By 1852, however, little Kate had blossomed into a beauty with the slender figure and perfect features of a heroine in a sentimental novel. She was moody, clouds crossing her brow when her sunny enthusiasms and tenderhearted affections were replaced by self-pity or frustration, but she radiated tremendous vulnerability and charm.

Maggie too had grown into a vital, attractive young woman who, while she lacked her sister's languishing grace, had eyes that shone with intelligence and wit, a warmly expressive face, and a petite, shapely figure. A friend later described her as "sparkling and irrepressible," her "buoyant glee . . . held in check but not dashed by the fear of breaking bounds, and possibly giving offense. . . ." By nature happy and impulsive, this friend testified, Maggie "had learned self-command from being frequently in the presence of persons uncongenial to her. . . ."[1]

A creature of controlled passions rather than of passing moods, Maggie, like Kate, was charismatic. Biology and maturity were transforming both sisters into truly terrifying beings: sexual women who could be perceived and portrayed as seductresses and, worse, ones with otherworldly powers.

This image of course is an old and familiar one: Eve, the temptress; Circe, the sorceress; the Sirens who used their wiles to lure men into danger. In the nineteenth century, however, women's sexuality became doubly suspect, a trait at odds with the era's idealized image of femininity.[2]

In the past in Christian America, men and women alike had been viewed as sexual creatures, and if fornication and adultery were forbidden, procreative sex within a happy marriage had been seen as an enjoyable, even blessed, activity. Premarital sex, while far from condoned, was often forgiven so long as the couple married or remained together. As the nineteenth century progressed, however, the economic incentive, if not the religious injunction, to be fruitful and multiply diminished, while new information about birth control made nonprocreative sex more of an option. For women, who endured the dangers of childbirth, the idea of sex for pleasure was at once alluring and guilt provoking. Carnal desire contrasted too sharply with the modesty and spirituality expected of those who inhabited the feminine sphere. Women who violated the ideal, in demeanor or behavior, might be labeled coarse, deviant, or seductive.

If respectable women were required to be—or look—demure, men had other problems. Success in the masculine sphere of the workplace seemed to require a level of aggressive, competitive energy that—medical doctors somberly warned—could easily be drained away in the careless expenditure of seminal fluid. Virtue and wasted energy, metaphors for America's hopes and fears, reflected quite literal concerns of the day.

If sexuality was viewed as unseemly in a woman, lust was conceived of as natural in a man. His sexual exploits were tolerated, evidence of his animal side. He might find relief in guilty pleasures, such as sex with prostitutes or, if single, in flirtations with girls who were livelier than the lady he might choose for his wife. Much as he might love the beguiling woman with whom he dallied, it was her reputation, of course, that was damaged if he failed to propose.

Although attitudes toward sex were more conflicted than in the past, passion expressed in words, not deeds, remained paradoxically acceptable. As mutual affection rather than economic factors became increasingly important in choosing a mate, many couples expressed their sentimental and even sexual yearnings in love letters. With rates of premarital sex in decline by 1850, yet with a premium newly placed on romance, love letters served as a release from the pent-up emotions inevitably stirred by courtship at a time when middle-class young people were marrying later.

For Maggie, now approaching the age of courtship and marriage, but also for Kate, the world of sexual mores and relationships was filled with contradictions. No longer just ciphers for the spirits, they were becoming women with their own earthly needs, whose behavior could be assessed and judged and whose position in society was complex. Although they moved easily among the great and famous of their day, they also worked for a living in a profession that brought them into contact with all sorts of men, a profession regarded by many as disreputable. Unconventional, charismatic, and filled with a hunger for life, they were at risk in a society that smiled on romance but blamed the woman for a couple's mutual indiscretions.

In October 1852, at the urging of Philadelphia's Spiritualist community, Maggie and her mother visited the City of Brotherly Love, where they rented the spacious bridal suite at Webb's Union Hotel. The sunny parlor was soon filled, as elsewhere, with men and women eager to investigate the spirits as well as to ogle the medium. One visitor, the noted explorer, author, and lecturer Elisha Kent Kane, quickly surrendered to Maggie's charms.[3]

"Once in the mornings of old," Kane wrote, later recalling his first meeting with Maggie and spinning it into a fable, "I read in a penny newspaper that for one dollar the inmates of another world would rap to me the secrets of this one; the deaths of my friends, the secret thoughts of my sweet-hearts; all things spirit-like and incomprehensible would be resolved into hard knocks, and all for one dollar! . . . With that, all alone, I wended my way to a hotel, and after the necessary forms of doorkeepers and tickets—by Jove, I saw the 'spirit.'"[4]

By the "spirit," Kane meant Maggie, of course, who appealed to him with her kindhearted warmth, youthful energy, and unusual beauty. But he also sensed other qualities in her that both attracted and disturbed him: her aura of mystery, her paradoxical double nature, "that strange mixture of child and woman, of simplicity and cunning, of passionate impulse and extreme self-control. . . ."

Equally unsettling to him was her profession. After briefly showing interest in the spirits, he quickly pronounced himself adamantly opposed to the rapping—declared it altogether a fraud—although he couldn't say for certain how the sounds were made.

"Take my advice and never talk of the spirits either to friends or strangers," he once scolded Kate. "You know that with all my intimacy with Maggie, after a whole month's trial, I could make nothing of them. Therefore they are a *great mystery*."

Kane, whom Maggie called "Lish," or sometimes "Ly," wrote letters suffused with the passionate sentimentality of the nineteenth-century gentleman, and these form the basis of a slim volume about the couple's courtship titled *The Love-Life of Dr. Kane*. The book was published on Maggie's initiative in 1866, but its contents have long been disputed for several reasons. The letters are linked by a narrative, labeled a memoir, whose anonymous author may have been either Joseph LaFumee, a newspaper editor with the *Brooklyn Eagle*, or Elizabeth Fries Lummis Ellet, a popular author, both of whom befriended Maggie.[5] Most likely at the Fox family's behest, this loyal friend and misleading author—LaFumee or Ellet—distorted facts, for example by portraying Maggie as a naive thirteen-year-old girl rather than as a nineteen-year-old woman when she first met Kane. In addition, some letters in the collection were edited for the book's publication. But other correspondence in archives and libraries substantiates the compelling story of the couple's love affair.

Kane, the indomitable, sentimental suitor who wooed Maggie in 1852, teasingly called her his "Circe," the enchantress whose wiles ensnared the hero of Homer's epic *Odyssey*. He meant the nickname affectionately, but it carried a bite.

His favorite poem was Tennyson's "Ulysses," and like the hero, Elisha Kent Kane was a wanderer, an explorer; however, Kane's most famous journeys took place in the frigid far north rather than under Mediterranean skies. The remote Arctic region with its winter-long nights, shimmering mirages, and miles-wide ice sheets had defeated intrepid sailors for centuries, even as the hope of finding a northwest passage from Europe to Asia had beckoned them onward. In the nineteenth century the hunt for an open polar sea through which ships could sail across the top of the Americas intensified. The effort came to be seen as more than a commercial enterprise; it acquired the symbolic power of a quest into the unknown, a challenge that could prove the courage and mettle of heroes.

In the late 1840s, just such an expedition of one hundred men, led by the seasoned British explorer Dr. John Franklin, vanished. Exploration, already fraught with emotion, quickly evolved into a humanitarian mission, and in 1850 thirty-year-old Kane joined one of several rescue expeditions that sailed in search of the missing men.

Slim, about 5'7" tall, with intense eyes and aristocratic, narrow features, he by no means looked the part of the daring adventurer, if by that one imagines the burly trapper who invaded the inland wilderness with his rifle on his back. Born to a well-to-do Philadelphia family in 1820, he was the oldest of seven children. His maternal grandfather, a wealthy manufacturer, had made his fortune in flour mills and counted Thomas Jefferson among his close friends. Kane's father, John Kintzing Kane, was a highly respected jurist and an intellectual with an abiding interest in science and natural philosophy. On both his mother's and his father's side, Elisha Kent Kane's family was a proud one, influential in local affairs and on the national scene.

Privilege offered no protection against disaster. In his late teens Kane contracted rheumatic fever, a disease that permanently weakened his heart. Despite recurring periods of depression and invalidism, he refused the role of victim. By the time he left for the Arctic in 1850, he had studied medicine at the University of Pennsylvania, been appointed to the post of assistant naval surgeon, and accompanied expeditions to China, India, Africa, and Europe as well as to Central and South America. His parents had been a source of encouragement but were now beginning to urge him to settle down.

By 1850 Kane also had left a few broken hearts behind him. One relationship almost certainly produced an illegitimate child, and he had developed a pattern of literally sailing away when a relationship became too close. He may simply have been a cad or a rake; more likely, he consciously or unconsciously wished to live what threatened to be a brief life to the fullest, whether in romance or adventure, no matter the consequences for others.

The Arctic rescue mission joined by Kane in 1850 returned in 1851 after sixteen months away with little positive news to report on the fate of Dr. Franklin's men. Only a small makeshift graveyard had been found; the survivors apparently had journeyed onward. Could anyone have remained alive after the passage of so many years? Most people who understood Arctic conditions felt justified in surrendering hope, but Dr. Franklin's widow and Elisha Kent Kane were not among them.

To save the long-lost Franklin, and certainly for other reasons as well—the thrill of discovery, the fame it bestowed—Kane was determined to return to the Arctic, this time as commander of his own expedition. Death had shadowed him for many years, and his name on a map of the world—as it appears today on Kane Basin, an ice-locked bay off the northwest coast of Greenland—must have promised a more assured immortality than any Spiritualist could offer.

He began an arduous process of fund-raising for the new expedition, writing a book about the first expedition (he hoped it would bankroll the second one), hounding government officials and private donors for money, and giving endless rounds of lectures. His energy and enthusiasm, his pleasant and agreeable speaking voice, and his endless store of information and anecdotes enchanted his listeners, somewhat to his discomfort. He wryly compared himself to "his rivals" who also performed for paying audiences. He named as his competitors the aging magician Blitz, the popular opera singer Alboni, and the philosopher Emerson.

"We are all of one feather," the explorer complained. "No matter: so that I get my money, I do not care."[6]

In the spring of 1851 he suffered a series of seizures—a family friend called the bouts a nervous collapse, but they more likely stemmed from his chronic disease—that physically and emotionally depleted him. That summer his beloved fifteen-year-old brother, Willie, died after a brief illness. Slowly, Kane recovered from stress and sorrow and resumed his work: writing, lecturing, and fund-raising.

It's not clear why he attended his first seance in the fall of 1852. He may have been curious about the manifestations or looking for an hour's entertainment or perhaps seeking relief from his suffering over Willie's death. Whatever his reasons, he was thunderstruck at first sight of Maggie and in the following months returned repeatedly to see her.

For a while Kane observed conventional rules of propriety. He invited Maggie out for carriage drives in the country, but he always brought along a female chaperone such as an older friend or favorite cousin on their outings. He sent gifts of flowers, books, and music, but he politely directed them to the attention of Margaret rather than to Maggie herself.

Maggie, thirteen years his junior, initially seems to have shown little interest in her new suitor and to have behaved with reserve, as genteel young women were expected to do. Perhaps she found other men more attractive or appealing, or she doubted his intentions. But Kane, as his life course had already demonstrated, was nothing if not determined, and he won her over.

Slowly his tone turned more proprietary, and his gifts grew more personal and lavish. In December 1852 he wrote to Margaret, "I could not resist the temptation of sending the accompanying little trifle of ermine for Miss Margaretta's throat. As I know you to be carefully fastidious as to forms, permit me to place it in your hands."[7] He gave Maggie a white camellia, comparing her delicacy to the flower's with the words, "like you, it must not be breathed upon."

He took her to visit the beautiful cemetery where his brother Willie lay buried in the Kane family vault, an intimate and sentimental journey. She was delighted by her worldly suitor, their trips through the rolling Pennsylvania countryside, and her pretty gifts.

Early in the new year 1853 he professed his love then admitted to being virtually engaged to a woman of his parents' choosing, a relationship he vowed to end. Maggie assumed she too would soon meet the Kanes, but this didn't happen. Kane undoubtedly realized that his proper Presbyterian parents would be scandalized by his romance with—in the heated opinion of some commentators—a notorious woman, and one whose family was beneath his in social class. In fact, John and Margaret's relatives were respectable middle-class farmers and artisans, but the Fox family boasted no influential professionals, wealthy manufacturers, or distinguished members of learned academies. It's also possible that the Kanes, if they knew about their son's previous romances, were impatient with what they regarded as his escapades. Kane kept his relationship with Maggie a secret from his parents.

Instead, he asked whether Maggie would be a trusting girl and place her future in his care. Soon afterward, he gave Maggie a diamond ring set in black enamel (she was said to have modestly declined a more extravagant one set in pearls), and the couple began to behave as if they were engaged. She took his arm when they went out for walks; under the not-so-watchful eye of mother Margaret, the lovers slipped one another private, teasing notes.

His friends, some for amusement and others perhaps for more serious reasons, consulted the spirits, and he sometimes did so himself, mostly as a ploy for seeing Maggie. The lure of forbidden fruit was powerful and the intrigue of the romance stimulating. For Kane, the excitement may have substituted for a different sort of danger that he had faced in the Arctic.

"I was unwilling to call upon you to-night for fear of *talk,*" he breathlessly wrote Maggie one evening, "but I told my brother if you had company to show my ring, so as to avoid mentioning names. Do not let him suppose that you have anything more than spirit business with me. I say this on your own account."

Undeniably a ladies' man, Kane probably had started the flirtation with Maggie as a lark, only to discover that he couldn't give her up. Enchanted by a woman who was unacceptable not only to his family but also to a part of himself, he expressed his frustration and ambivalence even in his compliments. After receiving one of her letters, he advised her, "I need hardly say [I] am gratified to find that you write so ably. You have more *brain* than I gave you credit for."

Then he went on to express unambivalent disapproval. The newspapers had linked Leah's name with the suicide of a man who had attended her seances, and the thought of Mrs. Fish's influence on her younger sisters outraged him.

"Oh, how much I wish that you would quit this life of dreary sameness and suspected deceit," he admonished Maggie. "We live in this world only for the opinions of the good and noble. How crushing it must be to occupy with them a position of ambiguous respect!"

Distressed by his vacillations and accusations, Maggie struggled with ambivalent feelings of her own, mistrust mingled with affection. One afternoon, anticipating that he might cancel one of his visits, she challenged him to explain himself.

"Now, Doctor—be candid!—am I not correct when I say that you are an enigma past finding out?" she demanded, her tone light but her question serious. She hinted at the similarities between them, the paradoxes each found at once unsettling and intriguing in the other, when she added provocatively, "You know I am." She had chosen a word, *enigma*, that symbolized their developing relationship. Just as the Arctic and spirit worlds were enigmatic, inviting exploration into their farthest regions, so too the lovers were to each other.

Her question riled him, for he viewed it less as an honest expression of her feelings than as manipulation: she was the clever one, he was her victim.

"You say 'that you do not understand me'—'I am a riddle'—'an enigma,' and all that nonsense. Dear Maggie," he seethed, "you understand me very well. You know that I am a poor, weak, easily deceived man, and you think that you are an astute, hardly seen-through woman, managing me as you please. Now tell me the truth—don't you?"

Fiercely asserting his masculine superiority, he thundered, "I am a man rather of facts and stern purposes, than of woman thoughts and dreamy indolence. . . . I will leave after me a name and a success."

"But with all this," he added gloomily, "I am a weak man and a fool, weak that I should be caught in the midst of my grave purposes by the gilded dust of a butterfly's wing; and a fool because, while thus caught, I smear my fingers with the perishable color."

In an effort to demolish the butterfly or half hoping to drive her away, he assured Maggie that she was unworthy of his permanent regard. "You could never lift yourself up to my thoughts and my objects," he wrote. "*I* could never bring myself *down* to yours."

But even as he emphasized the disparities between them, reminding her that his was a destiny different from hers, he too highlighted their similarities. He conceded that "just as you have your wearisome round of daily money-making, I have my own sad vanities to pursue. I am as devoted to my calling as you, poor child, can be to yours. Remember then, as a sort of dream, that Doctor Kane of the Arctic Seas loved Maggie Fox of the Spirit Rappings."

In Maggie, Kane had met his match. He understood intuitively, as did she, that there were powerful bonds between them. Both had dared to live outside the narrow confines of polite society, he as an Arctic explorer, she as a spirit medium. Both were ambitious for money and fame. And both were passionate, willful individuals, committed to the uncertain paths on which they traveled.

In January 1853 Margaret and Maggie left Philadelphia and returned to New York City, moving back into the house on Twenty-Sixth Street with Leah, Calvin, and Kate. Under Leah's suspicious eye, Maggie retreated from the relationship with Kane. Resentful of his criticism of Spiritualism, Leah must also have felt that he had compromised her sister, courting Maggie without making any public commitment to her. Leah, whose own situation had been ambiguous for many years, probably worried that Maggie would make the same mistakes.

Not surprisingly, distance stoked Kane's fires.

"Why do you not write to me?" he demanded. "Have you forgotten your friend? Or does your new life drive from you the recollection of old times?" Speaking of himself in the third person, he begged Maggie to "remember his warm hands, his glowing kisses, and his steadfast, trusting heart."

He followed this letter with a copy of the fable *Undine*, a popular novel about a sea nymph by that name. In the novel the whimsical, carefree Undine lacks what is most vital in a human being: a soul. She receives one on her marriage to her mortal suitor, but there's no happy ending. He betrays her, and she ultimately serves as the agent of his destruction. The book undoubtedly reflected Kane's views and fears of Maggie: despite Undine's innocent charm, as a sea nymph she was kin to the Siren.

One of Kane's New York friends, Cornelius Grinnell, son of the whaling tycoon who was helping to finance Kane's new venture, delivered the explorer's notes and gifts secretly, sometimes slipping them to Kate if Maggie was busy or holding a seance. A sophisticated New Yorker who enjoyed the social whirl of balls, dinner parties, and private theatricals, Grinnell surprised himself by finding the mediums interesting, the seances impressive, and the groups who attended the sittings an intriguing array of skeptics, converts, and those in search of education or entertainment.

When Kane himself visited New York on business, he tried to set up secret meetings with Maggie, on occasion using Kate as a decoy. "Maggie, do you know Satler's Cosmoramas in Broadway near Twelfth street, on the right hand side going down?" he asked. "If you and Kate will walk past it at exactly four o'clock on Saturday afternoon, I will be there."

Although he often succeeded in arranging tête-à-têtes, this time Maggie kept her distance, coolly responding, "You will pardon me, my dear friend, for not meeting you. Strange that I should have made such a promise—so imprudent!" She added that she would be happy to see him if he called for her at home.

Margaret, Kate, and Maggie spent February 1853 in Washington, where congressmen on working vacations from their families, government officials, and restless soldiers frequently sought advice from the spirits. Within a short time, so too would the wife of the nation's newly elected president. A few weeks earlier Franklin and Jane Pierce had been en route to Washington when their trail derailed, an accident that killed their eleven-year-old son before their eyes. In the aftermath of the tragedy, Mrs. Pierce sat in her room late at night writing notes to her dead son, and later in the year she met at least once with Maggie Fox.

Old friends and devoted Spiritualists visited the girls' suite for messages, but so too did others with less concern for the sisters' well-being. Some ostensible seekers of spiritual knowledge, as Kate discovered, were dissolute drunks and rakes out for a good time. Accustomed to men like Horace Greeley and Judge Edmonds, who treated her kindly, Kate found the place oppressive. "I am tired of my life," she sighed. Out of twelve "fine gentlemen" who had visited her the night before, ten had arrived drunk and subjected her to "mean, low remarks."

"Only imagine Maggie and me, and dear mother, before a crowd of drunken Senators," she wrote to Leah. One of the gentlemen had shown the gall to proclaim, "'This is all a humbug, but it is worth a dollar to sit in the sunlight of Miss Kate's eyes.'"[8]

These episodes upset her so much that, with a certain amount of characteristic drama, she swore that she wished to be laid in a peaceful grave, that she would live on a crust of bread to have a different life. "Washington is a mean city," she exclaimed.

Kane continued to barrage Maggie with love letters and complaints.

He lamented, "When I think of you, dear darling, wasting your time and youth and conscience for a few paltry dollars, and think of the crowds who come nightly to hear of the wild stories of the frozen north, I sometimes feel that we are not so far removed after all. My brain and your body are each the sources of attraction, and I confess that there is not so much difference."[9] He once again had acknowledged a similarity, although as always to her disadvantage. This time he placed her in a category akin to a prostitute.

Few of Maggie's letters to Kane from this period seem to have survived, but his letters to her paint a vivid portrait of a dazzlingly alive young woman. Her body obsessed him too, and his notes overflowed with sexual desire: "Is it any wonder that I long to look—only to look—at that dear little deceitful mouth of yours," he demanded, "to feel your hair tumbling over my cheeks." He lavished attention on her appearance and clothes, sending her sets of lace undersleeves and underhandkerchiefs, pretty lingerie designed to fill in a décolletage or to cover an arm laid bare by the fashionably wide sleeve of the day. He hounded Maggie to remember to wear them, for he wanted her to appear ladylike and well dressed. He had given a set to his sister and planned to send one to Kate as well.

Knowing that Maggie wasn't the sort of young woman to shyly retreat from the social scene, he also allowed distance to provoke his jealousy. "How does Washington come on?" he demanded. "Many beaux? Many believers? Many friends? Answer these questions you wicked little Maggie!"

And he continued to chastise her for her apparent indifference to his ardor and misery, complaining that he was the one who did all the writing and, he feared, all the loving too. He frequently signed his letters "Preacher," a tongue-in-cheek acknowledgment of his own frequently patronizing tone.

One rainy Sunday afternoon in Boston, he sank deeper than ever into a morass of self-pity. Recalling "lazy days" of "talking nonsense," he assured her that he was the one writing true spirit messages, "from another world—*our* world, Maggie—the world of love."

And then, exhausted by work and longing for her presence, he began to fantasize about a different future.

"Maggie," he said, "if I had my way with you, I would send you to school and learn you to live your life over again. . . . Once that, Maggie, and you would love me; not the sort of *half-affected* milk and water love which you now profess, but a genuine confiding affection. . . ."

Transformed into a proper prospect, an exemplar of womanly virtue, skilled in the arts of music and French, she would become a trusting girl, one acceptable to his parents and one who appreciated him at last.

"Now to you I am nothing but a cute, cunning dissembler," he acknowledged, "a sort of smart gentleman hypocrite, never really sincere, and amusing himself with a pretty face."

She was suspicious of his motives, he insisted, not because of anything he did but because of her own guilty conscience, "the suspicious, distrusting eyes which your short intercourse with the world—*your world*—has forced upon you." He assured her that he was altogether different from other young men who might make opportunistic promises to win a girl over.

Then he went on to place her in a classic double bind, threatening that "until you look deeper, you will never *love* me; and unless you love me I will soon cease to love you."

Kane's confusing courtship, his promises and retractions, his flattery and his threats, pained her. Both figuratively and literally, she was losing hold of her own world; he asked her to disconnect from her family, spirits and mortals alike, but he promised her no lasting bonds with his.

"This afternoon I went out to do some shopping and lost my way," she wrote. "I grew so frightened that I was obliged to ask a lady to show me the way home. When I entered the room I cried aloud; and looking up I saw General Hamilton, who asked me what was the matter. I told him that I had lost my way, and that I did not like Washington at all."

The general had laughed, instantly making the connection between her distress and the real reason for it, and had insisted that "No young lady could ever lose her way in Washington unless she had some '*affaire du coeur.*' I did not deny the charge," she told Kane, venturing to mention the subject closest to her heart. "Doctor, there is a rumor—so the General tells me—that you and I are to be married before you go to the Arctic." The rumor in fact was becoming widespread.

Margaret tried to discourage Kane's attentions to her daughter, but rather than respecting her wishes, he took up writing to Kate as well, stirring sibling rivalry under the guise of innocent affection. "Dear Miss Incomprehensible Kate," he teased, "I do not see why you should not take half of my correspondence." He told her about witnessing a scene that saddened him immensely. A medium's answer to a young man's question had been so painful that the "tender inquirer" had fainted.

Kane acknowledged that Maggie and his "dear little open-minded" Kate never went so far, but he warned Kate that she too was on the downward path to becoming "a hardened woman, gathering around you victims of a delusion. Think of that, Katy!"

His concerns about the practices of some mediums were legitimate, but his offers to transform Maggie's life remained ambiguous at best. On the one hand, he assured her of his determination to "raise her above her calling, even to his own level" and "cultivate her mind, give her compentence; her sister should be his care." On the other hand, he accused her of being too heartless and shallow to accept his offer.

"I saw that you loved me," he sighed, "but not enough. Dear child, it was not in your nature."

Maggie's tolerance for his behavior is puzzling. The child of a perennially absent and distant father, a man intoxicated with religion if no longer with alcohol, she may have been grateful for and flattered by Kane's attentions, whether negative or positive. But the couple's relationship surely wasn't such an anomaly; they were behaving as many other young men and women have been known to do in the throes of romantic love and in the heat of pursuit. At a time when emotional bonds had begun to replace financial ties in marriage, theirs was a relationship of high emotion.

Kane's courtship technique—accusatory seduction, a time-honored if largely unconscious dance of approach and withdrawal—eventually prevailed over Maggie's hesitations, Leah's dire warnings, and Margaret's weak attempts to exercise good judgment. On a fund-raising visit to Washington, Kane stayed, not at a hotel, but at the same boardinghouse where Maggie was living, hardly a wise move for a man who wished to safeguard the reputation of his beloved. Visits between floors, not surprisingly, were frequent, and his presence could not have gone unnoticed. He typically interrupted seances to demand her attention, on one occasion, for example, sending in a note that read, "Come out for a moment from those coarse people. . . . Surely you can rest a minute! Come dearest fluttering bird! Come!"

At this point, however, Maggie may have felt safe enough to commit indiscretions and to indulge his whims, for Kane had inched further toward what seemed to be a permanent bond. He had started to explore schools for her, something he made sound ominous even as he joked about it.

"Listen, Maggie," he teased, "instead of a life of cherished excitement you must settle down into one of quiet, commonplace repose. Instead of the fun . . . you will have the irksome regulations of a school, the strict formal precepts of a lady abbess, a *schoolmistress.*"

Intuitively, Kane grasped that Maggie was living a more expansive life than her class and gender otherwise permitted, just as he, through his Arctic adventures, had transcended the limits potentially imposed by his illness and by Philadelphia society. He also recognized that it was her wildness, the Circe in her, the unknown magic, that drew him to her. But he wanted and needed to tame her in order to make her respectable.

To tame her in every arena, that is, except the sexual one. And there, by allowing her to be seen and to participate in compromising situations, he encouraged her to venture far outside the boundaries of what was acceptable at the time. Although Maggie and Kane weren't formally engaged, the relationship had become obvious to many people, and at the very least it was physically intimate. Whether they ever sexually consummated the relationship remains controversial; given their mutual attraction, as well as their individual natures and joint opportunities, it seems unlikely they could have resisted each other for the duration of their affair.

He continued, however, to try to protect his own and his family's reputation. When Maggie returned to New York from Washington in the spring of 1853, Kane persisted in exploring schools for her but implied to those in authority that she was merely the recipient of his selfless charity. He may not have fooled anyone; still, he remained steadfast that any formal engagement had to wait until she had completed her education and given up the public practice of mediumship.

His dislike of Leah persisted, and the feelings were mutual. He called her "tigress." She despised him for his influence over Maggie, questioned the sincerity of his intentions, and undoubtedly worried as well about the impact on the Fox family's income and on Spiritualists' morale if her famous sister retired.

He in turn relapsed into fears that Maggie might be leading him on romantically, as he suspected she often led others on professionally when she gave seances even for her most devoted Spiritualist friends, men such as General Waddy Thompson and the former governor of Wisconsin, Nathaniel Tallmadge.

"Here sat dear loveable *whispering Waddy,*" Kane wrote, parodying what happened at seances, "with his *mental* questions; and here cute, but well believing Tallmadge, with his sharp, cunning eye, but foolish, credulous brain . . . and here I set up a devil of a thinking—as to whether this girl who could lead others would ever be led by me, or whether I too was not a Waddy Thompson of another sort, and Maggie only cheating me in a different way."

Not that he, even after so many months, seemed at all certain himself about the nature of the raps. "You know I am nervous about the 'rappings,'" he wrote. "I believe the only thing I ever was afraid of was this *confounded thing being found out.* I would not know it myself for ten thousand dollars."

Torn between her family and Kane, Maggie increasingly found the demanding routines of her daily life "tiresome," and she confided to him that she no longer wanted "to meet with all kind [sic] of people" daily. She had glimpsed the possibility of a different kind of life, one shared with him, and it powerfully attracted her.

"What have I ever done that I should be denied the pleasures of a quiet home, the blessings of love—the reward of virtue," she asked. "I have given my whole time to this subject [of the spirits] for six years." She added, "I think I have done my part—I feel that I have convinced this skeptical, unfeeling world that I am innocent of making these sounds. I ask no more."

He was the "only human being" that had ever urged her "to better things," she admitted. But his imminent departure terrified and saddened her. "What shall I do when you leave for your distant pilgrimage of danger," she asked. "Who then will extend to me a helping hand?"[10]

A sad event served to seal the couple's bond. On May 4, 1853, Calvin Brown died, having never fully regained his health after his illness in Cincinnati. Permitted to pay his respects, Kane reportedly took Maggie's hand in the presence of a small group of mourners and promised to marry her on his return from the Arctic. Although he still refused to make the engagement public, his vow at such a sorrowful hour, only weeks before his departure on a quixotic, dangerous mission, convinced Maggie of his sincerity. Her ambivalence about abandoning her familiar world vanished.[11]

Judge Edmonds delivered the eulogy at Calvin's funeral in New York. Then the family moved on to Rochester, where Isaac Post made the sad arrangements for a second memorial service.

"Bring on your dead," Isaac had telegraphed. "My house is at your service."

After Calvin's burial in Mt. Hope Cemetery, the mourners traveled to Arcadia. As their carriage turned into the lane leading to David Fox's farmhouse, his children raced to the gate to meet them. Seven-year-old Georgie, Leah wrote, "was wonderfully struck with the appearance of our deep mourning, and said [to Margaret], 'Grandma, what makes you all dress so black?'" The next day Georgie fell sick, and on May 12 he died.[12]

On May 30, 1853, Kane's brig, the *Advance,* left New York harbor, bound for the Arctic and what he hoped would be the discovery of an open polar sea, the legendary warm waters that, like the Spiritualists' vision of heaven, held forth the promise of infinite opportunity and boundless advancement. Unlike the earlier Arctic expedition in which he had served as a naval surgeon, this one was under Kane's command. The *Advance* stopped in Newfoundland in mid-June, then headed north toward the Arctic Circle, traveling up the west coast of Greenland. Not far beyond the last European settlement, Kane counted more than two hundred icebergs, and the *Advance* was still at the start of its journey.

He had arranged for Maggie to spend the summer under the watchful eye of his favorite aunt, Eliza Leiper, who lived near Crookville, a small manufacturing village about eighteen miles from Philadelphia. He urged his aunt that for Maggie's sake nothing be said "of the unfortunate connection with 'Spirits.'"[13] He graciously offered to give the money for Maggie's expenses directly to the Fox family to manage, but since Margaret was uncomfortable with the gesture, he asked his friend and intermediary Cornelius Grinnell to administer the fund. Seeing that the decision had been made and probably not wanting Kane to be her enemy forever, even Leah acquiesced, grumbling that she failed to understand why a young girl would choose to spend the most pleasant months of summer in school. Kane told Maggie that she was free to come and go as she wished and to decide in the fall whether to remain in Crookville or attend one of the fashionable boarding schools in Albany or Troy. Until then, she was to live with the Turner family, who were acquaintances of Eliza Leiper. Susannah Turner, wife and mother of the household, was known to be a kind, responsible woman, and her daughter, whom Kane jokingly but uncharitably called ugly, was to be Maggie's governess.

The message to Maggie was clear: if she was capable of transformation, she might become a suitable mate. Like a spirit, she was to emerge from her sensual, corporeal state a purified being.

Maggie was now triply bereaved: mourning a brother-in-law and nephew who had recently died, in seclusion from her old way of life, and bereft of her love who, for all she knew, might not survive his journey.

TWELVE

"MY DREAMS ALWAYS PROVE FALSE"

W ITH MAGGIE AWAY at school, supported by Kane and in retirement from public seances, the responsibilities for mediumship in the Fox family—both spiritual and financial—fell entirely to Kate and Leah. Sixteen-year-old Kate was hired by Horace H. Day, a wealthy businessman and the publisher of a magazine called the *Christian Spiritualist*, to hold free weekly meetings open to the public. The annual salary of twelve hundred dollars was excellent, but the work was hard, no longer fresh and exciting. Emma Hardinge, an English actress turned trance speaker and historian, also held meetings in the same building, and she sympathetically observed "poor patient Kate Fox, in the midst of a captious, grumbling crowd of investigators, repeating hour after hour the letters of the alphabet, whilst the no less *poor, patient* Spirits rapped out names, ages and dates to suit all-comers."[1] Yet compared to the weekly salary of three dollars made by a woman who worked in a textile factory, Kate was doing well.

Both Kate and Leah continued to hold seances for their private, paying clients, although now the two sisters lived and often worked separately, in part because the breach between Leah and Maggie over Kane had left scars. On her visits from Crookville, Maggie visited only her mother's house.

After Calvin's death in 1853, forty-year-old Leah moved first to Irving Street and then to Ludlow Street in Manhattan; Kate and fifty-seven-year-old Margaret took a home of their own on Tenth Street near Broadway. One visitor there, who called himself "A Searcher After Truth" waxed eloquent on the subject of Kate's appearance, commenting on her hair—black "as the wing of a raven" and parted "in two simple curls, after the Madonna style, giving striking effect to a fair forehead of an intellectual character"—and on her eyes, which he observed were a brilliant black, but pensive beneath long eyelashes. She was dressed modestly in black silk, he observed, with a gold cross at her neck.

His enthusiasm for her beauty didn't extend to her mediumship, however, for a spate of wrongly rapped answers dismayed him. Nevertheless, he remained curious enough to ask whether she had ever actually *seen* a spirit, and her answer seems to indicate that the spirits remained as alive to her, in reality or imagination, as they had been from the beginning. She replied that her grandfather, Jacob Smith, who had died in 1846, was often with her. Although she had never actually *seen* him, she knew by his characteristic actions, distinctive raps, and specific messages when he was close by.[2]

Jacob Smith seems to have been an influential spirit guide for Kate. For example, she once held a seance for the publisher and match manufacturer, Charles Partridge, at which a match boy's spirit complained in cruel detail about the hardships of his life. Partridge took pride in his business, one that employed hundreds of people and turned out millions of matches, and he demanded to know who had sent such a rude and accusatory being. In response, the match boy rapped "Jacob Smith," who apparently had lost none of the zeal for reform that had characterized some spirit messages from Hydesville on.

*   *   *

For a few months in the summer of 1853, Maggie dutifully remained at the Turners. Kane had consented to her wish to study German, joking, "You can scold me in German, flirt with country bumpkins in German, write naughty letters to me in German, and I'll be none the wiser."[3] He had advised her to concentrate on English history and literature and had asked her also to study music because he loved her beautiful voice.

The Turners' pleasant house stood behind a picket fence on an acre of land that smelled sweetly of roses and honeysuckle, and Maggie had a piano of her own in her bedroom. Daily life in the village of Crookville was as quiet as Kane hoped: he had imagined her "counting time by the village clock" or standing "under the shade of some drooping chestnut." For Maggie, though, the hush of this uneventful existence surely felt claustrophobic rather than comforting. If she had dreamed of a "quiet home," she had imagined sharing it with Kane.

When autumn came she delayed making a decision about schools, instead fleeing to New York. She avoided Leah, but she visited her mother and Kate often and lived at the Clinton Place home of Ellen Walter, an acquaintance Kane had handpicked as Maggie's city chaperone. Her absence from Crookville grew so long that in November 1853 Susannah Turner sent a concerned letter care of Walter, who replied that Maggie had been too ill to travel or even to write. Suffering from colds, coughs, headaches, earaches, and fevers, Maggie was under the care of Edward Bayard, a noted homeopathic physician from a prominent family.

When Maggie finally returned to Crookville around Christmas, she studied hard and in a neat schoolgirl's hand politely advised Cornelius Grinnell of her wants and needs. In one note she asked for eighty dollars, apologizing in a follow-up letter for not submitting a complete account of her expenses: money owed for board to Mrs. Turner and to Mrs. Walter along with reimbursement for her travel, French books, drawing materials, a bonnet, cape, dress, and doctor's bills for the treatment of her neuralgia. Other notes followed: an apologetic request for fifteen dollars one month, sixty another. Both Grinnell and Turner worried that Maggie spent money extravagantly, a tendency she shared with Leah, who had a liking not only for fine houses but also for pretty furnishings and clothes.

By February 1854 Maggie had already spent the money left for her care, and Grinnell approached Robert Patterson Kane for advice. Robert, Elisha's brother and lawyer, agreed to further support in deference to his brother's wishes, so long as Grinnell took the opportunity to put Maggie in her place. Remind her, Robert wrote, that she was known to them "only as a dependent, as one to whom the doctor bears the relation of a kind hearted friend whose interest in the young lady shows itself by furnishing her with the means of leading an honest life. . . ." He advised Grinnell that although they both wished to honor Kane's wishes, "Mlle. is not his mistress and holds to him no other relation than that of the recipient of his charity. . . ."[4]

Whaling ships and other expeditions headed north toward Greenland carried letters and provisions for Kane in the off chance of meeting up with the *Advance*. Maggie, who had heard false rumors of his imminent return, funneled her letters via Walter to Grinnell, and the contents of one are particularly revealing. After telling "Lish" her bits of news—what friends Mrs. Turner and Mrs. Leiper had been to her, how she was hoping to start her German lessons soon—she begged him to hurry home, reminding him that she often thought of his "sacred promise." Couldn't she share the secret of their engagement with Mrs. Walter? she asked.

"Some lady asked Mrs. Walter if she thought that you had any idea of marrying me. Mrs. Walter told her that she thought not. If any one should ask me that question, what shall I say?" She mischievously scolded the "Preacher" for hypocrisy by adding, "You say and I know it is very wrong to tell stories. I think I had better not answer the question at all." She seems to have harbored no doubts about Kane's plans to introduce her to his parents, for she mentioned feeling shy about meeting his father.

She also added a telling anecdote.

"I have visited Mrs. Walter. And while there," she wrote, "the Spirits directed Kathy and Mrs. Walter and myself to magnetize Dr. Bayard. He was suffering very much with the neuralgia in his face." Dr. Bayard, apparently, had become the patient.

"He had no pain for three or four weeks after that," Maggie continued. "But I am sorry to hear that it has returned again. Spiritual manifestations are spreading all over the world. Some of the greatest men in the world have become believers in the Spirits."[5]

Apparently she had never entirely disavowed her faith, even to her beloved Lish, who made such a show of disapproval.

During Maggie's stay in Crookville, Kane's book about his first Arctic expedition, *The United States Grinnell Expedition in Search of Sir John Franklin,* was published to wide acclaim, and she requested a copy of her own. When she finally received it, she thanked Grinnell effusively and confessed with a proprietary air that she was very pleased with her famous lover and his bold accomplishments. "Is he not brave to meet so many dangers face to face?" she demanded with heartfelt pride in the explorer.[6]

That spring of 1854 the British admiralty formally acknowledged Franklin's death, and Maggie must have wondered if the news would reach her lover and if it would speed his return. Lonely for those she cared about and perhaps frustrated as well by the apparent futility of Kane's mission, Maggie requested another chance to visit New York, promising that she would stay at Mrs. Walter's home rather than with her own family and study every day.

It had been almost a year since Kane had set off into uncharted territory, convinced that Franklin, in defiance of the British admiralty's orders, had headed north in search of the open polar sea. Following this projected route, one of Kane's scouting parties came upon a natural wonder that rivaled even the dream of open water: previously known only to the indigenous inhabitants of the Arctic region, it was the largest glacier on earth. From this slow-moving mountain of ice on Greenland's northwest coast, bergs as large as cathedrals floated off into the sea. Kane called the glacier a "crystal bridge" between two landmasses, and he named it the Humboldt glacier after a German scientist and explorer whom he admired.

Scientific discovery came at a price. Two of his men died. Wracked with scurvy, his other crew members were near mutiny against the commander who had led them far north with no sign of Franklin to show for the effort. The *Advance* remained ice locked in August, and a scouting party found no openings in that frozen world to sail south. With their second Arctic winter already on its way, Kane and his crew were trapped. At the end of October the light vanished.

That month another Franklin rescue party discovered a cache of artifacts: a gold chain, part of a telescope, a key. The Inuit recounted tales of starving men who had dropped dead in their tracks as they hauled their longboats across the ice. It was clear that the stories described some of Franklin's men and that he had traveled a different route from Kane's, far to the south, where he almost certainly had perished.

This news quickly reached the United States. Maggie, who had spent the summer of 1854 in New York but had returned to Crookville for the fall, was back in the city by Christmas. "I suppose all further Search for Sir John or Crew will be unnecessary," she remarked hopefully to Grinnell.[7] He, however, understood that as Kane had not already returned, the future of the *Advance* was in doubt.

Writing in his journal on Christmas Day, Kane described a vision so intense that today it might be called an out-of-body experience. In his waking dream he was no longer on the *Advance* but in his family's festive dining room, watching his parents, friends, and other relatives enjoying themselves around the holiday dinner table. Though he disdained seances, Kane wasn't altogether immune from the pull of the seemingly inexplicable, and the vision was so apt in every detail that it stunned and distressed him. As a self-described pragmatic man of action, he denounced his own tendency to fall subject to what he called magnetism.

On New Year's Eve 1854, outside in the icy, dark night, Kane had another unsettling experience. This time, as he struggled to light a fire, he saw an amorphous, phosphorescent glow envelop his hand. Even more disturbing, the man with him also witnessed the light. The impossible halo glimmered until the fire finally caught and outshone it, inaugurating the year 1855.[8]

If the American public was united in its admiration for and fascination with Kane's story—a brave man with a debilitating illness, risking his own life on a heroic voyage for the sake of knowledge and to save another man's life—it remained critically divided on issues at home. In 1854 Congress effectively erased the borderline it had established thirty years earlier to limit slavery's expansion north. Instead, the settlers of the newly organized territories of Kansas and Nebraska were granted the right to decide the issue of slavery for themselves upon petitioning for statehood.

The Kansas-Nebraska Act, as the new law was known, constituted a stunning blow to antislavery forces and continued the nation's march toward civil war. Kansas became known as "bleeding Kansas" for the violence that erupted between pro- and antislavery settlers there, some of it incited by outside agitators. The Whig Party, moribund after recent defeats, was replaced by the new Republican Party, which consisted largely of members opposed to slavery or at least to its further expansion in the territories. A lawyer and Whig from Illinois—soon to become a Republican—named Abraham Lincoln began to make a national reputation for himself by criticizing the provisions of the Kansas-Nebraska Act.

Many antislavery Spiritualists worked for abolition through organizations dedicated to the cause, but there's no evidence that the Fox sisters actively participated in any of these or spoke out in public about the developing crisis. The personal, especially bereavement, rather than the political usually predominated at their private seances. The sisters' longtime friendship with reformers such as the Posts and Frederick Douglass, however, clearly points to their political sympathies, and the spirits who spoke through them seem to have used their influence, if subtly, on behalf of abolition and other reforms. The little girl—Kate—who had once urged George Willets to attend the antislavery fair in Rochester and who introduced Charles Partridge to the unhappy match boy's spirit undoubtedly passed along similar messages to others.

During the middle years of the 1850s the Spiritualist movement itself continued to grow, like the nation spanning the continent from the East Coast to California. But controversy surrounded its adherents. Under pressure for his unorthodox beliefs, Judge Edmonds resigned from the bench; he later issued a statement that brusquely reminded his colleagues that he was nobody's fool and that in fact he had used the same skills to investigate the spirits as those he had employed in his thirty years of successful practice at the bar.[9]

Edmonds's prominence and the attention he received provoked

envy among some of his fellow Spiritualists. "He talked well," commented one acerbic critic after a lecture, "but said nothing but what was & is familiar to inteligent [sic] Spiritualists, but as it was Judge Edmonds it created a good deal of excitement, filled a large Hall and was no doubt productive of some good."[10]

The former judge estimated that the number of Spiritualists in the United States had risen to several hundred thousand. In 1854, convinced of strong popular interest, Nathaniel Tallmadge, former governor of Wisconsin and a friend of the Fox family, presented a petition to Senator James Shields, Democrat from Illinois, and asked him to sponsor it in Congress. Signed by more than a thousand people, the petition proposed the creation of an official government committee to examine Spiritualist phenomena. Shields, however, betrayed Tallmadge, first by making a public joke of the document, then by calling Spiritualism an "occult science," a label that believers vehemently rejected, insisting that there was nothing arcane or supernatural about their faith. The bill died.[11]

Attempts to create stable organizations also marked these years, although the democratic and individualist nature of Spiritualism presented obstacles. In June 1854 Edmonds, Tallmadge, and Horace H. Day—Kate's employer—helped found the Society for the Diffusion of Spiritual Knowledge. In a book published a year later, *Modern Spiritualism: Its Facts and Fantasies, Its Consistencies and Contradictions,* Eliab Capron dismissed the society as a pompous group of intellectually pretentious newcomers, stating that they had called their first meeting in secret and excluded "old and tried friends"—himself among them.

Capron's *Modern Spiritualism* was a seminal work, the first substantial history of the movement. Although the author didn't hesitate to criticize some of his fellow believers, in general the book constitutes an unabashed ode to spirit communication. He remained a loyal promoter of the Fox sisters, whose reputations he in fact had helped to create, and stressed their unique position among the hundreds of mediums who followed them. Kate, as always, seemed to interest him most, for he wrote that it was she who in 1848 "seemed to be required in order to obtain the communications. . . . This was the first discovery of mediumship in that family."[12]

Capron, always the promoter, drew on every theatrical story or colorful rumor that had surfaced since Hydesville. The peddler, for instance, had produced not only raps but other, far more horrifying, noises: "A sound like the death struggle, the gurgling in the throat . . . of a man whose throat was cut; then the sound of dragging a lifeless body across the room, down the stairs, the feet striking on each step . . . then a sound as if shoveling dirt in the cellar, the nailing of boards, and the filling up of the hastily-made grave. . . ."[13]

During the winter and spring of 1855, Maggie ricocheted back and forth between Susannah Turner's house in Crookville and Ellen Walter's in New York. She often visited Kate, whose own routines—generally a matter of holding seances at Tenth Street—also remained largely unchanged from the previous year. With a touch of flattery and nostalgia, Kate wrote to Amy Post, "I am very lonely: oh, how I do wish that you were here, you know we always loved you. I can not think of you as a mere friend but as something dearer."[14] But she was equally eager to relay her pleasure with both the spirits and her new friends. She was always happiest when with trusted comrades, and she felt she had found a warm circle in New York.

"Last evening the Bayard family met at our house for spiritual manifestations," Kate said. "The piano was sweetly played upon by spirit fingers, the guitar was played, then taken up and carried above our heads, each person in the circle was touched. The room was perfectly dark and *all hands held*. Dr. Bayard and family said that they had never passed a happier evening in all their lives." Kate cheerfully confided that her headaches had been cured by a healing medium and that she was planning to attend the opera with Mrs. Walter that night.

Although the Turners were hesitant to allow Maggie to take another trip, in July they agreed to one at Ellen Walter's request. As usual, much to Susannah Turner's frustration, Maggie postponed her return. In August the prodigal student accompanied her mother and Kate to Wayne County for a weeklong reunion with family: her father, David and Elizabeth Fox, Maria and Stephen Smith, and a half-dozen nieces and nephews. Joseph Post, Amy's son, came along. "We do have merry times enough," he wrote to his mother, commenting also that "David is one of the kindest souls. . . ."[15]

Kate added a postscript: Maggie and Joseph tried to play a prank on gullible David by pretending to be married. How the couple planned to convince him, with what pantomime of affection, can only be imagined, but the presence of "an old Methodist lady" who wore "a face nearly as long as a steeple" inhibited the jokesters and spoiled the joke. The anecdote suggests that Maggie, much as she may have missed Kane, could still be flirtatious and enjoy herself.

That August of 1855, twenty-seven months after their departure, Elisha Kent Kane and his men were rescued by a merchant ship off the southern coast of Greenland, more than a thousand miles from where they finally had abandoned the *Advance*. They had spent the previous winter living in the shell of the brig, which had been crushed by collisions with icebergs and ground between ice floes that had locked it in place, then carried it north as they drifted. With the *Advance* unfit for sailing, Kane and his crew had set out in late May to travel by foot and longboat across thirteen hundred miles of Arctic ice, hauling their supplies on sledges, which also carried the sick, until they could launch their boats in open water. One-sixth of his party had died in the attempt to find Franklin, but Kane had mapped regions never charted before, in the process accumulating a wealth of new information on the Arctic and its people.

His return was preceded by a spate of newspaper articles that not only announced his rescue but also reported the rumor that "the celebrated Dr. Kane would shortly lead to the altar Miss Margaret Fox, of spirit-rapping celebrity." Cornelius Grinnell suspected the items had been planted by Leah in a determined effort to force Kane's hand. If Kane's parents had turned a blind eye to the relationship before, they certainly couldn't do so any longer.

On October 11, 1855, Maggie learned that Kane was aboard a steamer entering New York Harbor. She had spent September in Crookville, but she was back in New York by the time he returned. She waited at Ellen Walter's, certain that he would visit. No word came the first day, and none the second. She crept to the house on Tenth Street to be with her mother and Kate. Later that evening Walter sent a message and carriage for her: a visitor was at the door of her Clinton Place home, and Walter was sure he was Kane.

Walter unfortunately had jumped to conclusions, for her guest wasn't Kane at all but his loyal friend, Grinnell, sent to retrieve the explorer's love letters. Walter apologized to Maggie, hiding the truth from her and saying that the guest had been some gentlemen on business.

Dressed in full naval regalia, Kane himself arrived the next day and asked Maggie to sign a document disclaiming any romantic relationship between them. Understandably wretched but dignified, she did so. Apparently stirred by the sight of her, Kane found his resolve evaporating. He didn't go so far as to renew their engagement, but he returned the following morning, handed the document back to her, and told her to tear it up.

And the cycle of approach and withdrawal began again with a battery of letters that castigated her even as they surely titillated them both. Since Kane had reneged on his commitment, Maggie returned to holding seances, an act that, not surprisingly, provoked him.

"Do keep out of spirit-circles," Kane begged, but his reasons now had less to do with ethics and duplicity and more to do with sex. "I can't bear the idea of your sitting in the dark, squeezing other people's hands," he wrote. "I touch no hands but yours; press no lips but yours; think of no thoughts that I would not share with you; and do no deeds that I would conceal from you. Can you say as much? Will the spirit answer?"[16]

Dressed in her glamorous white silk cloak, she accompanied him to the opera; bundled beneath buffalo robes, they went for sleigh rides in the country. He apparently was a marvelous mimic, with a boyish charm that delighted her. During one of their frequent separations, she wrote, "Lish', I have not laughed since we parted. By the time we meet again I fear I shall quite have forgotten to laugh; and then you will clothe me in the habiliments of a nun, and send me to a convent to count my rosary."

Once, after her temperamental poodle had nipped Kane's hand, she responded with a tongue-in-cheek twist on the notion of supernatural powers.

"I am very sorry that little Tommie bit your hand," she apologized, clearly amused instead. "I hope it does not give you pain. Tommie is very cross to many. You must not be superstitious, and attribute his unkindness to any fault of his mistress. Dogs are very strange things, and Tommie is very sagacious, and thinks himself *very* smart."

When work consumed him and he couldn't get away, she wrote to him in bittersweet, sentimental cadences. "What duties have you, my Ly, which claim your presence in Philadelphia this evening?" she asked in one letter, adding a few sentences later, "I shall surely expect to see you Monday evening, and now as the 'shadows lengthen' and the hours grow sad and dull, my soul will leave New York and fly to its treasured love."[17]

The newspapers had seized on the story of the love affair and wouldn't let it go. Horace Greeley grumbled avuncularly that the couple should be left alone. In a passage that points to the stunning celebrity of both Maggie and Kane, he demanded, "What right has the public to know anything about an 'engagement' or non-engagement between these young people? If this were a monarchy, and one or both of them were of the blood royal, there would be an excuse for reports and speculation with regard to their relations to each other. . . ."[18]

Appropriately, Maggie nicknamed Kane's parents, whom she had never met, "The Royal Family."

Margaret Fox was less sanguine about the relationship than her daughter and tried to discourage Kane, but he stubbornly persisted in visiting two to three times a day. Then a crisis occurred, possibly precipitated by old rumors of Kane's illegitimate child. As friends pressed Margaret to end her daughter's relationship, she finally erupted in a maternal rage at the explorer, threatening that she would "publish" him to the world if he didn't leave her daughter alone. She cried, "I from this moment *forbid* you ever again entering my house. I *forbid* my daughter ever receiving you while she is under my care . . . my child is as pure as an angel, and if you are seen coming here the world will censure her."[19]

Kane responded by writing to Maggie that he would never believe such a ban unless it came directly from her own lips.

She firmly replied, "I must either give you up from this moment and forever, or give up those who are very dear to me, and who hold my name and reputation as sacred."[20]

But the story wasn't over. In April 1856, six months after Kane's return from the Arctic, he attended the funeral of one of his friends and was left feeling sad and depressed. That day he demanded to see Maggie, set siege to the house, and wouldn't be turned away. As at Calvin Brown's funeral three years earlier, he apparently had been moved to action by loss: he reiterated his offer of marriage.

According to the Fox family's account, Kane sealed the engagement by placing a cherished ring from the Arctic on her finger and by giving her a locket that contained a few strands of his deceased brother Willie's hair. Yet Kane continued to insist that no one other than Maggie's family and a few close friends be told about the engagement until he had finished his book and started earning an income. Until then, he was dependent on his parents' financial support.

A few weeks later Maggie, Kate, and their mother moved from the Tenth Street house to a more spacious residence on Twenty-Second Street. By then, Margaret's ambivalence and concern seem to have lessened, the change propelled no doubt by Kane's promise to marry her daughter. Maggie was permitted to have her own private domain on the third floor, with a bedroom and pretty parlor to herself. There, despite Margaret's objections, Kane became a frequent visitor to Maggie's unchaperoned quarters.

"Tell your mother not to distress herself about the third story room," he reassured her. "I regard it as a sort of sanctuary: a retreat to which we are driven by mischief-making eyes and tongues."

But his thoughts weren't always so pure; he concluded one of his notes to Maggie by reminding her that "there is not a single naughty word, and what is better, not a single naughty thought, in all this letter."

The Victorians approved of flirtation, courtship, and declarations of passion, but they expected women to remain chaste until marriage. Given the blatant appearance of impropriety, Maggie's reputation—what was left of it—was surely as good as ruined. Up to a point, the Kanes may have recognized their son's responsibility for pursuing the romance. But he, of course, was their much-loved child: easier for them to imagine him as the innocent who had been seduced by a social climber with a sorceress's powers than as the seducer.

Through the spring and summer of 1856 Kane worked day and night on his book. Although he'd returned from the Arctic looking healthier than ever except for more gray in his hair, now the long hours of lecturing and writing left him pale and sick. His manuscript, called *Arctic Explorations: the Second Grinnell Expedition in Search of Sir John Franklin,* was completed in August 1856. It was a "centre-table book" with magnificent illustrations and a text that was evocative and poetic as well as scientific. It was wildly popular—second in popularity that year, it was said, only to the Bible.[21]

Kane planned to go to England to present a copy of the book to John Franklin's widow and to plan another expedition. In August Maggie accompanied Kate and her mother to Canada to visit her sister Elizabeth, and she wasn't certain that she'd return in time to see him before he sailed. In a letter from Canada she teased him about the dances and balls to which she'd been invited, then struck a more serious note.

"I have often dreamt of you since I left, and have twice dreamt that you were *very* ill, and wakened each time weeping bitterly," she said, "but fortunately my dreams always prove false, unless they are of a pleasing character.

"I am no great believer in dreams whether pleasant or unpleasant," she added.[22]

A postponement of Kane's trip gave the lovers a few weeks for a brief, happy, reunion. From Philadelphia he wrote affectionate notes, calling her his "dear, darling little 'spirit!'"[23] On his visits to New York they took drives, went to the opera, and spent time in the privacy of the third floor. He bought her a diamond bracelet from Tiffany's and arranged to have a photograph taken of her, joking about subjects that once had distressed him.

"Don't be afraid of your neck and shoulders," he told her, advising her on how to dress for the portrait. "I want you to look like a Circe, for you have already changed me into a wild Boar." She attached the locket that he had given her to his watch chain so that it would go with him, a powerful reminder of the bond between them.

According to Maggie, one evening he suddenly summoned Kate, Margaret, and another witness into the parlor and swore in their presence, "Maggie is my wife, and I am her husband. Wherever we are, she is mine, and I am hers. Do you understand and consent to this, Maggie." Although no longer common, the custom of marriage by mutual consent had a long history, and Kane may have felt that he had happened upon a romantic solution to a problem that, on the eve of his imminent departure, he had been unable to resolve in any other way.

Afterward, he called Maggie "wife" and assured her that she would be taken care of should anything happen to him. He left the United States for England soon after this secret little ceremony.

By the time Kane reached England he was so ill that Lady Franklin dropped any plans she had except to nurse him. When he didn't recover, his doctors exiled him to the tropics, where it was hoped that the warm weather would cure him.

"I am quite sick, and have gone to Havana; only one week from New York," he wrote to Maggie. "I have received no letters from you. . . ."

She sent back a note immediately, writing with caution, as she usually did with letters that threatened to fall into his family's hands.

"Could I only see you," she said, "I would say much that I cannot write."

He didn't answer; perhaps her letter was never delivered or he was too weak to respond. On February 16, 1857, thirty-seven-year-old Elisha Kent Kane died. His flag-draped coffin was received in state at the port of New Orleans, carried by steamboat up the Mississippi, then transported by locomotive across the country to Philadelphia. Crowds of weeping men and women saluted the fallen hero along the way. His exploration of the Arctic, a world as mythic in its foreboding beauty and mystery as the spirit world, had captured the public's imagination; his courage in confronting his own lifelong illness and his indomitable determination in facing the perils of his journey had won him admiration and devotion. In all but his love life, Elisha Kent Kane had been a brave man.[24]

His family not only denied that Kane had ever intended to marry Maggie, they also claimed that his only motives for helping her had been fraternal and benevolent, the impulse to rescue an unfortunate girl.

In the wake of Kane's death, Maggie experienced what can only be described as a total breakdown. Later she remembered her condition as "brain fever." Often ill with headaches and neuralgia under less stressful circumstances, she now fell into a depression and nervous collapse no doubt exacerbated by the narcotic medicines of the day; she was in a state of near delirium.

For Kate, who early on had acted as Kane's go-between and who had been his "dear open-minded" girl, the explorer's death must also have been crushing. He had promised to save her too from the tiresome rounds of seances with strangers and to provide her with a life that as she grew older would be satisfying and fulfilling, to raise her up to his own level of secure upper-middle-class gentility, even as he had vowed to raise Maggie. The hopes Kate had harbored for her sister undoubtedly had seemed bright for her own future. Content to be with those in whose affections she felt safe, she must have thought about a time when she'd be valued, not necessarily as a medium, invisible behind the spirits, but as a woman loved for who she was, as Maggie was loved by Kane.

What message was Kate sent, not by Kane's immortal spirit, but by the reality of his death? Surely it was one about false promises and betrayal. Although she may have mourned the loss of Elisha Kent Kane, her grief certainly was more intense for Maggie and herself.

In April 1857 Margaret Fox wrote to one of Kane's brothers, Robert, telling him that their mutual acquaintance, Mrs. Cornelius Grinnell, had implied that a small bequest had been left to Maggie. Robert, a lawyer, had helped arrange his brother's affairs.

"Her trials have been (as you must already know) greater than she could bear," wrote Margaret, "and we fear that unless changes soon take place she cannot survive them much longer."[25]

Although Kane had willed almost everything to his family, he had placed five thousand dollars separately in Robert's care. Kane's family swiftly denied that the explorer had intended the money for Maggie.

By May Maggie was strong enough to write to Robert herself, asking not for money but for some posthumous word. "I know the Dr. must have left some message for me," she said, "and know that you will not refuse to deliver it even though it gives you much pain in recalling the name of him whose memory is and ever will be sacred. I have always held a religious faith in the deep sincerity of the Dr.'s love and his memory will always remain a beautiful green in my unchanged affections."[26]

PART IV

WORLDLY TRIALS
1857–1888

THIRTEEN

"SO MANY UPS AND DOWNS IN THIS WEARY WORLD"

FOR ALL KANE'S OBSESSION with secrecy, the newspapers, hungry for gossip about two celebrities and happy to print rumors side by side with facts, had tracked the romance at every stage. Although many people who knew Maggie, and some who didn't, sympathized with her situation, the outcome was not only a tragedy but also an embarrassment, as Leah had long feared. At the sight of her sister's misery, however, Leah relented, and for the present they forgave one another for their mutual recriminations.

And life in this world went on. In 1857 Leah was still holding seances on Ludlow Street, where she was visited on at least one occasion by the lawyer George Templeton Strong. A diarist who wrote about almost every aspect of life in the city, Strong had met the Fox sisters in 1850 and continued to be interested in Spiritualism, although his ideas changed through the years. He initially had believed a natural cause such as electricity might produce the manifestations, then a year or two later had suggested that "opium, drink, and mental excitement" played a role. When a respected chemist, Robert Hare, converted to Spiritualism in the mid-1850s Strong commented, "Hare seems as mad as one of his quadrupedal namesakes in the month of March."[1]

When Strong emerged from his visit to Leah, he was sure she practiced what he called "mind-reading." He had posed questions "about an imaginary transaction, fixing my thoughts on an answer—and that answer was given with great precision."

Strong wasn't the only person to grow increasingly skeptical about Spiritualism, or at least about the Fox sisters, as the years went by. Even some of the sisters' old Rochester friends, among them George Willets, developed doubts. By 1857 he had moved to New Jersey, where Leah agreed to hold regular seances for a group of his friends and relatives, a circle that included Daniel Underhill, a widowed businessman who may have been distantly related to the Post family.

After witnessing luminous orbs floating around the room, some members of the group became suspicious that Leah had coated her hands with granules of phosphorus. She in turn protested that the spirits themselves had produced the granules, much to her surprise. Not everyone was convinced by her explanation, but Daniel Underhill was. His interest soon turned from otherworldly to earthly matters, and he began to court her. He was a desirable suitor in every way: a committed Spiritualist, well-to-do, from an old and respected family, president of an important insurance company, and about eight years younger than forty-four-year-old Leah.[2]

In June 1857, four months after Kane's death, Leah and Kate accepted a challenge that, for the sake both of Spiritualism and the Fox family's name, they felt they couldn't ignore. The Boston Courier had offered a reward of five hundred dollars to any medium who could prove the existence of spirit communication to a panel of four distinguished Harvard professors, including the renowned mathematician and astronomer Benjamin Peirce and Louis Agassiz, the most famous natural scientist of his day. A proponent of the theory of an Ice Age, the latter was the man for whom Elisha Kent Kane had named a remote Arctic promontory, calling the point Cape Agassiz.[3] The scientist, however, wasn't universally loved; the philosopher William James, who studied under him, later described Agassiz as "such a politician & so self-seeking and illiberal to others that it sadly diminishes one's respect for him."[4]

In sponsoring the investigation, the *Courier* was capitalizing on an earlier controversy. A Harvard engineering professor, after attending a few seances conducted by a divinity student, had accused the medium of fraud. The student was expelled, but arguments over the case raged on.

The Harvard professors and the reporter assigned by the *Courier* all found the mediums—about ten in all—entirely unconvincing. Two of them, the young Davenport brothers, were called "Cabinet Mediums" for exhibitions in which they allowed themselves to be tightly bound head and foot, then locked inside a portable cabinet along with an assortment of musical instruments. While the two teenagers presumably sat immobile within the cabinet, listeners on the outside could hear rapturous melodies being played behind its locked doors.

This time, however, the Harvard professors assigned Benjamin Peirce to join the brothers in the cabinet. Once the Davenports had been tied up, Peirce entered, grabbed up all the instruments—two tambourines, a fiddle, a banjo, and a horn—and clutched the items between his knees.

The *Courier's* reporter described the scene with undisguised delight:

"Before the last jet of gas was turned off, the aspect of Prof. Peirce, looking out from the shadows of the tabernacle, with the spiritual youngsters on each side of him, and vigilantly guarding the instruments which were soon to be toned by the supernatural orchestra, was something pictorial to behold."[5]

After ten minutes of silence, during which the spirit ensemble played no music, the jets were relit and the gloating professor emerged from the cabinet.

At the conclusion of the two-day investigation, the reporter wrote that only the Fox sisters had produced manifestations, and these he and the professors chose to dismiss as just "a little rapping by the Foxes, easily traceable to their persons and easily done by others without the pretense of spirits; not a table or piano lifted or anything moved a single hair's breath. . . . So ends this ridiculous and infamous imposture."

The mediums claimed that the manifestations had been predictably weak because of the investigators' hostility, and they organized a second set of demonstrations for a different group of reporters, who turned out to be more enthusiastic. The Harvard professors, however, remained steadfast and fierce in their denunciation of what they considered out-and-out fraud, signing a statement that argued that "any connection with spiritualist circles, so called, corrupts the morals and degrades the intellect." The panel members deemed it "their solemn duty to warn the community against this contaminating influence, which surely tends to lessen the truth of man and the purity of woman."[6] Although Spiritualism had long been accused by its opponents of causing everything from adultery to insanity, this denunciation may have more personal, expressing in part Louis Agassiz's attitude toward Maggie Fox for her "contaminating" influence on "the truth" of a man who had named a geographical promontory in his honor: Elisha Kent Kane.

By the autumn of 1858 Maggie had forged an erratic relationship with Kane's brother—and lawyer—Robert Patterson Kane. His family had asked him to retrieve the explorer's love letters, and whether for that reason alone or because of genuine affection for her, Robert occasionally visited and brought gifts. She often responded flirtatiously, as though trying to reassure herself that she had lost none of Circe's old powers. But sometimes, when he pushed too hard, she reacted with understandable rancor over his family's attitude toward her.

"The letters are mine to guard and cherish so long as I live and when I am no longer able to guard them, I will place them with you," she wrote. "But do not think me so lost as to ever allow them to be published—"[7]

She insisted on her own and Kane's integrity, no matter the ambiguities that had clouded the sad situation. "The private marriage you can think of as you please," she told Robert, admitting that she herself thought "a private marriage is quite as disgraceful as to stand in another light. . . ." But she added—bravely if unrealistically—that neither Robert nor his parents could ever deny Kane's honorable intentions, at least not to her.[8]

In devotion to his memory, in August 1858 Maggie converted to

Catholicism, explaining that even before his death Kane had urged her to do so. His choice for her is puzzling since he himself had been baptized a Presbyterian. Moreover, anti-Catholic feeling, largely associated with a virulent nativism sparked by fears of immigration, was running high in the United States in the 1850s. Kane had been a Mason too, and the antagonism between Freemasons and Catholics was no secret.

Perhaps Catholicism, which at the time seemed to some Protestants to be imbued with medieval mystery and drama, had appealed to Kane's romantic nature, and he had come to believe that the church's pomp and splendor would suit the passionate Maggie. Catholicism also provided firm, paternal guidance in moral and religious matters, along with the frequent opportunity for the parishioner to confess sins and to be granted absolution. The church may have seemed to Kane ideally capable of fulfilling the role of stern but compassionate and loving teacher, a part in which he so often had cast himself.

Maggie's baptism sparked a warm response and the gift of a rosary from Robert Kane. Newspapers reported on the event sympathetically, but they offered different interpretations of it. Did Maggie's conversion to Catholicism mean that Spiritualism was insufficient to sustain her or that the spirits themselves were nonexistent? Horace Greeley tried to separate her conversion from any overall judgement on Spiritualism, emphasizing that she had "never dreamed of saying or implying that any of her family were guilty of fraud or deception in the matter of the 'Rappings.' "

He was right in his attempt to distinguish the two. Maggie renounced her association with Spiritualism without publicly denouncing either the spirits or her family. Whatever Catholicism may have meant to Kane, to Maggie it meant absolute deference to his wishes, those desires of his that, for a host of reasons, some under her control and some not, she often had defied in his lifetime: by playing truant from Crookville, by participating in seances, by seeming to him to be too dangerously alluring, by seeming to him to be not loving enough. In accepting Catholicism, she rejected Spiritualism as Kane had asked her to do and as in her guilt and despair she surely wished she had done years earlier.

The house at 50 East Twenty-Second Street now seemed expensive, all the more so with Maggie dependent and in seclusion, and the third-floor apartment especially was filled with sad memories. Horace Greeley came to the rescue, inviting Kate, Maggie, and Margaret to move into the home he maintained at 35 East Nineteenth Street. The Greeleys, who traveled and also spent time at their country residence, were grateful to have caretakers there, and the situation was a boon to the Fox family. The house on Nineteenth Street, moreover, soon became the site of the one joyous event that took place during this sad time.

It was with Robert Kane that Maggie shared the good news, confiding that Leah planned to marry Daniel Underhill. "Now I am going to tell you the best news you have listened to for many years," Maggie glowed, apparently without envy that Leah's romance was to end more happily than her own.

"Leah poor Leah that has had so many ups and downs in this weary world is to be married *honorably* and by a minister at this house next Wednesday Nov. 3rd—Her husband is wealthy, his family are Quakers, and there is no end to his relations here and in Philadelphia. . . ." Maggie admitted that the "Doctor disliked Leah and for that reason I almost despised her; but she has been very kind to me since he died, and has talked so affectionately of him that I have forgiven her."[10]

John Fox attended the wedding, which was held in the Greeleys' parlor, and then stayed on. His little house next to David's in Wayne County had been destroyed by fire; he also may have had other reasons for making the change. Old and frail, he may have wanted his wife's companionship in his last years or believed he could be of some comfort to the grieving Maggie.

The newlyweds, Leah Fox Fish Brown Underhill and her husband, Daniel, moved into a home at 232 West Thirty-Seventh Street in Manhattan, and she retired from public seances. She was now in her mid-forties, stout, enlarged to formidable proportions by the huge petticoats popular in her day. Her square, open face had thickened with age but retained its pleasing expression, so much like her mother's. She had found herself a husband who was dignified and attractive, with a wavy abundance of fair hair, whose fire insurance business supported her in style, who treated her siblings and parents kindly.[11] Leah's nieces and nephews—the children of her brother David and her sister Maria—visited the house on Thirty-Seventh Street so frequently that Leah urged them to call her "Ma." Eventually she and Daniel, either formally or informally, adopted a daughter named Lillie, who also may have been David's or another relative's child.[12]

Leah had become the bourgeois housewife that she had yearned for so long to be, a life very different from the one she had led as a single mother in Rochester or as the doyenne of mediums in New York. She was as stodgily respectable as any of the notorious Fox sisters could hope to be. Her house reflected the then-current version of the American dream, its two adjoining parlors a warren of carved rosewood chairs, polished side tables, gilt mirrors, ornately framed paintings, bric-a-brac, dizzily patterned area rugs, and lace and velvet draperies. The centerpiece, of course, was her piano, as it had been since her days as a music teacher. Birds warbled in the nearby aviary, a sunny space that she used to entertain and that blossomed with flowering plants all year long. The Underhills' home in Manhattan was a perfect Victorian showplace.

Despite the newfound calm and security of her marriage, Leah wasn't about to surrender her hold on spirit communication entirely, perhaps because she thoroughly enjoyed the personal power and pleasure it gave her. In private and for free, she continued to dazzle family and friends with her mediumistic prowess. Emma Hardinge called her "the best test, rapping, and physical medium I ever met, as well as one of the kindest and most noble-hearted of women," pleased perhaps to have a more socially substantial member of the Fox family to praise than the increasingly woebegone Kate or Catholic Maggie.

Leah had an enthusiastic audience in Robert Dale Owen, an American philosopher, diplomat, and social reformer who, by the time he met her in 1859, had abandoned atheism to investigate Spiritualism. In his first book on the movement, *Footfalls on the Boundary of Another World*, published in 1860, Owen examined phenomena such as poltergeists and apparitions, and he retold the story of the Fox family in a version undoubtedly influenced by Leah. Kate was only nine and Maggie twelve in 1848, he asserted, making the girls not only more childlike when the raps began but also more innocent in 1852, when Maggie met Kane.

Other revisions heightened the Fox family's genteel respectability. As children, according to Owen, Kate and Maggie had slept in their own bedroom rather than in their parents'. By 1860 middle-class families valued the privacy—and demonstrable appearance of financial well-being—afforded by separate bedrooms.

In October 1860 Owen accompanied Kate, Leah, Daniel, and several other friends on a mission that would have satisfied the thrill-seeking ghost hunter hidden in the heart of any dignified Spiritualist. The group visited a large old house in the country, a rambling and decrepit place reputedly haunted by a former owner, Peter Livingston. In life, Owen wrote, Livingston had been lame and had used a small invalid's carriage to propel himself about. It was whispered that his carriage now careened through the house's dark corridors at night.

That evening Owen, Leah, and their little group huddled around a small table in the ghost's former bedroom and put out the lights. A minute afterward, "such a clatter began," as if "heavy substances of iron, such as ponderous dumb-bells or weights," were rolling across the floor. Pounding, like that made by a heavy mallet, followed.

"Then," Owen wrote, "was heard a sound precisely resembling the rolling of a small carriage on a plank floor." As the invisible carriage raced frantically around the floor, someone suddenly, without warning, lit a candle. The room fell instantly silent.

The group tried the experiment again and again, always with the same result. "The sudden transition, without apparent cause, from such a babel of noises to a dead silence," Owen wrote, "was an experience such as few have had, in this world."[13]

Three nights later, on October 25—two and a half years after her conversion to Catholicism—Maggie joined Owen, Kate, and her mother for a private seance. With windows and doors locked and the room dark, Owen felt the power of "a tremendous blow on the centre of the table; a blow so violent that we all instinctively started back. By the sound it was such a stroke, apparently dealt by a strong man with a heavy bludgeon, as would have killed any one. . . ."[14]

Perhaps the blow reflected Maggie's growing rage at the Kane family or the anger of lower spirits on her behalf. To drown her grief and frustration over the course her life had taken, she had started drinking heavily, and her letters to Robert Kane were becoming more aggressive and desperate. Although he was still sending occasional gifts of money, her gratitude had turned to frustration at feeling she had to beg.

Maggie felt trapped. She had no husband or inheritance, and few options were available to her for earning a living unless she resumed holding public seances. But she desperately wished to honor Kane's wishes, so powerful was the hold he exercised over her even after his death. For their part, the Kanes continued not only to demand Elisha's love letters back but also to refuse to pay her the five-thousand-dollar inheritance that she believed had been left specifically for her care.

A few months before attending the seance with Owen, Maggie had begged Robert Kane to bring her the little locket engraved with Willie's name that Elisha had carried with him to England. "I will remember the kindness eternally," she said. "The Doctor gave me the locket and I fastened it again to his watch chain."[15]

Denied that, she had asked Robert for a lock of her lover's hair, sending along one of Elisha's letters "that you may know how sacred the love between the doctor & myself was. . . ."[16]

In September 1860, a month before she attended the seance with Owen, she had scrawled a note to Robert Kane in huge drunken letters, promising to deliver all of his brother's letters if he would only help her out and send her a little more money.[17]

By now Maggie had moved from the Greeleys' house to a small apartment of her own on West Forty-Sixth Street in Manhattan. There, more like a traditional mourner than a medium, she established what others later called a shrine to her dead lover, a place filled with mementos of what, despite the painful turmoil of her romance, she chose to remember as happier days. She remained relatively isolated, seeing only her family and close friends, and passionately denied rumors that she still held seances. Kane had despised everything associated with Spiritualism, she said, and now so did she.

*   *   *

Robert Dale Owen required one final piece of evidence to convince him of the spirits' authenticity. One summer afternoon, on an excursion with the Underhills and another friend, he drove to a seaside village, and from there the foursome set out for a walk along the nearby rocky beach. The view was a sublime one of the sort that many painters of the day tried to capture.

"The portion of rock whither we repaired was not an isolated block, detached from the rest," Owen explained, "but part of a large, flat mass of rock, covering at least half an acre and running back into a bluff bank that rose beyond it: there were also several underlying ledges. We were about thirty feet from the sea and, as there was a moderate breeze, the surf broke on the rocks below us.

"But yet," he continued, "standing on the ledge beside Mrs. Underhill and asking for the raps, I heard them quite distinctly above the noise produced by the surf. This was several times repeated, with the same result."

He clambered over the boulders, down to a lower ledge, and placed his ear against the bottom of the outcrop on which Leah and her companions were seated. "I felt," he wrote, "simultaneously with each rap, a slight but *unmistakably distinct vibration or concussion of the rock*."[18]

In the vastness of that natural setting, in a location that no medium could control, the spirits seemed to Owen at that moment to have provided authoritative proof of their existence. From then on he found it unnecessary to conduct further tests.

FOURTEEN

"A MEDIUM OF REFLECTING OTHERS"

O F THE THREE FOX SISTERS, Kate alone now held seances for paying clients; indeed, her life had grown increasingly dedicated to, or circumscribed by, her work on the spirits' behalf. In 1861 she was almost twenty-four years old, five years older than Maggie had been on first meeting Elisha Kent Kane. Apart from her schoolgirl crush on John E. Robinson, Kate had never shown any sign of interest in a suitor, and in fact no public suitor had courted her. She lived with her parents at the Greeleys' house, she met with clients, and she visited Maggie, whose drunken despair terrified and saddened her. Only in her work did Kate seem to move forward. The most astonishing manifestations yet to appear in the history of Modern Spiritualism were about to be produced through her mediumship. These were accomplished in her sessions with Charles Livermore, a wealthy thirty-one-year-old banker in mourning for his wife.

A man on whom fortune seemed to shine, the handsome Livermore had cofounded the powerful financial firm of Livermore, Clews, and Company in 1859.[1] But tragedy struck soon enough; within a year his wife, Estelle, was on her deathbed, where she wondered aloud whether she could promise her grief-stricken husband she would return. Her physician, the prominent Spiritualist Dr. John Gray, eventually grew so concerned about the intensity of Livermore's suffering in the months after Estelle's death that in January 1861 he urged the banker to seek Kate's help.

She was now translating messages in a variety of ways: by spelling words aloud, letter after letter, as the invisibles rapped; through automatic writing, transcribing messages with her left hand in reverse script; sometimes communicating two messages simultaneously, scrawling one in large, looped letters while speaking the other. In her sessions with Livermore she also brought blank cards on which spirit writing seemed to materialize spontaneously.

During their first meetings, which were sometimes held at the Greeleys' house and sometimes at Livermore's, the banker experienced phenomena that had become routine to many Spiritualists: loud raps, the touch of spirit hands, the levitation of a heavy table. At his twelfth session he received a message purporting to come from Estelle and promising that she would soon be visible if he persevered. A meteor shower of dazzling phosphorescent lights followed. Several weeks later, at his twenty-fourth sitting in mid-March, Livermore glimpsed the faint outlines of a face and figure that he took to be Estelle's, the form illumined only by the crackling glow of spirit lights.[2]

Kate and Livermore had been meeting on average every other day. His forty-third sitting, held on April 18, most likely took place in the Greeleys' parlor, since he often noted specifically when he was at home.

"Having absolutely secured the doors and windows," he wrote in his journal, "we sat in perfect quiet for half an hour, my faith becoming weak. Then we were startled by a tremendous rap on the heavy mahogany centre-table which, at the same time, rose and fell. The door was violently shaken, the windows opened and shut: in fact everything in the room seemed in motion."[3]

His patience and desire appeared to have triumphed, as the awestruck Livermore wrote, "Then an illuminated substance like gauze rose from the floor behind us, moved about the room and finally came in front of us.

Vigorous electrical sounds were heard. The gauze-like substance assumed the form of a human head covered, the covering drawn close around the neck."

The luminous substance evolved into a recognizable figure that touched him, then "receded and again approached. . . . it was Estelle herself—eyes, forehead, and expression in perfection."

Estelle laid her head on his; he felt his wife's long hair cascading over his face. As she moved away, a brilliant light was projected against one of the walls. In its glow he saw "an entire female figure facing that side of the room, the light apparently in one of her hands." After remaining there, fully in sight, for more than half an hour, Estelle sent the message: " 'Now see me rise. . . .' "

"And immediately," Livermore wrote, "in full brightness, the figure rose to the ceiling, remained there a few moments suspended; then gently descending, disappeared."

Estelle returned again and again; in Livermore's eyes she grew ever more like herself. In the darkness and excitement, Kate sometimes seemed to fade away as if she were the ghost and the shining Estelle the vital woman.

At one sitting in June, in response to a kiss on his forehead, Livermore looked up to see Estelle's radiant face poised in front of a light that "now vibrated rapidly, throwing its fitful gleams upon such beauty as, in beings of this world, it is not possible to witness."[4] Kate reacted with exclamations of "wonder and delight," a reaction that seemed to perturb the figure, for it retreated until the medium grew calm.

On another occasion, however, Kate responded with apparent alarm. As Estelle approached Livermore, a second figure materialized behind her: a short, thickset man, dressed in black even to his velvet cap.

"Here the medium became very nervous," Livermore reported, "and I have no doubt prevented his making his face more distinctly visible."[5] The dark figure returned a number of times and soon announced by writing on a card that he was Benjamin Franklin.

Often Livermore and Kate sat in silence and darkness for close to an hour before even a single spirit light was seen. Yet when the manifestations began, they more than fulfilled his expectations. On October 20,

1861, Estelle stood in front of him, enveloped in her gossamer robes, her arm bare except for its transparent drapery.

"I asked to be touched," Livermore told Benjamin Coleman, an English Spiritualist with whom he maintained a correspondence, "[and] when she advanced, [she] laid the arm across my forehead and permitted me to kiss it. I found it as large and as real in weight as a living arm. . . . She held up the little finger and moved it characteristically and while we were looking at that—let her hair fall loosely down her back. The manifestation was concluded by her writing a card, resting it *upon my shoulder,* caressing me upon the head and temple and kissing me for good night."[6]

Estelle surprised him with a gift an evening or two later. After draping a veil over his face, she held up spirit flowers—she often wore a white rose in her hair—allowing him to inhale their sweet perfume, far more exquisite than any earthly blossom that he knew. Before returning to the spirit world, she placed "her finger enveloped in gossamer several times" in his mouth, an erotic and intimate gesture.[7]

On a Wednesday evening shortly before Thanksgiving, Kate and Livermore waited patiently in the parlor, the room warmed by a coal fire and with the last hint of daylight seeping through the curtains. The bulk of the mahogany table, the chandelier and lamps, the couch and side chairs stood out in gray relief. Then a brilliant light rose from the floor, brighter than the natural illumination of the fire and the waning day; bathed in its glow was a disembodied hand. It seemed to him to be "as perfect a human hand as was ever created."[8] Although the hand was covered in gossamer, and Livermore wore a glove, touch rekindled love.

"And thus," he wrote, "we again grasped hands with all the fervor of long parted friends, my wife in the spirit land and myself here. The expression of love and tenderness thus given cannot be described for it was a reality which lasted through nearly half an hour. . . . I examined carefully that spirit hand, squeezed it, felt the knuckle joints and nails, and kissed it, while it was constantly visible to my sight."[9]

In his journal Livermore often used language suggestive of a magic lantern show to evoke what he saw; for example, he described how the spirit light on one particular evening rose "in a cloud" across the heavily curtained windows, "a portion of [the light] overhanging from the top;

while the face and figure of my wife, from the waist, was projected upon it with stereoscopic effect. . . . We were told to notice her dress, which seemed tight-fitting. . . ."[9]

But just as often the figures who appeared seemed as tangible as any mortal being. Estelle took to wearing "a perfect bow-knot of white silk ribbon [that] was attached to her breast diagonally." The second time she wore this dramatic accessory, Livermore held it between his fingers, finding it as real as silk. As his hand moved across the fabric, he heard "a low murmuring sound . . . something like the buzzing of a bee.

"I listened carefully," he said, "and noticed that it came from the lips of the spirit. This was an unsuccessful attempt to speak. . . ." Or perhaps the soft murmurs he heard were those of an aroused spirit, responding to his caress.

It's possible, of course, that in the darkened room Kate herself sometimes impersonated Estelle. With his full attention riveted on the illuminated figure, Livermore may not always have noticed the medium. On those occasions, however, when Benjamin Franklin sharply chastised Kate for her exclamations of delight or surprise, she clearly was reacting genuinely. If a mortal collaborator created the apparitions, Kate either may have lost herself in the drama or perhaps was not always prepared for what happened next.

Livermore's brother witnessed some manifestations, as did Dr. Gray, who observed "the production of lights, odors and sounds; and also the formation of flowers, cloth textures, etc., and their disintegration and dispersion. These phenomena," Gray stated, "including the apparition of Dr. Franklin have all been shown me. . . . Mr. L. is a good observer of Spirit phenomena, brave, clear, and quick sighted. . . ." Gray complimented Kate as well, praising her for comporting herself "with patient integrity of conduct, evidently doing all in her power, at all times to promote a fair trial and just decision of each phenomenon as it occurred."[10]

The first year, 1861, that Kate and Livermore met in the half light of one parlor or another coincided with the start of the Civil War. The prominent medium Emma Hardinge recalled how spirits had warned her of the catastrophe months before it began, showing her a vision in which "innumerable forms who seemed to shiver and bend, as if in the whirl of a hidden tempest" had prophesied the "fratricidal struggle."[11] Her vision seems to have been more realistic than clairvoyant, however, evoking what to many mortals increasingly seemed inevitable. In 1859 John Brown had led his historic raid on Harper's Ferry, hoping to incite a slave insurrection but succeeding instead in making himself a martyr among abolitionists in the North and a demon to the slaveholding South. In the fall of 1860 Abraham Lincoln had been elected president of the United States on a Republican platform that promised not to interfere with slavery where it already existed but to limit its expansion in the territories. The next month South Carolina had seceded, followed by other Southern states, and in February 1861 the Confederacy had been born. In April—the same month the luminous apparition of Estelle first appeared to Livermore—Confederate guns fired on Fort Sumter, a federal garrison in Charleston harbor, South Carolina, and the war officially began.

Charles Livermore's firm boomed with the war fever and soon emerged as the second largest marketer of federal bonds. Known to be a busy man and a practical one, with heavy responsibilities weighing on him in the midst of the national crisis, the banker nevertheless found time for his sessions with Kate.

Most Spiritualists accepted Lincoln's leadership, although they regretted his failure to call for an unconditional ban on slavery throughout the nation. Horace Greeley, long a friend to the Spiritualist movement if not a believer himself, expressed the views of many reformers when he sharply criticized the president for his "mistaken deference to Rebel Slavery."

Lincoln famously replied, "My paramount object in this struggle *is* to save the Union, and is *not* either to save or to destroy slavery. If I could save the Union without freeing *any* slave I would do it, and if I could save it by freeing *all* the slaves I would do it; and if I could save it by freeing some and leaving others alone, I would also do that."[12]

The *Banner of Light*, eventually to become Spiritualism's longest running newspaper, urged readers to enlist on the side of the Union, and many apparently did so. Emma Hardinge lamented that no regiments were comprised entirely of Spiritualists but attributed that fact to a familiar cause. "In martial as in all other forms of associative action," she observed, "no organization could be effected among the Spiritualists." She did note that "Spiritualists' total unconcern on the subject of death made them the bravest of soldiers . . . ," an assertion of course difficult to prove.[13]

While Spiritualists worked for whichever cause they supported—Union or Confederate—in conventional roles such as officers and soldiers, doctors and nurses, fund-raisers and factory workers producing goods for the front, they also contributed in less tangible ways. Many forwarded letters, said to have been dictated by spirits, to officers in the field with suggestions for battle strategies and information on the enemy's plans. The spirits were credited too with influencing speeches and policies. When the president drafted the Emancipation Proclamation, freeing slaves in the Confederate states as of January 1863, it was suggested that otherworldly beings helped shape his eloquent message.[14]

In the South, where Spiritualists were suspected of abolitionist sympathy, their public meetings were largely curtailed. Of course, not all Spiritualists were against slavery, and neither did antislavery advocates even in the North, whatever their religion, necessarily promote full racial equality. Racism was to prove far more difficult to eradicate even than slavery. A few Spiritualists debated whether the spirits of black individuals would be able to advance sufficiently through the spheres to associate at the higher levels with otherworldly whites.

During the war, battle-torn communities witnessed slaughter on a massive and modern scale. With modern methods of embalming a new procedure, and transportation of bodies difficult to arrange, many soldiers were buried where they fell on the battlefields, rapidly and unceremoniously interred in communal graves before their corpses could breed and spread disease.

In July 1863 eight thousand soldiers died at Gettysburg in a three-day battle, corpses outnumbering the living residents of that small Pennsylvania town by more than two to one. The combined Union and Confederate casualties totaled fifty thousand, including the dead, wounded, missing, and captured. Prisoners of war, civilians, and soldiers worked together to bury bodies beneath a thin veil of earth, which protected neither the living nor the dead. The decaying corpses threatened to contaminate soil and water; relatives and thieves disinterred the bodies in search of loved ones or valuables.

That autumn a new cemetery at Gettysburg, where the fallen could be reburied with dignity, was dedicated by Abraham Lincoln. He spoke little of the individuals who had died there, focusing instead on the "new birth of freedom" that would result from their courage and suffering.

With bodies buried in distant cemeteries, elaborate private rituals and funerals held close to home for a time seemed meaningless, at least to sorrowing families. Belief in the spirits' return, by contrast, had a compelling power for those whose relatives went off to war and never came back. Increasing numbers of the grief-stricken found solace in seances as the war continued. It's likely too that some of the men and women who attended seances were mourning not only their individual dead but also the ravaged body of the founding fathers' republic, that ideal of sovereign states bound together in harmony and by choice. The spirit of national identity that survived the war would be vastly transformed.

As Charles Livermore's meetings with Kate demonstrate, however, not every seance during these years was directly related to the war, not even in Abraham Lincoln's White House. When ten-year-old Willie Lincoln died while his father was in office, the child's mother, Mary Todd Lincoln, turned to several different mediums in Washington to help her establish contact with her son. Although she became a devout believer, there's no evidence to suggest that her husband, who attended at least one seance and permitted several to be held at the White House, experienced anything other than compassionate curiosity on his wife's behalf.

During the war years Maggie remained torn between fury at the Kane family, self-loathing, and conflicted rage at all things associated with Spiritualism. She wrote to a Canadian friend, the author Susanna Moodie, about "how *utterly disgusting* and *abhorrent* to refinement" Spiritualism had seemed to Kane.

"I have scarcely ten letters from Dr. Kane," Maggie continued, "that do not tell his utter condemnation of a life as he calls Spiritualism of '*wickedness and Sin*. . . . I solemnly promised Dr. Kane at our third or fourth meeting that I would wholly and *forever* abandon Spiritualism, with that promise I was educated and considered *as dead* to Spiritualism and Spiritualists. I have *sacredly* kept my promise from that day—and will hold it sacred until I meet him in Heaven."[15]

Maggie's relationship with the Kane family continued to deteriorate; their refusal to treat her with dignity and to acknowledge the true nature of the romance infuriated her. Finally, in 1862 she retracted her promise never to publish the love letters and threatened instead to do so. At the urging of friends, she also brought suit against the Kanes in court. Calling herself Kane's widow and adopting his last name, she used the letters to prove the explorer's love and to force a settlement. Under pressure, the Kanes agreed to give Maggie the sum of two thousand dollars plus a small ongoing annuity. In exchange she placed Kane's letters with Dr. Edward Bayard, the homeopathic physician who was treating the elderly Margaret Fox and who belonged to a family important enough to suit the Kanes.

While Maggie fought her personal battles and soldiers fought the nation's, Leah and Daniel continued to hold occasional private seances in their comfortable home, but their thoughts were never far from the Union's struggle. Emma Hardinge and Robert Dale Owen attended one sitting that went on until four in the morning. As Hardinge played war songs on the piano, Owen wrote, "a high shrill voice piped out from above our heads, 'lower the lights.' This order was obeyed, and instantly the music was accompanied by sounds as of the marching of a heavy body of soldiers, then came repeated EXPLOSIONS as of the firing of musketry. . . ."[16]

Charles Livermore's sittings with Kate Fox continued through the war years, and he also kept up his correspondence with his English friend Benjamin Coleman, sending letters, pictures, even newspaper clippings. But slowly and unavoidably he found his own life changing as his firm expanded with the war effort.

"I am so engrossed by the tread mill duties of my constantly increasing business," he wrote to Coleman, "that I cannot bring myself to the task of elaborating the details of my experience. . . . I can only say that the power of the manifestations which I receive has augmented rather than diminished and that I see frequently the spirit of Dr. Franklin and of my wife as described to you—but with increased beauty and facility."[17]

In the summer of 1864 many well-known Spiritualists gathered in Chicago for the movement's First National Convention, although none of the Fox sisters attended. Perhaps not surprisingly, the event didn't go altogether smoothly. Influenced by the achievements of antislavery groups, the lecturers and writers who attended the convention, most of whom were male, tended to advocate a strong national organization with political goals achievable in this world, while mediums and trance speakers, most of them female, argued that Spiritualism's very nature necessitated a decentralized approach and otherworldly focus. On a note that surely seemed ominous to some mediums, the convention proposed a resolution stating that "American Spiritualism means something more than table-tipping and trumpet-blowing, trance-speaking, and sightseeing—that the highest conditions it imposes are not abnormal states of beatified unconsciousness . . . but a vigorous, healthful, working state for the practical attainment of physical and spiritual freedom, purity, and growth." Despite controversy, the convention endorsed Lincoln for a second term.[18]

Lincoln was elected in a landslide victory in the fall of 1864. In April 1865, a month after Lincoln's second inaugural, General Robert E. Lee surrendered to General Ulysses S. Grant at Appomattox, effectively ending the Civil War, although the official date announced as the "close of the Rebellion" was still a year away. By the war's close, one million Americans, Union and Confederate, had been wounded; more than six hundred thousand had died. The number of Civil War dead is shocking even in retrospect, higher than the number of Americans killed in battle during World Wars I and II combined.

Five days after Lee's surrender, President Lincoln was assassinated by John Wilkes Booth. One Union veteran spoke for many when he cried, "Our country that yesterday was a scene of universal rejoicing over the return of peace, is today immersed in gloom and clothed in mourning."[19] Lincoln's coffin was carried by train from city to city, where it was met, wrote the poet Walt Whitman, "With processions long and winding and the flambeaus of the night. . . ."[20] Lincoln's funeral was said to have been modeled on that of Elisha Kent Kane, and particularly in the North and among the newly freed slaves of the South, there was an outpouring of public grief over the president's death.

In 1865, the year the fighting drew to a close and the country suffered the shock of Lincoln's brutal death, the Fox sisters experienced two devastating personal losses. In January frail, seventy-six-year-old John Fox passed away; in August Margaret died of typhoid fever. Having lived apart for most of their marriage, John and Margaret were buried separately as well, she in the family vault of Leah's in-laws at Greenwood Cemetery in Brooklyn, New York, he in Arcadia, near the homes of his more conventional children, David Fox and Maria Smith.[21]

Leah idolized her mother but at least had Daniel Underhill on whom to rely for emotional support. For Kate and Maggie, their mother's death was an event of an altogether different magnitude. Kind Margaret, her plump face wreathed in smiles, her gray head topped with her little lace cap, had been the one constant in her two youngest daughters' lives. Her spirit must have seemed insubstantial indeed compared with the comfort of her mortal, maternal self.

There was more hardship to come for the Fox sisters. The Kanes, claiming financial difficulties, halted the annuity they had agreed to pay Maggie only a few years before. Thus legally enabled to regain the love letters she had placed in trust, Maggie arranged for them to be published at last in 1866. In the book *The Love-Life of Dr. Kane* she unequivocally identified herself as her beloved Lish's widow: Margaret Fox Kane.

Whether Maggie released the letters for revenge, to prove Kane's love for her, or in the hope of some small royalty, the act failed to relieve either her financial or emotional suffering. Instead, it made her vulnerable to a new round of scathing accusations. Leah, humiliated by the reopening of the scandal as well as by Maggie's evident alcoholism, withdrew from any contact with either of her younger sisters.

Estelle Livermore last appeared to Charles Livermore through Kate Fox's mediumship in April 1866, then she returned to the Summerland—the phrase Spiritualists use to describe heaven—there to await her husband. Not long afterward Livermore retired, a very rich man who no longer worried about his name being used in connection with Spiritualism. The days when he could be publicly shamed for his beliefs by conservative banking colleagues were over. He wrote less often to Coleman, but the two continued to correspond, and both remained helpful friends to Kate in the years to come.

Charles Livermore's letters and journal entries about the return of his Estelle were printed in Spiritualist books and journals; he regarded the sittings with Kate Fox as vital documentation of the spirit's eternal life. Reading Livermore's notes today, one finds oneself immersed in the story of a remarkable romance, although who the parties were—in reality, in memory, and in fantasy—can never be entirely clear.

At the end of the war New York, the city of excess, erupted in an orgy of celebration and display. Who could give the most extravagant ball, build the showiest mansion, summer at the most desirable spa, serve the most—and the most costly—champagne? It was a brand-new era, the Flash Age, when money was flaunted shamelessly as never before and stuffy respectability, at least in some circles, was only to be mocked. Henry Clews, Livermore's former partner, was one of the small coterie of men who set the pace for the razzle-dazzle.[22]

The victory of the industrialized North over the agrarian South placed immense power in the hands of captains of finance and industry such as Vanderbilt, Belmont, Gould, and Morgan, builders of railroad and banking empires. Victoria Woodhull, flamboyant medium and woman's rights advocate, made her reputation by offering astute stock tips to Vanderbilt, providing him with the sort of practical suggestions that spirits in the past had steadfastly abjured. The spirits of deceased financiers became increasingly popular at other mediums' seances, ready to dispense financial advice.

The nation, try though it might to forget, also had to come to terms with its grief over Lincoln's assassination and the hundreds of thousands who had died in the war. Loss had affected almost every home and family; concern about the afterlife was pervasive, reflected not just in politics and religion but even in popular forms of entertainment. Throughout the late 1860s audiences flocked to see plays about ghosts and spirits, deriving some comfort from the luminous, spectral figures onstage, many of the illusions created with technology no more complex than mirrors.

Not surprisingly, Civil War monuments across the country proliferated to honor soldiers who had died; burying the dead, as it had been at the start of the century, once again became a matter of community concern and support rather than just an opportunity for expressing individual and familial grief.

Emma Hardinge wrote that the war added two million new believers to Spiritualism. If the war stirred even one friend or family member of each dead or wounded soldier to think about spirit communication, it's hardly surprising that interest grew. Over the next quarter century, estimates of the numbers of Spiritualists in the United States would range from one million to a highly inflated eleven million. Even the lower figure, however, took into account those who sympathized with the movement as well as those who identified themselves as committed Spiritualists.

The movement's growth did not necessarily predict its long-term health. The intense idealism that had characterized so much of American life before the war, the perfectionist longing for reform, was much subdued in the postwar age, and the change held true to some degree in the Spiritualist movement as well. Over the next decade disillusionment blanketed the nation. Reconstruction became a bitter struggle between those who urged swift reconciliation with the former Confederate states and those who sought justice and equality for African Americans; Congress demanded the impeachment of President Andrew Johnson; scandal pervaded the administration of his successor, Ulysses S. Grant; and mutual recriminations divided women's rights advocates from their former allies in the abolitionist movement when the vote was made available to men, whatever their race, but denied to women. The seance room increasingly became a private retreat from the realities of the outside world rather than, as it had been in the past, a gathering place for mortals actively seeking to understand the relationship between the concerns of this world and the next.

Just as extravagant, outward manifestations of wealth—a marble mansion, expensive clothes, an extensive art collection—were longed for in the decades after the Civil War, so too were extravagant, outward manifestations of the spirits. The full-form apparition of Estelle, which appeared through the mediumship of Kate Fox, set a standard for what was expected and desired at seances, a standard that would become increasingly difficult for mediums to meet without engaging in blatant acts of fraud. In the decades after the war, the pressure on mediums to perform miracles at every seance, exerted by Spiritualists and skeptics alike, gradually began to take a toll not only on Kate but on the movement itself.

Kate, in the wake of her parents' death, followed Maggie's tragic example by turning to alcohol for comfort or release. There's a theory that mediums are prone to alcohol and drug addiction; it's been suggested that they turn to these substances to block out the overwhelming stimulation of sensations that bombard them from without and within and against which they have no defenses. Others argue that alcoholic spirits, far from being a sedative, have always been used and abused in the search for spiritual knowledge when other, higher paths have remained elusive or closed. Kate's and Maggie's alcoholism most likely originated in a predisposition inherited from their father, but it was a condition exacerbated by the tensions, longings, temptations, and disappointments of their lives as mediums.

Although Leah had turned her back on her sisters, evidencing little compassion for their problems, many of Kate's old friends tried to help her, blaming her rapid descent into alcoholism on the postwar age and on the rise of increasingly wealthy curiosity seekers who trifled with her powers and courted her with champagne. As early as the 1850s, however, Elisha Kent Kane had noticed that both sisters had a taste for liquor and had warned Maggie, "Tell Katie to drink no champagne, and do you follow the same advice. It makes your nose red and is a bad custom for young ladies. . . ."[23]

To keep Kate from deteriorating as severely as Maggie, Dr. Edward Bayard, former trustee of the Kane love letters, arranged for her to board as a patient at Dr. George Taylor's Swedish Movement Cure, a situation that either Bayard himself, the Underhills, or Charles Livermore discreetly paid for. Taylor and his wife now became Kate's second family. He was a craggy-faced medical practitioner in his midforties who had studied at Harvard and New York University. His wife, Sarah, was about a decade younger than her husband and an impressive figure in her own right, having served as a high school principal before her marriage. She was plump and pretty, with a determined set to her chin rather like Leah's and a motherly manner not unlike Margaret's.[24]

In 1858 George Taylor had visited Sweden to investigate techniques of massage or "passive gymnastics," methods that he understood could relieve the symptoms of chronically ill patients. On his return he had opened his own establishment. Housed in two handsome, adjacent town-houses on Sixth Avenue and West Thirty-Eighth Street, Dr. Taylor's health sanitarium became one of the most popular and respected institutions of its day, a time when the wealthier middle classes, much like those of today, retreated to spas to benefit from regimens of water cures, exercise, massage, vegetarian diets, and—something that is offered rarely today—vibratory stimulation. Many of the treatments spawned by the craze for health reform were designed to cure neurasthenia and hysteria, along with symptoms such as listlessness and paralysis.

Victorian attitudes toward sexuality were one factor contributing to a range of nervous disorders, as both women and men wrestled with conflicting messages and feelings. Most ministers of mainstream churches continued to advise that sex was for purposes of procreation only. In response—and for many other reasons too—some middle-class women tended to abjure intercourse while their husbands sought guilty pleasure in masturbation or with prostitutes. Both sexes found that healthful pursuits such as hydrotherapy and exercise—activities that sometimes served as substitutes for, or alternative means to, sexual release—expended nervous energy and relaxed tension.

It was one of Dr. George Taylor's contributions to the health of the nation to create new and improved steam-powered massage and vibratory equipment for curative purposes. Many of his machines were intended to treat "female pelvic complaints." One piece of equipment consisted of a padded table with a large opening through which a vibrating sphere massaged the patient's pelvis. The healthful afterglow generally left patients invigorated, although it's not entirely clear they always acknowledged to themselves the exact nature of the relief they felt.[25]

Kate began to board and receive treatments at the Taylors soon after her parents died in 1865, her stay sometimes interrupted by days or even weeks when she would disappear without warning. No one knew where she went, but she generally returned gravely ill, and Sarah worried with good reason that Kate kept bad company. The wealthy and fashionable people who lived in Fifth Avenue mansions, Sarah complained, plied the medium with liquor.

Although a resident at the Taylors' for many years, Kate was never allowed to take her meals at the public table shared by the other boarders. Her isolation may have been to protect her delicate health or to prevent the Taylors' other clients either from witnessing her dissolution or succumbing to her spell.

When financial support for Kate was withdrawn in 1867, the Taylors allowed her to stay on for free as their own charge. Later the situation changed again: Kate began holding seances for Sarah and George Taylor in 1869, an arrangement that may not have served exactly as a quid pro quo but that worked for all concerned. Kate retained access to the Taylors, their comfortable home, their companionship, and presumably occasional treatments. In lieu of a fee, they received communications from their two dead children: Frankie, who had died several years before at age three of tubercular meningitis, and Leila, who had contracted scarlet fever in 1867 at eighteen months old. Kate had known Leila for most of the child's short life and surely felt personal grief over the little girl's death as well as compassion for the bereaved parents.

The Taylors also had another son, William Langworthy, who was ten when the seances began. He often took part in the sittings and, more than half a century later, reflected as an aging man of seventy on the wonders he had witnessed as a boy.

According to the Taylors' accounts, Kate conveyed messages to them not just from their departed children, but also from a whole circle of otherworldly beings: the mysterious Professor K., Uncle Albert, the ubiquitous Benjamin Franklin, various grandparents, Sarah's brother Olin, and others. Olin served as a guide, ushering the spirits in and out, summarizing their thoughts, organizing the sittings, imparting wisdom, and gently overseeing Frankie and Leila.

The children remained as mischievous and charming in immortal dress as they had been in their mortal bodies.

"The children played about us," Sarah wrote after one sitting. "Frankie pulled his Papa's long beard. . . . The Doctor spoke of it and wondered what the child was doing. . . . When we opened our eyes we saw the Doctor's beard had been and was then braided in three separate, three stranded braids, and a comical sight it was. We believed Frankie then laughing over his exploit."[26]

When more than one spirit was present, a lively ensemble of raps, which the Taylors called echoes, ensued. Kate usually transcribed the messages with her left hand, writing in reverse on long sheets of brown paper. Dr. Taylor or another mortal participant would then read the reverse writing aloud by holding a hand mirror up to it, as Sarah Taylor faithfully copied the messages into legible journals.

The combined troupe of visible and invisible beings often behaved exactly like a squabbling tribe of old friends and relatives. The professor's spirit kindly advised Sarah that she needed to hire more household help. His wife, on the other hand, treated Sarah rudely, and Kate didn't care for either of the two spirits. "When I described [the professor]," Sarah wrote, "[Kate] finally recalled having seen him here and said that she did not like him."

The Swedish Movement Cure overflowed with mortals—sick and well—who came for the treatment and who were eager on discovering Kate's presence to benefit from her services too. Harriet Beecher Stowe, one of Dr. Taylor's occasional patients, attended several sittings and confessed a few years later to the author George Eliot that Kate was "a very peculiar beautiful interesting girl" who astonished her.

Stowe compared Kate to Undine, the sea nymph who could acquire a soul only on her marriage to a mortal man. The comparison in retrospect seems more poignant than Stowe could have known, for Undine was also the heroine of the book that Elisha Kent Kane had sent to Maggie more than a decade before.

"[Kate] is apparently without a nature of her own but is only a medium of reflecting others," Stowe wrote, but at the same time she described the traits of a real-life woman: Kate was "Sensitive, wilful, irritable, affectionate."[27]

Then Stowe reiterated, "She fulfills my idea of a fay or wood sprite." Even in the eyes of the sympathetic and caring author, Kate was nonexistent apart from her role as a cipher.

Stowe described in detail a sitting that took place one evening in Sarah Taylor's sewing room. Seven people were present, including Stowe's husband, Calvin. As the participants held hands around a center table, Stowe recalled, "Phosphorescent lights arose and floated about among us—They were like the dear light of a glow worm. They touched me on my arm and I felt that they had a strong resistant force—one of them struck the table with a loud report like the firing of a pistol. . . ."

Her husband, Calvin, was asked to hold a handkerchief in his hand; to his surprise, "one of those globes of light rested in it—in this glove was a hand which displayed itself first on one side and then on the other. . . ." Then the disembodied hand—playfully, one has to assume—snatched the renowned author's pencil and paper and used them to write a message. Equally astonishing, two-hundred-pound Calvin "was moved back from the table four feet to the wall, chair and all, and then placed again at the table." It confounded Harriet that these feats were accomplished in a room she knew well, in a boardinghouse occupied upstairs and down "by boarders who knew nothing of what we were doing, and while Katie was held between two of us."

As to what produced the manifestations, Harriet Beecher Stowe could offer no answers, although the demonstrations seemed to her to be "matters quite beyond doubt as facts." Adopting a line of reasoning that went back to Spiritualism's earliest days, she suggested that a scientific explanation would one day be discovered, and in this she compared the manifestations to the aurora borealis and Darwin's studies on natural selection.

Just as Kate had produced an innovation for Livermore—two full-form apparitions at once—she added a new manifestation to her personal repertoire for the Taylors: spirit pictures that emerged on blank paper. Accomplishing the task, however, proved excruciatingly difficult; spirits and sitters collaborated on the project for almost two months early in 1870. The routine remained much the same at each session. A clear, electrical atmosphere was the first requirement. Nothing could be accomplished in damp weather.

The mortals usually sat in double darkness—eyes closed, gaslights turned down—for several hours. They were advised not to listen to anything that transpired during that time. Night after night Sarah, George, and Kate valiantly struggled to keep up a conversation. Chatter helped them avoid listening to the spirits' rustlings and rattlings.

At the end of this waiting period, the spirits would command the sitters to take a variety of repetitive actions, ones that were bound to distract mortals from anything else that was happening: to rise and go to the door, to return to the table, to go back and forth to the window, to open and close it. The sitters were often asked by the spirits to move about the room four or five different times as well as to fetch specific items such as pencils, knives to sharpen them, crayon board, and linen handkerchiefs. All of these objects would mysteriously vanish from the room.

Finally, on February 10, the process neared completion; a missing sheet of crayon paper, neatly covered with a cloth, was returned to the seance table. As instructed by the spirits, Sarah dutifully tucked the paper away, still covered, in a bureau drawer. The next day, "echoes" told her that the time had come for unveiling the portrait. "Meet tonight at eight," Benjamin Franklin commanded.[28]

That evening, despite rain, there was activity.

"At eight," Sarah wrote, "I placed the crayon paper with the cloth upon it, on the little table, turned off the gas, and before I could get to my seat was told to open the window. Scarcely was the sash entirely up, when the pencils touched the Doctor and Katie and rattled upon the table. We now sat for a little time when the Doctor and Katie were sent by the door as usual. There was a good deal of moving of the table and the treading about of feet not our own."

The Taylors and Kate sang hymns until, at last, the echoes said, "Get light."

With joyful anticipation, Sarah uncovered the crayon paper and saw "the purest, sweetest, most spiritual likeness" of her little son, "who had been more than five years in heaven." She and her husband gazed upon the image "through fast falling tears and in speechless wonder."

Olin ordered Sarah to bring more drawing paper and pencils to the next session; the process would resume with Leila.

The day after the picture of Frankie appeared, however, Sarah wrote a disturbing entry about Kate's health: "Katie was very sick and the air was thick with dampness, still the echoes would have us sit. We sat down by the table, Katie resting in my arms. They as usual sent the 'Doctor and Katie by the door.' He had to about carry her she was so very sick, he brought her back and put her in the chair and my arms, she *perfectly unconscious.*"

In June Katie visited Maggie and found her sister drunk. Maggie's condition threw her into a depression; she returned to the Taylors exhausted and irritated. When she was about to leave, she removed her gloves and wrote a message. Holding it up to a mirror, she read it as though she indeed had no knowledge of its contents.

"It is about me," Kate announced. "I know my name is written there."

Throughout Kate's seances with the Taylors, messages sometimes seemed to be addressed to the medium herself, urging her to find another, better way. During a visit from Robert Dale Owen, who was greatly distressed by Kate's condition, the spirit of Professor K. sent a communication. It was conveyed by raps, with Kate writing down the words.

"We are happy to have Mr. Owen here this morning," Professor K. acknowledged, "and we will register Katie's promise in heaven, in the home of her Mother: we will register it in flowers and her eyes shall some day behold it. Mr. Owen we will tell you how Katie can be kept from touching wine; by keeping her from temptation.

"Now go and rejoice Katie, and live," the spirit counseled. "There are two paths, one happiness and peace, one misery and death! Choose the former and great will be your golden reward."

FIFTEEN

"EACH HAD HIS SECRET HEARTACHE"

KEEPING KATE FROM temptation was on everyone's mind, and in June 1871 Benjamin Franklin's spirit gave the Taylors fair warning: it was time for Kate to go abroad, to seek a fresh start. The spirits tried to reassure Sarah, terrified as she was of losing her mortal link to her immortal children, that a change of scene was necessary.

The spirits too were "deprived of a sacred privilege," they commiserated, "that of visiting you life-like and almost human. But time flies rapidly and we shall have Katie back, a new being. She will be benefited and changed, not only in habits, but in strength."[1]

A week before thirty-four-year-old Kate was to sail that fall, Margaret Fox—now in the spirit world more than five years—used her daughter's hand to thank Sarah Taylor, perhaps for being a more protective parent than she herself had managed to be. As raps echoed around her, Kate scribbled on her mother's behalf, "When Cathy is with you I am happy and can enjoy the sunlight of heaven. Oh, would that she could ever be under the mantle with which you have so often covered her."

Kate sailed for England on October 7, 1871, her spacious stateroom crowded before departure with well-wishers. Most were strangers to Sarah, but she guessed that they shared her painful feelings on that occasion, "that each had his secret heartache, not only at parting with Katie, but at seeing the very means of communication between them and some loved one, dearer to them than their own lives, the readable link between the two worlds, the key that opens the gates of heaven to mortals, borne far, far away."

Kate was little more than an "unconscious, thoughtless child," Sarah mused from her own self-absorbed standpoint, a child who "little realized the deprivations her best friends were imposing upon themselves, voluntarily for her sake!" Sarah added in resignation, "She is gone. The magnificent ship has left its moorings and Katie is riding the billows."

Was setting out across the Atlantic Ocean for a foreign country an adventure for Kate or a terror? Did she look forward to meeting fellow Spiritualists there, or was she frightened of their scrutiny? Traveling with one of Charles Livermore's relatives, Blanche Ogden, Kate arrived in England safely, only to leave for France immediately. It's possible that she was "unwell"—a euphemism frequently attached to her binges—and that Ogden had hurried her off to recover in Paris before meeting London's influential Spiritualists.[2]

First introduced to England in 1852 by Mrs. W. R. Hayden, an American medium and journalist's wife, Modern Spiritualism had sparked a furor of table tilting that rapidly spread. The next year, the scientist Michael Faraday, lauded for his research on electricity, had conducted investigations into the matter and concluded that the sitters' involuntary movements, rather than the spirits' strength, pushed ordinarily stolid tables into action. Despite his findings, table tilting continued to be practiced as a parlor entertainment, and a new device—the planchette, a precursor to the Ouija board—rivaled its popularity. For a time these activities were so engrossing that other serious investigations lagged.[3]

The medium Daniel Dunglas Home did more than anyone else to intensify interest in Spiritualism throughout Great Britain and Europe. Born in Scotland in 1833, Home later claimed to have experienced clairvoyant visions already when he moved to the United States at age nine.

By the time he visited England in 1855, he had conducted seances that featured raps, strains of ghostly music, and the sight of spectral hands, often with the gaslights turned up in the seance room. He also had exhibited, according to many witnesses, a startling ability to levitate as well as to shrink and elongate his body.

Slim and striking, Home was a dandy with a mane of curly hair and a reputation for extraordinary charm, although one of his fellow mediums commented that his "intellectual ability is not high." While Home never accepted payment for a seance, he didn't really need to. He stayed as a welcome guest—others called him a shameless freeloader—at the homes of his frequently wealthy fans. The poet Elizabeth Barrett Browning was intrigued by him, even as her poet-husband, Robert, found the whole subject of Spiritualism so distasteful that he wrote a poem called "Mr. Sludge, the Medium," bitterly satirizing the barely disguised Home.

Sticks and stones did little to quell enthusiasm for Home, though, who continued to levitate his way through England and Europe. In the late 1860s he performed his most amazing feat by appearing, in the presence of witnesses, to drift horizontally out one window and, a moment or two later, to float back through the window of an adjoining room.

As in the United States, Spiritualism was hotly debated in the press and dismissed by many scientists, but it was rumored that Queen Victoria was no stranger to seances after the death of her husband, Prince Albert, and the subject had captured the attention also of the renowned physicist and chemist William Crookes. Later knighted for his discoveries in the field of vacuum physics, Crookes had become interested in investigating the afterlife in the late 1860s, perhaps not just for science's sake but also because of a brother's death. With Kate and D. D. Home both in London in 1871, Crookes hoped to hold seances jointly with the two of them.

Through no fault of his own, his initial contact with Kate was erratic at best. Crookes's index of the letters he received from her in the six months after her arrival is a shorthand record of her broken appointments, bouts of illness, lies, abject apologies, and occasional temper tantrums.[4] In late April 1872 Kate promised to reserve evenings entirely for his test seances, coupling her offer with the wistful request "Let us be friends." But her resolve turned out to be fleeting. A more ominous entry in his index appeared a few days later: "Fox, K. Ill. Sick. Glasgow. Mr. Livermore." The connection between her illness and the banker's name may not have been altogether random. She had recently learned that Charles Livermore was in love, and she was soon to find out that he was planning to marry a woman twenty years his junior, news that surely had a powerful emotional impact on the medium, who for so many years had identified herself with Estelle's spirit.

Whether in response to Livermore's engagement or to the call of her own heart, thirty-five-year-old Kate entered at last into a serious courtship of her own. Her suitor, Henry Dietrich Jencken, was a friend of Crookes whom she had met at a reception on her arrival in England the previous fall. Tall, fair, and imposing in appearance, Henry was a man Kate later lovingly described to her fellow medium D. D. Home as "good and kind." He was in his late forties and a widower, although his previous marriage had been an unhappy one. A respected barrister, he also had edited a compendium of Roman law used by many of his professional colleagues.[5]

Spiritualism was a firm bond between Kate and Henry: his parents believed in spirit communication, and so too did their son. Moreover, Henry's family, like Kate's, was far from conventional. His father, a brilliant doctor, had fallen in love with a patient and an already married baroness—the woman who would become Henry's mother—in their native land of Estonia in the years shortly after the Napoleonic wars. She had left the baron and alienated their grown children to be with Dr. Jencken; the two of them subsequently had sons of their own. Eventually the couple moved to England but didn't find life there easy. Since the baroness had been disowned, and the non-English-speaking doctor initially had to struggle to find patients, Henry had grown up in a relatively poor household.

On September 1, 1872, three months after Charles Livermore wed his young bride, Henry asked Kate to marry him, a proposal she promptly accepted. That afternoon, as though buoyed up by good fortune, she sent Crookes a letter in which she promised to attend a seance with him every day for six months. But trouble followed immediately and continued through the fall. She quarreled with Livermore's relative, Blanche Ogden, and announced that she no longer would share quarters with her companion. Notes in Crookes's index of letters refer to Kate on two consecutive days, not as "sick" or "ill" but as "drugged," suggesting that she may have been under the influence of opium or another narcotic.

Henry Jencken apparently helped calm and stabilize his distraught fiancée, for on December 14, 1872, they were married as planned at St. Marylebone Parish Church in London, where Elizabeth Barrett and Robert Browning had been wed a quarter century before. An imposing neoclassic building, the church had supplanted older structures on a site rich in history. The philosopher Francis Bacon had been married there, the poet Byron baptized there, and Charles Wesley buried there.[6] Although Kate's guests included the Duke of Wellington's son and a German prince, the departed notables threatened to outshine the living.

The wedding party itself was small. None of Kate's siblings came; it was a long distance, and they had families and responsibilities, although Leah might have enjoyed the excitement. Having emerged at last from her younger sisters' long shadows, she may have preferred to avoid celebrations where she couldn't command center stage.

Maggie, of course, was very frail. Kate also may have worried that her sister's addiction to alcohol would either ruin the occasion or disrupt her own valiant efforts at control.

The bride, groom, and wedding party arrived at the church at 11 AM in three carriages drawn by milk white horses. Kate wore a simple white dress with a gold brooch at her neck and a half wreath of flowers brightening her black hair. According to the Spiritualist press, gentle raps during the ceremony announced the spirits' approval of the union, raps that grew louder and yet more jubilant later at the wedding breakfast. It was a chorus said to have been led by Margaret Fox, whose spirit, if indeed present, must have been overcome with relief and gratitude that her youngest child no longer faced alone the trials of the mortal world. Some guests also reported seeing the banquet table, laden with the wedding feast, levitate several inches as though to gambol in delight.

At the party's end the couple returned to Henry's fine home to begin married life and to start a family. Kate became pregnant almost immediately. Settled at last, with a child on the way, she seemed free from her addictions for the moment. Although her newfound security and lifestyle might have permitted her complete retirement, she and Henry, like Leah and Daniel, continued to participate selectively in private circles and test seances.

In the spring of 1873 Kate and Henry attended four sittings with the medium William Stainton Moses, who had studied for a time at Oxford and been ordained a minister in 1863. Moses, who kept notes, provided possibly the only description of Kate's voice, commenting that she spoke rapidly, rather sharply, and with a slight Yankee accent. Her past troubles must have shown in her face, for it was so thin that he commented on how pronounced her nose and brow looked and how tightly compressed her mouth. But with her thick, dark hair and piercing purple-black eyes, she impressed him as "altogether a person out of the common." He also noted with interest the powerful, peculiar "treble rap" that followed her.[7]

However intermittently from 1872 on, she had been holding seances with Crookes as well, sometimes with Daniel Dunglas Home or other mediums present. Crookes established what he considered strict test conditions. Investigations generally took place in the light, unless darkness was necessary to frame a luminous apparition, and they were conducted in Crookes's own laboratory, among witnesses he had chosen personally for their reliability.[8]

In an article later published in the *Quarterly Journal of Science*, Crookes discussed these seances in detail. Among the phenomena he witnessed, he listed "the movement of a heavy table in full light" when no one was touching it; the buoyancy of a fan that circled a table "without contact with any person"; floating, glowing orbs; the touch and sighting of spectral hands; and spirit writing.

Like other investigators before him, Crookes marveled at Kate's versatility, her capacity, he testified, to give a message via automatic writing to one person "whilst a message to another person on another subject was being given alphabetically by means of 'raps,' and the whole time she was conversing freely with a third person on a subject totally different from either." Home, famous for his levitations, in fact produced some of the most startling manifestations. "On three separate occasions have I seen him raised completely from the floor of the room," Crookes wrote, "once sitting in an easy chair, once kneeling on his chair, and once standing up." But Kate outshone everyone in the "percussive sounds" that followed her.

"For power and certainty" of the sounds, Crookes asserted, "[I have] met with no one who at all approached Miss Kate Fox." Other mediums, he explained, required the familiar setting of a formal seance, but not so Kate. She needed only to "place her hand on any substance" for sounds to ring out "like a triple pulsation," loud enough to be heard several rooms away.

Crookes maintained, "I have heard [the sounds] in a living tree—on a sheet of glass—on a stretched iron wire—on a stretched membrane—a tambourine—on the roof of a cab—and on the floor of a theater.

"I have had these sounds, proceeding from the floor, walls, &, when the medium's hands and feet were held—when she was standing on a chair—when she was suspended in a swing from the ceiling—when she was enclosed in a wire cage—and when she had fallen fainting on a sofa.

"I have heard them on a glass harmonicon—I have felt them on my own shoulder and under my own hands. I have heard them on a sheet of paper, held between the fingers by a piece of thread passed through one corner."

Crookes's experiments point out, once again, both the precautions that investigators took to eliminate the possibility of fraud and the humiliations to which such tests frequently subjected the mediums—humiliations they endured for the sake of fame, money, attention, or truth.

The scientist concluded that the manifestations he had witnessed were "facts" that were neither the product of fraud nor of his own delusions. He admitted, however, that determining the causes required still further experimentation. Crookes conjectured that what sometimes was called the "Psychic Force" or the "Mind of Man" could account for the extraordinary occurrences.

"But I, and all who adopt this theory of Psychic Force as being the agent through which the phenomena are produced," Crookes added, "do not thereby intend to assert that this Psychic Force may not be sometimes seized and directed by some other Intelligence than the Mind of the Psychic." The spirits, in other words, remained part of the picture.

Although he advocated new trials and tests, Crookes, Home, and Kate never again collaborated with one another so closely. In the fall of 1873 Crookes turned his attention to "other matters of scientific and practical interest," Home was ill, and Kate became preoccupied with an altogether new role, that of mother.

She and Henry had spent the summer at the seaside, where she suffered miserably in the late stages of her pregnancy. In September, nine months after her marriage, she gave birth, in what was a painfully long and difficult delivery, to a son she named for her husband's brothers: Ferdinand Dietrich Lowenstein Jencken.

The little baby with the long name, affectionately called Ferdie or "boysie," was immediately rumored to be blessed with gifts of mediumship, and England's Spiritualist press spread the news. Nursemaids reported encounters with veiled white figures in Ferdie's room; Henry himself was said to boast that little Ferdie, at six months old, grasped a pencil in his tiny hand to write a message in Greek. Whatever Henry actually claimed, and despite Spiritualists' passion to meet the gifted child, the happy father steadily insisted on protecting his son from the celebrity that had once surrounded his wife.[9]

The stories that swirled around Ferdie, like the accounts of the events at Hydesville, became part of the ongoing mystery or series of puzzles that surrounded the Fox sisters then and that continue to surround them today. Had Kate's first baby become part of a ruse to fool the credulous into believing in the spirits? Was Henry Jencken, dignified and kind, practical and respected, a collaborator in fraud or his wife's dupe? Did Kate have visions in which her son accomplished astonishing feats, and did others around the child fall into such fantasies and expectations as well? Or was the supernatural or psychic legacy of Ferdie's great-great-grandmother, Margaret Rutan, at work again?

Kate quickly became pregnant a second time; shortly before her child was due, she decided to return home to her sisters. In October 1874 she and Ferdie sailed for New York. Since Henry remained behind in England, detained on business, his namesake, Henry Jr., was born far from his father's comforting arms, at Leah Underhill's home early in 1875. During their visit Kate and her boys of course spent time with Maggie, the sister with whom she had shared so many childhood hours and adventures. Now in her early forties, Maggie looked drawn but had regained some of her former magnetism. Although she seems to have remained absolutely faithful to Elisha Kent Kane's memory, she was flattered by the attentions of two men who found her as vibrant as the explorer once had. Joseph LaFumee, editor of the *Brooklyn Eagle,* and Wilson McDonald, a noted sculptor, reportedly were her devoted admirers and friends.

Reconciled to receiving no further income either from the Kanes or her book, she had finally managed to cut back on her drinking and had resumed holding public seances. One of her clients, the mineralogist Henry Seybert, was a wealthy philanthropist known for donating the Liberty Bell to Philadelphia's Independence Hall. Maggie's return to professional mediumship, however, must have felt on one level like a betrayal of Kane, causing her to experience some anger both at herself and at those unwitting fellow Spiritualists who required her services.[10]

A few of the old friends Kate might have visited during her stay in the United States had passed away in her absence, including Horace Greeley, whose death in 1872 was a particularly tragic one. So outraged had Greeley been by Grant's scandal-plagued Republican administration that he himself had campaigned for the presidency on the third-party Liberal Republican ticket, only to find himself endorsed by Democrats and tarred by Republicans as a Southern sympathizer who would sacrifice the rights of African Americans in the interests of sectional harmony. His humiliating defeat, coupled with his wife's death earlier that same year, had caused him to suffer a nervous breakdown. He had died soon afterward in a mental institution.

To the embarrassment of some Spiritualists and to the pride of others, the medium and free love advocate Victoria Woodhull had run in the same election on the Equal Rights ticket, the first female candidate for president of the United States.

In March 1875 Kate and her boys left Leah's house and moved to the Taylors' for four months. The Swedish Movement Cure had switched its quarters to a new location, the Hotel Branting on Madison Avenue, and financial reversals had hurt Dr. Taylor's business, for Sarah worried constantly about money matters. Benjamin Franklin's spirit kindly interceded with practical suggestions.

"Let me say sell," Franklin urged the Taylors, "but sell to advantage. You can sell this place for twice the money you gave for it. So I say sell, do not delay, do not delay. . . . Then you can purchase a house of your own, a private house and enjoy your children. . . ."[11]

With his injunction to "enjoy your children," Franklin may have been gently prodding Sarah, who had recently given birth to a little girl, to remember to cherish her mortal as well as her immortal babies. Kate had no such difficulty, and Sarah complained that the medium's maternal duties too often limited the time for seances; the older woman felt that their gatherings were never quite the same as they had been: "the baby would cry or [Ferdinand] would awaken or something would surely mar the smoothness of the chain that held us in communication."

Benjamin Franklin did what he could to console Sarah about the situation, enthusiastically booming, "And so we have Katy back again, not Katy alone, but Katy with two beautiful children, two blessings that she can see and feel and touch and feel the little hand touch her back." Sarah, the spirit seemed to imply, be *happy* for Kate!

In May 1875, after a separation of seven months, Henry Jencken finally arrived in the United States to meet his new son and his wife's relatives, and in July he and his family returned home to London. Maggie soon followed to spend time with her sister, afterward traveling there for extensive visits and eventually establishing her own following among English Spiritualists.

The next few years were happy ones for Kate's marriage, but she worried constantly about Ferdie and Henry, both of whom were frail children who suffered frequent bouts of illness. In an account later written by the wife of a Fox family descendant, Henry Jr. was said to have suffered from epilepsy, a possibility that raises intriguing questions about Kate. Although epilepsy isn't necessarily genetic, and there seem to be no other signs of the disease on either the Fox or Jencken side, it's tempting to think about Kate's early trances, and the "commotion" of snapping and cracking noises once commented upon by her childhood family doctor, in relation to seizures. Epilepsy in ancient times was little understood and often associated with religious ecstasy or demonic possession. Although more was known about the disease by the nineteenth century, the relationship between temporal lobe epilepsy and altered states of consciousness continues to be studied today.[12]

Relatively stable though Kate's home life was during these years, a storm was brewing in Spiritualist circles, for the medium Daniel Dunglas Home had decided to write a book about his fellow mediums, a work rumored to be unflattering at best. Some mediums responded to word of Home's potential betrayal with fury, but Kate took a gentler route, albeit one that was consciously or unconsciously manipulative. In a letter written in response to one of his in February 1876, she reminded Home of their friendship, stressed forgiveness as a virtue, and shared confidences about her personal life.

"I was very happy to hear from you and to learn that you were writing such an important book," she began, adding with a characteristic flourish that "some good spirit must have admonished you to do it!!!"[13]

His letter, she continued, showed that he had a kind heart and "as for listening to tale bearers it is simply a waste of time. . . . I have never said an unkind word of you for I never had one unkind thought towards you, and I do not believe those who have said that you have spoken harshly of me."

Her letter doesn't identify the cause of the breach that had occurred with Home in years past, but it's revelatory of Kate's feelings toward her sisters and her children. "You know that I have had severe trials," she told Home. "My sister Mrs. Underhill who is more than twenty-three years older than myself was always jealous of me, and when my blessed mother died we were not on speaking terms." Nevertheless, Kate continued in her letter, Home should avoid criticizing Leah in his book, for "Mrs. Underhill" was at last "trying to make up for past injustice to my sister and myself."

By the term *injustice*, Kate may have meant any one of a number of old wounds: the hurdles Leah had set for her sisters in the early 1850s; the harshness she had shown to Maggie over the affair with Kane; the lack of compassion she had demonstrated in response to her sisters' alcoholism in the 1860s. Margaret Fox had been an indulgent, loving woman if not always a wise one; Leah, the other maternal figure in Kate's life, had been tough, a demanding though arguably misguided taskmaster. Kate, who as a little girl far from home used to weep with longing for her mother, felt overwhelmingly grateful for Leah's recent solicitousness.

"She writes to me now," Kate confided with some poignancy, "calling me her dear child, which she never did before and when I was in America some months ago, she did everything that a mother could do so I forgive her, and although at times I find the shadows of her unkindness lingering in my heart, I try to remember that she is a changed woman and a good woman. . . ."

Powerfully attached to her true mother, flawed though Margaret might have been, Kate also was struggling desperately with her own maternal role.

"My little ones have been very ill. You are aware, I suppose," she wrote, "that my youngest child was born in America, in Mrs. Underhill's house. He has been very ill and I have nursed him day and night seldom taking time to step out of the room. What a hold a child has upon a mother's heart and oh, what a care they are. I want you to see my children."

Home's book, *Lights and Shadows of Spiritualism,* a work that castigated a number of mediums for faking manifestations and duping clients out of their fortunes, said not a word that was disparaging of Kate or Maggie Fox.

The children's health seemed to stabilize, and Kate's and Henry's relationship, both with one another and their children, flourished. Writing in 1880 to his brother in Australia, Henry noted with a touch of pride, "In my home, my 2 little boys Ferdinand and Henry are growing up into boyhood and offer me much pleasure. The day of schooling is almost at the door."[14] But he was destined not to see that day arrive, at least not for his younger son; in November 1881 Henry suffered a stroke and died three days later. After a marriage that had lasted almost ten years, his grief-stricken wife was left with their two little boys of six and eight and with whatever comfort the contemplation of the spirit world could offer.

SIXTEEN

"I LEAVE OTHERS TO JUDGE FOR THEMSELVES"

FOR A DECADE Henry Jencken had provided well for his family, but he wasn't a wealthy man; his personal estate at the time of his sudden death, excluding real estate, amounted to less than two hundred pounds. Like her sister Maggie, Kate now had to face life without a husband to support her and without any reliable means of earning an income except to hold seances.

Still, Kate remained one of the world's most famous mediums, and even after her long retirement, opportunities came her way. In January 1882 A. Aksakoff, a Russian bureaucrat and a dedicated investigator of Spiritualist phenomena, wrote Kate to offer condolences on her husband's death. Since he had recently suffered a similar loss—although not one that placed him in financial straits—he found himself sympathizing with her sorrow and eager to assist her if he could.[1]

Certain that he could help both Kate and the cause of Spiritualism, Aksakoff invited her to his country on a mission: to convert skeptics

·through her mediumship and also, in consultation with the spirits, to design safety measures for the coronation of Czar Alexander III, thereby enabling the new ruler to avoid his father's fate of assassination. For her services, Aksakoff offered her a hundred pounds plus expenses for the first month. Although he sharply warned that a frigid climate, unfamiliar food, and a tense political situation made Russia an inhospitable place for delicate boys raised in London, Kate took them with her anyway. She couldn't bear to be parted from Ferdie and Henry so soon after their father's death.

The popular movement that had started with raps trailing two charismatic young girls and that had grown despite, or in part because of, the controversy that followed the Fox sisters to Rochester and beyond, could now claim to have swept across two continents. Kate later took pride in showing off the jewels and other gifts she received in St. Petersburg and in having held seances for the royal family. According to the historian Emma Hardinge, the spirits once again played the role of conciliator and adviser, urging the czar to steer clear of political oppression and to favor liberal reforms. The immortal visitors who had first come calling during the heady days of agitation for abolition and woman's suffrage in the 1840s apparently hadn't forgotten their social agenda.

As international interest in Spiritualism continued to burgeon, so too did the number of organized groups dedicated to the systematic investigation of paranormal phenomena such as extrasensory perception. One of the most important, the Society for Psychical Research, known as the SPR, was started in 1882 at Cambridge University in England. Its impressive founders included Henry Sidgwick, a professor of philosophy at Cambridge; his wife, Eleanor, who later founded a women's college there; her brother, Arthur Balfour, future prime minister of England; and William Barrett, who taught physics at the Royal College of Science in Dublin.

Mrs. Sidgwick recalled first meeting Kate in 1874 during a seance at which the medium had "obtained a word written on a sheet of our own paper, under the table in light which I believed would have been good enough to read ordinary print by." But Mrs. Sidgwick suspected that Kate might have written the word with her foot, a common trick among fraudulent mediums.

Under the auspices of the SPR, Mrs. Sidgwick retested Kate a decade later, determining nothing conclusive but noting that the medium sometimes seemed to ask leading questions and that she occasionally claimed a coincidence as the work of the spirits. Mrs. Sidgwick admitted that Kate's raps were "peculiar—quite unlike what one can produce oneself by rapping with the foot." But she subsequently recanted even this statement. After reading the thirty-year-old report issued by the Buffalo doctors in 1851, she mused that Kate's "peculiar" raps might have been due after all to toe snapping. It was a conclusion shaped largely by hindsight.[2]

In the United States, Maggie too became caught up in the new round of organized investigations. Henry Seybert, the Philadelphia philanthropist, had willed funds to the University of Pennsylvania for an impartial inquiry into the nature of Spiritualist phenomena. In November 1884, not long after the philanthropist's death, Maggie met with the doubting and daunting members of the Seybert Commission at the Philadelphia home of its chairman, Horace Howard Furness. According to transcripts, the raps on both evenings were erratic, as were the answers to questions.

"This investigation is of great importance to us," noted Chairman Furness, a renowned Shakespearean scholar. "There is no question about it—we have heard these curious sounds." The issue for the committee, of course, as it had been for other investigators for more than thirty-five years, was whether the sounds emanated from the medium or from the spirits.

"I think you are entirely at one with us in every possible desire to have this phenomenon investigated," he told Maggie, who assured him that she was. She wearily refused to claim that the sounds were either otherworldly or independent of herself, observing that she would "leave others to judge for themselves."[3]

After hearing faint raps and loud ones, Furness placed his hand on Maggie's foot, announcing jubilantly, "This is the most wonderful thing of all, Mrs. Kane, I distinctly feel them in your foot. There is not a particle of motion in your foot, but there is an unusual pulsation." Certain that Maggie made the raps but unsure as to whether she did so consciously and deliberately, he invited her back for a third session, but she declined, pleading poor health and adding politely that she would be happy to return when she felt stronger. She never did. Her attitude throughout had been one of mild acquiescence.

A month later the American Society for Psychical Research, the ASPR, was formed, largely through the efforts and interest of the Harvard philosopher and psychologist William James, brother of the novelist, Henry. From the late 1860s William had been fascinated by psychic phenomena, and he had attended many seances. Most had turned out to be depressing demonstrations of fraud, but he remained committed to the idea that "there is no source of deception in the investigation of nature which can compare with a fixed belief that certain kinds of phenomenon are *impossible*."[4] His words can be seen as a motto for those who joined organizations such as the ASPR.

With circumscribed resources and no compelling reasons to remain in England, Kate and her sons returned to the United States in 1885. She moved in with Leah and Daniel, then in July called on George and Sarah Taylor, who hadn't seen her for a decade. Thrilled by her visit, Sarah wrote, "My joy can better be imagined than described. Here was Katie looking well and happy, though ten years older, with two nice healthy looking English boys."[5]

The medium and the spirits were equally ecstatic. "We shall have such sweet meetings again, as of old," Olin assured Sarah, with Kate scribbling each word. "We shall talk of the past, present, and future. We shall advise. We will bring all the loved ones back to whisper their loving greetings in your ear."

Later that summer Kate left Leah's and moved to her brother David's farm in Wayne County. She may have found it difficult to play the role of Leah's little sister again after having been a matron in charge of her own household. Moreover, Leah had come to view her various nieces and nephews as if they were her own, and she probably felt entitled to comparable maternal prerogatives with Ferdie and Henry, an attitude that the boys and their mother might well have resented.

There was surely another reason for the tension: the publication of

Leah's book, *The Missing Link in Modern Spiritualism,* in 1885. The book, padded with many newspaper articles and letters, reviewed the history of the Fox family, burnished to a sheen, and recounted the trials and triumphs of Spiritualism's first decades, focusing on events in which Leah's role was prominent. The work undoubtedly stirred bitter questions in the hearts of her sisters. How had Leah managed to protect herself from obloquy and to emerge from their ordeals unscathed? The thrill of the seances, the money and the gifts, even a sense of helping others, perhaps had once compensated Kate and Maggie for the pressures of their lives, but no longer. And here was Leah, capitalizing once again on the fame of her sisters.

The tone of *The Missing Link* tends to veer between nostalgia and bombast, but in places Leah's account evidences a distinctly wry and even subversive wit. Like her sisters, she remains an enigma in her own right. Her book, a mixed bundle of distortions and truths, is self-aggrandizing at the same time that it's faintly scandalous. While claiming middle-class respectability, she pokes fun at bourgeois gentility with references to the money she's made and the number of times she's been stripped naked. Referring discreetly to herself in the third person, she wrote of one investigation by a committee of women:

"They took the mediums into a room, bolted the door, and erected a platform of tables, on which [the mediums] were compelled to stand. Here, piece by piece, they were disrobed by the committee, and every article of wearing apparel examined and laid aside."[6]

She added the titillating detail that "a large number of gentlemen and others waiting to hear the report of the committee" were standing impatiently just outside the door. Leah's book, indeed, is a little like a seance: sparkling effects, intimate confidences, false family histories, a few startling facts, and a shiver of the erotic.

Kate stayed at David's farm until the late fall of 1885, then rented a ground-floor apartment for herself and her boys on East Eighty-Fourth Street in New York City. Here she conducted private seances and hosted one public gathering a week. Sometimes as many as fifteen people attended Kate's "Public Evenings," among them her surrogate mother, Sarah Taylor, who wrote of manifestations that were as startling as of old:

objects floating, tables levitating, and invisible hands that caressed, tugged, and poked.

With Henry Jencken no longer in Kate's life to protect her from temptation, however, she succumbed to her old enemy, alcohol. On June 2, 1886, George Taylor found her drunk in a saloon. "He had heard that something was wrong and had searched her out," Sarah wrote. "She was taken to her rooms and all the miseries of her old life of ten and fifteen years ago were repeated."[7]

Kate struggled on for two years, until her drinking precipitated a crisis with long-term ramifications for her family and for the Spiritualist movement: on May 4, 1888, Kate was arrested and held for three hundred dollars' bail at the Harlem Police Court on charges of neglecting fourteen-year-old Ferdie and twelve-year-old Henry. The Society for the Prevention of Cruelty to Children, otherwise known as the Gerry Society after its founder, had arranged for the indictment. Ferdie and Henry were tall, lean young men who looked well cared for and bright eyed to the arresting officers, but Kate was undeniably drunk. The boys were sent to the Juvenile Asylum, an establishment for children who were deemed to have no better home.

The day after her arraignment, Kate gave an interview to the New York newspaper the *World* in which she broke down and sobbed. She told the reporter that the boys had been in school at Rochester and had been visiting her for only two weeks. After fiercely denying that she ill-treated her children, she sadly admitted to what she called "intemperate habits." These habits showed in her once-handsome face, the reporter wrote, which was lined with worry, age, and dissipation.

Kate made no reference to her father's alcoholism in talking about her own. When she and her sister Maggie were young and famous, she confided, the two of them had been wined and dined everywhere; people had sent them baskets of champagne. And so the drinking habit, she said, had been born.[8]

The Fox sisters' weakness for alcohol and—it was rumored—drugs too had embarrassed Spiritualists for some time; many conservative, middle-class adherents of the movement, concerned about their own credibility, had become uneasy with other aspects of the movement as well, including the radical ideas often associated with Spiritualism and extravagant manifestations such as materializations. Everyone was uncomfortable with what seemed to be rampant fraud. A notorious medium was on trial that very spring for allegedly duping a wealthy patron out of his fortune.

Trying to position herself in the most respectable light, Kate criticized the "fanatics who hire halls and preach universal belief in everything." She was a firm believer in some manifestations, she asserted, but not in all. Then the old Kate flamed up through her tears, and she invited the reporter to return on another day to visit with the spirits.

Word of her nephews' detention quickly reached Maggie, who had been visiting friends in England since the previous March. Her devotion to Kate surfaced immediately, and she formed a plan: she sent a cable signed, not with her own name, but with that of Edward Jencken, Henry's brother in Australia, whom she claimed was the boys' legal guardian. The cable ordered Henry and Ferdie's release, and the ruse worked.

With her boys again by her side, Kate immediately booked passage to England. According to Maggie, on their arrival in London her nephews greeted her joyfully, and she threw her arms around them, joking, "Here's your Uncle Edward boys."

"Hello Uncle Edward!" they shouted in unison.[9]

Then Maggie struck again in defense of Kate, this time with a stunning blow aimed at the entire Spiritualist movement. She sent a letter to the *New York Herald* that appeared under the headline "The Curse of Spiritualism"; in it she denounced the rise of fake mediums, and as Kate had, she lambasted "fanatics" who blindly believed anything. Hundreds of men and women, Maggie seethed with self-serving wrath, ignored harmless messages such as the ones she delivered to "rush madly after the glaring humbugs that flood New York."[10]

Such fanatics, she continued, wanted "the 'spirit' to come to them in full form, to walk before them, to embrace them, and all such nonsense, and what is the result? Like old Judge Edmonds and Mr. Seybert of Philadelphia, they become crazed. . . ."

The fools, she concluded, lost their money, their sanity, and often enough their lives.

Clearly she blamed her own and Kate's misfortunes as much on members of the Spiritualist movement as on outsiders. Between some Spiritualists' obsession with ever more explosive effects, the willingness of unscrupulous mediums to produce the desired pyrotechnics, and other Spiritualists' dread of scandal, there was little call, it seemed, for rapping spirits. The pressure to work effectively in such an atmosphere, Maggie intimated, could drive even an honest, sober medium to drink or to deception.

Maggie was far from finished with her denunciation of the Spiritualist movement, and she girded for a new attack. She and Kate suspected that Leah had been behind the zealous Gerry Society's seizure of Ferdie and Henry. Although Leah certainly had legitimate concerns about Kate's alcoholism, her younger sisters believed that she had acted purely out of jealousy and spite in an attempt to gain control of the boys and that she might dare to do so again. They also worried that other Spiritualists, friends of Leah's, had supported her. These alleged confederates, Maggie stated, were afraid she'd expose them in fraud and were using the boys as blackmail. The time had come, Maggie and Kate felt, to destroy Leah's power over their lives.

Maggie sailed for home in September 1888, arriving in New York late in the month. But before she could take any action, Kate got herself into more trouble by conducting a seance in England that non-Spiritualists mocked and that the Spiritualist establishment in London condemned, turning viciously on one of its own.

The seance was held at the house that had been Thomas Carlyle's before he died in 1881 and that had been purchased recently by a Spiritualist. A reporter who had known Carlyle in life attended the event and found the literary luminary's spirit messages unrecognizably insipid. He proceeded to describe the seance in a tongue-in-cheek article published in the popular magazine *Pall Mall*.

An important Spiritualist publication in Great Britain, *Light*, promptly struck back, taking aim, however, not at the reporter but at Kate, arguing that for "the credit of Spiritualism" loyal Spiritualists had to disavow the kind of "pseudo-messages" printed by *Pall Mall*. These sorts of communications, *Light* chastised, amounted to "clumsy parody," even though they came through "the famous American medium."[11]

Blows and counterblows. Now Kate and Maggie, long slighted by many middle-class Spiritualists for their alcoholism, had come under explicit attack from the British establishment if not yet from the American.

Back in the United States the drama continued to unfold. On Sunday, September 23, 1888, a reporter for the *New York Herald* visited Maggie in her apartment on West Forty-Fourth Street. Although he confessed to knowing little about her or her history—he was, after all, simply on assignment—he was struck by her intensity and magnetism. He also commented on her careless dress: the breezy negligence that Kane might have recognized and criticized, as he had chastised the beautiful young girl for forgetting to wear her undersleeves thirty years before.

Her face showed "sorrow and world-wide experience," the reporter wrote. Despite her notoriety, he said, she had retained friends on both sides of the Atlantic, and in London she was "entertained by some of the best-to-do of the great and comprehensive middle class."[12]

As Maggie talked to him she paced rapidly back and forth, sometimes covering her face with her hands, sometimes sitting down suddenly at the piano to play "wild incoherent tunes." Perhaps they were angry versions of the music that Leah had once taught her students or that the spirits had played on bells or guitars at long-ago seances.

The reporter's story about the sisters, published the next day under the headline "A Celebrated Medium Says the Spirits Never Return," consisted of a lengthy interview with Maggie, one in which she took direct aim at Leah and the deceased Margaret Fox.

"When Spiritualism first began," Maggie said, "Katie and I were little children, and this old woman, my other sister, made us her tools. Mother was a silly woman. She was a fanatic. I call her that because she was honest. She believed in these things.

"We were but innocent little children," Maggie continued. "What did we know? Ah we grew to know too much. Our sister used us in her exhibitions, and we made money for her. Now she turns upon us because she's the wife of a rich man, and she opposes us both wherever she can. Oh, I am after her! You can kill sometimes without using weapons, you know."

To the reporter's surprise, Maggie demonstrated the raps, which he heard underneath the table, on the outside of the door, and rippling across the floor.

"How do you do it?" he demanded with a touch of admiration.

She told him that she wanted to keep her explanation a secret until the night she gave her lecture. But it was all trickery, she insisted, then turned the question around by asking with a twinkle, "Spirits, is he not easily fooled?"

A moment before she dazzled him with raps, Maggie presented him with a strange paradox. Though she knew how to make the raps—apparently had done so since childhood—her own knowledge and abilities hadn't been the source of her disbelief. She now knew for certain that spirits do not return, she said, only after trying futilely again and again to contact the dead. Like the people who came to her seances, she was a seeker herself; she had wished desperately for comfort after Kane's death.

"Why, I have explored the unknown as far as human will can," she cried. "I have gone to the dead so that I might get from them some little token. Nothing came of it—nothing, nothing." Her denunciation of Spiritualism, the animus of it, came not just from her rage at Leah and at her fellow Spiritualists, but also from her own profound disappointment at the spirits' failure to respond.

SEVENTEEN

"THE DEATH-BLOW"

KATE RETURNED to the United States from England in mid-October 1888, unquestionably to present a common front with Maggie in attacking Leah and Spiritualism, although she denied knowing anything about the brouhaha created by the article in the *Herald*. A reporter who followed her to Maggie's wrote that the two women "fell on each other's necks, in an ecstasy of affection and delight at being together once more." Kate looked quite "comely," he noted, adding that she had vowed "with heartfelt earnestness" that she "was done forever with her once-besetting vice."[1]

Kate echoed Maggie's denunciation of Spiritualism as a tissue of lies, calling it "a humbug from beginning to end." It was true that Horace Greeley had educated her, Kate told the reporter, but otherwise Leah's book on the Fox sisters' lives and work had been altogether a fiction.

Maggie had promised to make a public appearance exposing Spiritualism as a fraud, and the much-publicized event was held at the New York Academy of Music on October 21, 1888. That morning the *World* published a full-page story on the Fox sisters, accompanied by a lengthy first-person statement by Maggie. Like the stories recounted in *The Love-Life of Dr. Kane* and in Leah's *The Missing Link in Modern Spiritualism,* the substance of Maggie's confession was a confusion of fact, fabrication, and obfuscation.

One of its main goals was to discredit her oldest sister. Leah had dared to call Kate an unfit mother who mistreated her children? With all the zeal of the Gerry Society's child welfare reformers, Maggie turned the tables as adeptly as any spirit. It was Leah who abused innocent children, she claimed, who manipulated babes who knew no better and who were helpless under the treacherous influence of cruel and self-serving adults.

"My sister Katie and myself were very young children when this horrible deception began. I was eight, and just a year and a half older than she," Maggie stated, subtracting about five years from their true ages at the time.

She and Kate were mischievous, she acknowledged, and liked to terrify their mother, who was a good woman and easily frightened. Later, Maggie would recall that they also had loved to tease Leah's daughter, the serious Lizzie.

How could such very *young* children, the medium implied, be responsible for their own behavior? Having established her mythic state of innocence, Maggie gave her version of how the raps began.

"At night when we went to bed," she said, "we used to tie an apple on a string and move the string up and down, causing the apple to bump on the floor, or we would drop the apple on the floor, making a strange noise every time it would rebound."

Apple dropping was most likely an actual game played by the girls. It also was an image rich in irony, although Maggie may not have intended the twist. Newton's discovery of gravity had been a seminal moment in the history of science and in the conception of a mechanical universe, a universe antithetical to the notion of supernatural intervention. The discovery of gravity had occurred, according to legend, after Newton had witnessed an apple—dropping. Mary Baker Eddy, the founder of Christian Science, famous by the 1880s both as a religious leader and as a sworn enemy of Spiritualism, had adopted the legendary image. She said that the inspiration for her faith had hit her like an apple—dropping.[2]

Apple dropping, however, wasn't the only trick up the Fox sisters' proverbial sleeve, at least not according to Maggie's statement in the *World*. From apple dropping, Maggie continued, they had advanced to rapping with their knuckles and joints, a discovery that Kate had made first with her fingers and that both girls soon learned to reproduce with their toes.

"The rappings are simply the result of a perfect control of the muscles of the leg below the knee," Maggie said, echoing the ponderous lingo of the Buffalo doctors and other exponents of the joint- and bone-cracking theory, "which govern the tendons of the foot and allow action of the toe and ankle bones that are not commonly known."

The family's neighbors in Hydesville and Rochester had come to investigate the raps, Maggie recalled, but to no avail. "No one suspected us of any trick because we were such young children," she stated in the *World*. "We were led on by my sister purposely, and by my mother unintentionally. We often heard her say, 'Is this a disembodied spirit that has taken possession of my dear children?'"

Although she and Kate certainly had relished fooling the adults, Maggie insisted that Leah was the one who had forced them to continue doing so, taking them to Rochester, where they "were exhibited to a lot of Spiritualist fanatics. . . . Mrs. Underhill made as much as $100 to $150 dollars a night. She pocketed this."

Leah had wanted to start a new religion, Maggie revealed. To that end, she not only had assured her younger sisters that she herself received spirit messages, but she also had tried to instill her professed belief in supernatural visitations in them. Yet at the same time, Maggie explained—and here she pointed out a bewildering contradiction—Leah had conspired in trickery, even supplying cues about when to rap yes or no at seances.

When she was thirteen, Maggie continued, turning to a new chapter in her life story, she had met Dr. Kane, to whom she had instantly confided her hatred of Spiritualism. Calling herself Kane's widow, as she had now for many years, she expressed her hope that if "those we love who have passed away before us can look down upon us from heaven—if we are ever to meet again—I know my dead husband is looking on me now and blessing me for my work."

After his death, she said, poverty had driven her back to her life as a medium. She had seen so much deception, she concluded in her statement to the *World*, that she had made up her mind "to positively state Spiritualism is a fraud of the worst description." And she owed all her misfortune to Leah.

That night, October 21, 1888, the Academy of Music was packed to the roof with obstreperous combatants: staunch Spiritualists versus those who had come in triumph to hear the internationally famous medium, Margaret Fox Kane, deal what was being called a "death-blow" to the movement.[3]

One of the event's promoters, Dr. C. M. Richmond, a portly dentist whose avocation was magic, also served as the evening's lecturer, assigned to speak on Spiritualism's evils, to expose common tricks of the trade, and to introduce Maggie. He was extremely nervous, never having faced such a large crowd. Mustering his courage, he performed various tricks for more than an hour, explaining how slate writing, spirit painting, and mind reading could be done as adeptly by a skilled magician as by an alleged supernatural being. The audience, rowdy to begin with, eventually grew impatient for the main event and started shouting for Maggie, rudely urging the dentist to "go and pull teeth."

At last Maggie ascended the stage, described by one reporter "as a little compact woman, dark-eyed and dark-haired." Kate was seated in a box in the audience, lending silent approval to what her sister was about to do.

Maggie was wearing a black dress and flowered hat. She was far more nervous even than Dr. Richmond and kept taking her eyeglasses on and off as she alternately read from her statement, then glanced up at the audience to repeat each sentence. Different contingents cheered and booed her as she spoke in an excited voice, denouncing Spiritualism.

When she finished her statement Dr. Richmond called several physicians onto the stage. Maggie slipped off one of her shoes and placed her stocking-clad foot on a small pine table. Sharp raps were heard resounding throughout the theater. The reporter for the *New York Tribune* wrote that the noises increased from faint to loud, "traveling up the wall and along the roof of the Academy."

While the raps continued, the doctors solemnly examined Maggie's feet, a procedure that the audience met with suggestive laughter and ribald remarks. Then Maggie stood on the table for another examination, after which the doctors pronounced that the raps were indeed made by her big toe.

Nobody seemed to question whether the raps produced by Maggie's toe were supplemented by other means: whether Dr. Richmond himself might have had confederates in the audience willing to mount the kind of symphony for which the spirits had become famous.

The Buffalo doctors and C. Chauncey Burr in the 1850s had been right about the joints and muscles, ligaments and tendons, of the human leg and foot. Properly manipulated, they can certainly be noisy. In a theater with good acoustics, audience members sitting at the back of the balcony can hear actors crack their joints. But exactly how much noise does the human body have to make to evoke a chorus of spirit voices?

Just as elements of Maggie's confession can be questioned, it's tempting to ask whether Maggie, or Dr. Richmond, actually revealed at long last *all* of the exciting secrets of the mysterious noises.

Maggie's confession supplies important new pieces of the puzzle. Which pieces click into place with a satisfying snap? Which ones will not be coaxed into place at all? Did the Fox sisters in fact indulge over a forty-year period in deliberate fraud? If so, what were their motives, and how did they pull it off so well?

Maggie alleged in her confession that she and Kate were the victims of Leah's ambition and greed. There's no question that both children deserved to be better protected, but questions as to who could or should have provided that protection, and from what forces in an era of rapid change, remain more complex.

The girls' father, John Fox, failed his youngest daughters as he had failed in most other activities in his life. Recent speculation suggests that he may have reverted to alcoholism, perhaps even physically abused Kate and Maggie, a theory based in part on the idea that the spirits represented the sisters' imaginative response to mistreatment. The accounts of his contemporaries, however, seem to indicate that John did not drink after reconciling with his wife. More likely the devoutly religious John, while an avowed enemy of the spirits, was too self-absorbed to intervene in his daughters' careers.

The most serious accusation that Maggie hurled at her mother may not have been that Margaret was superstitious but rather that she was a foolish and frightened woman. Margaret Fox always yielded to whomever pushed the hardest: the persistent poltergeist; her determined oldest daughter; the ambitious Eliab Capron; the charming Elisha Kent Kane. Although her devotion to her children was admirable and unquestionable, she failed to realize that times had changed since her own adventurous journey westward in her youth; in an era that valued modesty and gentility in its daughters, Margaret allowed Kate and Maggie a dangerous, if at times liberating, freedom.

Leah, closer in age to her mother than to Kate or Maggie, had grown up in the 1820s in a boomtown. Leah yearned for security, and she was willing to take risks to earn it. What she seems to have glimpsed in her two charming, inventive, and perhaps extraordinary younger sisters was the chance to create herself anew: the opportunity to trade in the marginal respectability of a single mother in Rochester, first for fame and fortune and then for a life of bourgeois comfort.

In the 1840s and 1850s, without a father or husband she could count on, strong-willed Leah did exactly what many men of her day were doing: she promoted a cause and made money as she did so. Women such as Amy Post surely gave her the impetus to conceive of herself as the leader of a movement; men like the mesmerist Stanley Grimes supplied the model for staging a performance and charging a fee. Leah lived in an age of enthusiastic prophets and quick profits; the word *speculate* means not only "to wonder about" but also "to take a risk on." She managed to tap in to her era's appetite for both.

By promoting her younger sisters' gifts, Leah may not have envisioned herself as exploiting the girls or at least not solely for her own benefit. Instead, she may well have imagined she was rescuing them from the dismal alternatives that faced many a young woman without money or prospects: the existence of a farmer's wife or a factory worker. Inventing a religion was a grand scheme in the American tradition of dreaming large, even if a little humbug was required to make the dream come true.

It's hard not to admire Leah for sheer gumption. However ironically and disdainfully, Emerson in 1855 had placed the profession of medium in the same category as that of railroad man, landscape gardener, lecturer, and daguerreotypist: all were careers newly minted in the nineteenth century.[4] The Fox sisters helped not only to found a new religion but also to establish a new line of work.

While no one can say for certain, it's likely that one or all of the Fox sisters at some point believed that the spirits of the departed manifest themselves to the living. As children, the three of them were told of relatives who possessed paranormal abilities such as precognition. From early childhood, Kate and Maggie had observed their Methodist father's daily prayers, watching in awe and amusement as he appealed to a deity who could summarily exile him to hell if he returned to his dissolute ways. The children may have heard tales of "Old Jeffrey," the Wesley family poltergeist, or seen any one of a number of charlatans, performers, and visionaries at work on a circus stage or a Rochester street corner: a mesmerist magnetizing a subject, a clairvoyant extolling the spirits, or a magician creating illusions.

There's no reason to assume, however, that Leah, Kate, and Maggie all felt precisely the same way either about the spirits or about their own powers as mediums; neither is it likely that their ideas remained fixed over a period of forty years. As Kate and Maggie responded to their friends' desires for messages and manifestations that noisily denied death's silence, they may have convinced themselves that their powers had a supernatural dimension. Could they do so even as they delighted in fooling others, even as Leah taught them cues and tricks? Sometimes rational adults experience irrational fears of the dark; children clustered around a campfire may frighten themselves by telling ghost stories of their own invention. Most of us are familiar with the uncomfortable sensation of being of two minds, of holding two or more conflicting ideas at once.

Maggie, in her confession, tried to position herself as a young, innocent child when the raps began, but in fact she was already an adolescent with a will of her own. She surely wasn't entirely subject to Leah's wishes—or the spirits'—in continuing to hold seances for friends and strangers, first in Rochester and then in New York. She also relished and needed the excitement that came with her life as a medium, and she enjoyed the financial rewards too.

Until, that is, she encountered Elisha Kent Kane and began to dream about what she called "the pleasures of a quiet home, the blessings of love—the reward of virtue." Then the world of the spirits and those who called upon them seemed tedious and dismal indeed.

Like Leah, in becoming a public medium, Maggie chose to invent a new self, to accept the designation of high priestess (or to defy the label con artist). What destroyed her was her failure to do what Leah later managed to accomplish: to create a third self. In the end she was unable to transform herself into the genteel, upper-class girl who could be accepted by Elisha Kent Kane and his family. If self-invention is in the American tradition, so too is the failure to succeed and the desperation that can follow.

Kate, only eleven years old when the raps began, early on seems to have lost the sense of a self she could shape. More than either of her sisters, she came to be viewed as a cipher; others looked through her to the reflection of their own needs and desires. Elisha Kent Kane saw in Kate his lover's sister, a girl to use as a go-between; Charles Livermore saw the essence of his beloved Estelle; Sarah Taylor saw her children happy in heaven. Everyone who cared about Kate believed that they protected her, but it's possible that no one, not even Maggie, ever did.

The intensely personal quality of Kate's spirit messages inevitably raises the possibility that the invisible beings who spoke through her represented a part of herself, that she developed what later came to be called a split personality or multiple personality disorder. But in the field of psychology the existence of such an illness is controversial; moreover, perhaps the only entity as elusive as a spirit is the unconscious.

Merry and mischievous as a child, Kate seems to have grown increasingly self-effacing, her demeanor not unlike that of a sweet-faced, genteel heroine. With her ethereal presence, she became the prototype of the passive medium, a role that allowed women to assume a measure of power while seeming to remain powerless. In embodying this role, Kate may have exerted more influence over the course of Spiritualism and the nature of mediumship than either of her more forceful sisters. But as the century wore on, many women, even mediums, sought to exercise their power in the wider world more directly, leaving Kate behind.

Kate is central to the mystery of the Fox sisters. The first one, according to her sister Maggie, who made the raps. The original medium, said her mother, Capron, and Leah. The Fox sister who drew the most attention from investigators such as Partridge and Greeley. Mischief maker, magician, medium.

PART V

AFTERLIFE

1888 to the Present

EIGHTEEN

"UNCOMMON POWERS"

THE MAINSTREAM PAPERS called Maggie's confession a "death-blow," and a book titled *The Death-Blow to Spiritualism: Being the True Story of the Fox Sisters, As Revealed by Authority of Margaret Fox Kane and Catherine Fox Jencken* came out shortly after Maggie's appearance at the Academy of Music in the fall of 1888. Written by Reuben Briggs Davenport, a professional author whose other books were unrelated to Spiritualism, *The Death-Blow to Spiritualism* featured a frontispiece authorizing it as "a true account of the origin of Spiritualism," signed by Maggie and Kate. The book essentially repeated and enlarged upon Maggie's confession, adding a few sensational points. According to Maggie, some if not all seances had moved wide of their original purpose: they were no longer gatherings of a religious or scientific nature but bacchanals at which nude females, wearing the sheerest of gauze, pretended to be apparitions and at which purported spirits gave their imprimatur to sexual orgies in the dark.

Some Spiritualists reacted to Maggie's confession and accusations with compassion. Several weeks after her appearance at the Academy of

Music, the spirit of Samuel B. Brittan, formerly the publisher of the *Spiritual Telegraph,* delivered his views at a seance, allegedly communicating them from the other world—the Summerland, as Spiritualists call it.

"Life has not been full of sunshine," for the Fox sisters, the spirit acknowledged. Although Maggie was a genuine medium with wonderful powers, "the band of spirits attending Margaret Fox during the early part of her career" no longer followed her. Instead, "*other* unseen intelligences, who are not scrupulous in their dealings with humanity" had become her untrustworthy companions. The Fox sisters, Brittan's spirit warned, had become "false witnesses."[1]

Other Spiritualists, mortal ones, charged that Maggie had switched sides simply for financial reasons. Since she had ceased to make a decent living as a medium, they argued, she had decided to support herself as one of the movement's fiercest critics. The *Banner of Light* reported that she was touring with the dentist and magician, Dr. Richmond, to make money on her toe-snapping demonstrations but that at one stop she had looked so unwell that a hotel clerk assumed she was "a victim of dipsomania."[2]

A third strategy adopted by Spiritualists was to remind one another and the world that Kate and Maggie were only incidental to the history of the movement. In a statement made at the Boston Spiritual Temple Society, the medium Mrs. R. S. Lillie reminded her audience that "these girls were no more the founders of Spiritualism than the chair, tables, or turnips that were thrown from room to room of the [Hydesville] house."[3]

Lest her listeners miss the point, Mrs. Lillie stressed that Kate and Maggie "were but the means in the hands of invisible intelligences at work earlier than this through Andrew Jackson Davis and others who were mesmerized, he, however, giving to the public the most prominent spiritual results."

Leah kept her head down and managed to avoid the conflict and to sidestep blame, at least from other Spiritualists. She and her husband, Daniel, continued the pattern they had established when they married in 1858, more than thirty years before. They entertained their host of friends in their comfortable home, their parlor filled with the sound of lively mortal conversation and perhaps still with the occasional immortal rap. A friend later recalled that Leah's table, the same one at which the Fox sisters had held their early seances in Rochester, was a large one that "rarely showed a vacant chair around it."[4]

In the months immediately after the events at the Academy of Music, Kate occasionally toured to repeat the accusations against Spiritualism, even appearing in Rochester, the city where she and Maggie had first made their name. One dramatic billboard, illustrated with a picture of Kate rapping for the Russian czar, announced:

MODERN SPIRITUALISM
Born March 31, 1848
Died at Rochester, Nov. 15, 1888
Aged 40 years, 7 months and 15 Days
Born of Mischief and
Gone to the Mischief[5]

In January 1889, however, Kate wrote to a friend that she thought there was money to be made by proving that the knockings were *not* made with the toes. "So many people come to me to ask me about this exposure of Maggie's that I have to deny myself to them," she complained. "They are hard at work to expose the whole thing *if they can,*" she observed, then added without explanation, "but they certainly cannot."[6]

A reporter for the *Rochester Democrat and Chronicle* commented that Kate was "in the hands of a professional exposer of Spiritualism" and that she spoke in a practiced, inauthentic manner, from rote rather than from the heart. The reporter didn't indicate whether or not she gave a demonstration of the toe-cracking technique along with delivering her statement, but he concluded that Kate hadn't lost faith in the spirits.[7]

It seemed to some Spiritualists that Maggie's war against the spirits also hadn't been authentic. On November 16, 1889, a year after her public confession, Maggie recanted that devastating attack in an interview conducted in the presence of Henry J. Newton, the president of the First Society of Spiritualists of New York and a fellow of the New York Academy of Science. His wife and two other witnesses were in the room.[8]

"Would to God that I could undo the injustice I did the cause of Spiritualism under the strong psychological influence of persons who were opposed to it," Maggie admitted. "I gave expression to utterances that had no foundation in fact and that would at the time throw discredit on the Spiritual phenomena."

Her decision to recant, she said, was not made of her own volition but was an impulse that came from her spirit guides. Otherwise, she herself might have wished to avoid the insults she expected to be hurled at her from all sides—by those who had encouraged her first confession as well as by those Spiritualists she was now hoping to appease.

Asked whether her motive for recanting was to take revenge on those who had promised her a profit for exposing Spiritualism, Maggie insisted that she only wanted to set the record straight. She vaguely attributed part of the blame for the original exposé to powerful Catholics who had pressured her into rejecting Spiritualism. It's likely that, since she claimed to have converted to Catholicism, the church indeed frowned on her continued practice of holding seances. Talking to the dead in the Catholic Church was considered a matter more suited to exorcism than to celebration.

She testified that she hadn't been bribed to recant by wealthy Spiritualists. But she candidly admitted that she hoped to earn an income by resuming her lecture tour, this time on Spiritualism's behalf.

"My great ambition is to repair the wrong I have done," she said, "but you know that even a mortal instrument in the hands of the spirit must have the maintenance of life."

Above all, the spirits remained powerful forces in her life, she told her listeners. Far from abandoning her for her treachery, they sometimes rapped so loudly that they even woke her neighbors.

Word of Maggie's recantation spread, and just as she had predicted, her reversal didn't protect her from the slings and arrows hurled at her from all sides. A well-known magician, Joseph Rinn, maintained that one evening he smuggled her under the assumed name of Mrs. Spencer into a debate about Spiritualism, a well-attended event held at the Manhattan Liberal Club, one of New York's political and dining clubs for gentlemen. She looked so worn and dissipated, Rinn asserted, that even her oldest friends didn't recognize her. "Mrs. Spencer," whoever she was, revealed many tricks of the trade, explaining how mediums wrote messages on blank slates by using either their teeth or their feet.

Leah continued to be lauded by Spiritualists as a kind of queen mother. At a gathering of the First Society of Spiritualists at Apollo Hall in the spring of 1889, she delivered "touching remarks" beneath a portrait of Margaret, her mother, which she had loaned to the society for the occasion.[9]

On November 1, 1890, Leah died at her home in New York City. According to her death certificate, she had been suffering from carditis, an inflammation of the heart that had been exacerbated by "nervous excitability." Her age was listed as a girlish seventy-two instead of the more realistic seventy-seven or seventy-eight. She was buried in the Underhill plot at Greenwood Cemetery in Brooklyn, New York, where she was followed the next summer by Daniel.

A few months before Leah's death, Kate had visited her old friends George and Sarah Taylor, who had recently returned from Europe. It was the first time she had seen them in three years, but within a few minutes she had picked up a pencil and paper and produced a message.

"My Dear Sarah," the message read, "How happy we are to talk with you in this way. We have been with you often, Sarah, so often, and helped you at all times."[10]

The message was signed "Olin." Frankie and Leila soon crowded into the room, their characteristic little jokes and laughter inaudible to all but the medium's ear, as showers of raps announced the children's presence. Within a few weeks, even the venerable Dr. Franklin had returned. But after visiting the Taylors sporadically for a year, Kate dropped from sight completely in March 1891. George Taylor tried to find her, but she had moved and left no forwarding address.

Another year passed before they heard from her again. In February 1892 Kate invited the Taylors to visit her at 609 Columbus Avenue in New York, her new home. For the next three months Sarah and George occasionally called on her there, and they received many messages about their troubled finances. On June 1, 1892, Benjamin Franklin kindly advised Sarah and George not to worry about practical burdens.

"All that you have to do is keep a watchful eye with us, and there will be no loss," he counseled. "Management will soon be better. I see . . . bright changes. . . . God bless you, now and forever."[11]

This was the last message that George and Sarah Taylor received through the mediumship of Kate Fox. A month later they received a telegram from Ferdie informing them that his mother had died on July 2 and asking them to come to him immediately. "And so it was!" Sarah wrote in her journal, adding that Kate had been on her last drinking spree when she died.

Sarah Taylor had met with the medium intermittently over a period approaching a quarter of a century, and she had assembled a detailed thousand-page record of their seances. Sarah's notes were later published by her son, William Langworthy Taylor, under the title *Fox-Taylor Automatic Writing 1869–1892: Unabridged Record,* a work that represents an invaluable contribution to the history of Modern Spiritualism and the Fox sisters.

Kate's death certificate listed her age as fifty-three, most likely two years younger than her actual age, and the cause of death as "chronic diffuse nephritis," a disease of the kidneys. Her occupation was registered for posterity simply as "housewife." Greenwood Cemetery was the intended burial place, but perhaps someone in the Underhill family objected, or there was no money for the internment. Kate's body was placed in a temporary vault.

Sarah's mourning was deep, but it was not for Kate alone. "The loss of this vehicle of communication between my loved [ones], to whom I cannot speak directly, and ourselves is very great and at present seems irreparable," she wrote soon after Kate's death.[12]

At the time Maggie was penniless, living in an apartment at 456 West Fifty-Seventh Street that had been loaned to her by Henry J. Newton, president of the First Society of Spiritualists. On March 4, 1893, her old friend Titus Merritt, a Spiritualist bookseller who had known her family since the 1860s, was notified that she was ill. Two days later he arranged for her to be moved to the home of another loyal friend, Emily Ruggles, who lived on State Street in Brooklyn.

Ruggles took care of Maggie that night, March 6, and Merritt stayed with her the following night, March 7. A few hours before dawn, at 4:30 AM on March 8, 1893, fifty-nine-year-old Maggie died. She went peacefully, Merritt later wrote, without a struggle. Her heart had given out. Kate's body was removed from its temporary vault, and through the kindness of another old friend, Joseph LaFumee, Maggie and her younger sister were buried at Cypress Hills Cemetery in Brooklyn, New York, together in death as in life.[13]

The *Banner of Light* marked Maggie's transition to the Summerland with articles and letters. One writer, Mrs. Willis, noted that it seemed "but a few years since that Margaret and Katie Fox were sought for and interviewed, and could command almost any sums for the simple exercise of uncommon powers." They had failed "to hold themselves to a high standard," she continued, "and both of them lost prestige and power."[14]

Mrs. Willis discussed their rise and fall, however, without the vituperative disappointment that Spiritualists had directed so often at the Fox sisters in their later years. Instead, she cautioned that "we have yet to learn over again this lesson, sensitives are subject to conditions.

"When the nations of ancient times called on their mediums they made them feel their importance by consecration, and by preparing for them suitable abodes and temples.... But we of modern times take the blessing of mediumship and forget the mediator."

She concluded, "Therefore no word of censure or reproach can be cast on this mortal career...."

NINETEEN

"WE OF MODERN TIMES"

THE YEAR MAGGIE DIED, 1893, Spiritualists formed the National Spiritualist Association, an enduring institution that today is known as the National Spiritualist Association of Churches. Lily Dale, one of the many summer retreats organized by Spiritualists in the 1870s, is still in existence after more than a century. A picturesque Victorian town near Buffalo, New York, Lily Dale is now a year-round community of Spiritualists. Nonresident mediums and others concerned with spiritual matters visit from around the world to socialize, study, and attend seminars and seances in a peaceful lakeside setting. With its reputation as a town that talks to the dead, Lily Dale also attracts thousands of curious tourists annually.[1]

Lily Dale, the National Spiritualist Association of Churches, and other Spiritualist organizations notwithstanding, by the end of the nineteenth century the movement known as Modern Spiritualism, defined in part by the precept that "communication with the so-called dead is a fact, scientifically proven by the phenomena of Spiritualism," was already on the wane in the United States. At the movement's fortieth anniversary cele- .

bration in 1888—also the year of Maggie's confession—one speaker lamented that "though there are many millions of nominal Spiritualists in America, the active, faithful workers number but a few thousand."[2]

There are many reasons for the movement's decline. Perhaps most important, life expectancy increased and infant mortality rates dropped after 1880, a dramatic change produced in part by improvements in preventive medicine, public health, and sanitation. As more children lived on into adulthood, there were fewer tragic and untimely deaths to be mourned.[3]

Insofar as mediumship provided an interesting and lucrative living, women had more varied opportunities by the end of the century both to go to college and to find work. They were hired for positions once exclusively male, such as salesclerks, and for jobs newly created, such as typists. Although women wouldn't be granted the vote until 1920, magazines touted the new "working woman" who enjoyed stepping out to her job.

Spiritualists' own resistance to organization also contributed to the decline of the movement. Under the outside world's scrutiny, many Spiritualists in the last quarter of the nineteenth century disavowed phenomena such as the raps and materializations. Socially conservative Spiritualists criticized their more radical colleagues for their positions on issues such as free love and marriage reform. Theological differences and debates on subjects such as Christianity's view of the spirits also divided the membership.

Some of what had seemed most exciting about the movement came to seem less revolutionary in due course. Liberal ministers of mainstream churches co-opted some of Spiritualism's teachings, not only promising salvation to those who did their best to earn it, but also, in some instances, banishing hell altogether. The conflict between science and religion endured, but the dilution of Calvinist doctrine and the temporary lessening of evangelical fervor made the contradictions seem less acute.

The love affair with technology that helped give rise to Spiritualism may have played a role as well in its decline. Although Thomas Alva Edison was so intrigued by the movement that he hoped to build a machine to facilitate communication between the worlds, the invention of electric lights slowly but steadily began to banish shadows from the corners of many seance rooms. Metaphorically and literally, it became easier to exile many ghosts simply by illuminating the cause of the haunting.[4]

The American Medical Association, in concert with crusading journalists and federal bureaucrats, eventually restricted the availability of previously legal drugs such as morphine and opium. Insofar as these played a role directly or indirectly in creating altered states of consciousness or visionary dreams, the opportunity to indulge grew less frequent.[5]

The Society for Psychical Research and the American Society for Psychical Research clearly had an impact on the fortunes of Spiritualism. The investigations these groups conducted became more rigorous and methodical, and increasing numbers of mediums were trapped in acts of outright fraud. Cabinet mediums, their trick knots untied, were caught playing musical instruments with their own mortal fingers; apparitions turned out to be real people garbed in gauze and slipping about in the dark; spirit hands changed into flesh-and-blood appendages, coated with phosphorescent paint; mediums were found to be using their feet to lift objects while unwitting investigators confidently held tight to empty shoes, ones weighted for verisimilitude with lead. Investigators increasingly made a distinction between mental mediumship, which included feats of clairvoyance and telepathy, and physical mediumship, which involved manifestations such as raps, table levitations, and apparitions. Physical mediumship fell out of favor not only among Spiritualists but also with the public, and even mental mediumship became suspect.

When Spiritualism began, with its murdered peddler and its poltergeists, it had fed on an older fascination with occult powers. But Spiritualism as shaped by and in response to the Fox sisters had emerged as something sunnier, more democratic: one did not, after all, summon up the spirits by manipulating secret bodies of knowledge; one gathered a group of friends or hired a large hall to welcome the immortal beings. While benign spirit guides weren't necessarily unknown in other parts of the world, they descended like uninvited but cheery guests on nineteenth-century Christian America, whose inhabitants generally believed that miracles only happened in the long ago and that any spirit who spoke to a mortal had to be either a demon or a delusion.

As Spiritualism lost its hold on people's imaginations, however, the movement—even as it waned—helped revitalize interest in occultism. And as the nineteenth-century revolutions in transportation and communication diminished distances between continents, the religious traditions of other cultures increasingly influenced American thought.

One of the individuals responsible for creating both an occult revival and a cosmopolitan spiritual synthesis was Madame Helena Petrovna Blavatsky. A charismatic Russian immigrant who came to the United States in 1873, she claimed to have traveled around the world and to have studied under Tibetan masters. After flirting briefly with Spiritualism—she was said to have been gifted in the arts of physical and mental mediumship—she formed a lifelong friendship with a government official turned lawyer named Colonel Henry Steel Olcott, a man of enough stature to have served as one of three investigators appointed by the government to look into Lincoln's assassination.

Together Blavatsky and Olcott founded the Theosophical Society in 1875. Unlike Spiritualist institutions, the society was hierarchical in structure and esoteric in approach. The mysteries taught by its masters were said to take years to learn, and rituals included a secret handshake and a password. But a more important aspect of the organization, one that influenced the direction of popular religion in the twentieth century, was its integration of Eastern mysticism with traditions of Western spirituality.[6]

In the early part of the twentieth century the educated middle class in Europe and England remained deeply engaged with the question of paranormal abilities. The poet William Butler Yeats, briefly a member of the Theosophical Society and later of the Society for Psychical Research, belonged to the Hermetic Order of the Golden Dawn, an organization that attracted mystics and others devoted to the study and practice of medieval and Renaissance magic. Yeats and his wife, Georgie, filled volumes of notebooks with automatic writing, which they claimed flowed from the spirits.[7] Another influential figure, the psychologist Carl Jung, attended seances as a young man and believed that consciousness—or the unconscious—was potentially capable of extraordinary powers such as telepathy and that the claim to such powers did not necessarily represent delusion or mental illness.

Just as the carnage of the Civil War produced a surge of interest in Spiritualism in the United States, so too did World War I in England. More than seven hundred thousand British soldiers—almost one in eight—died under brutal circumstances, some of the men blown to bits on the battlefield. They were the "unburial bodies," wrote the poet Wilfred Owen, that "sit outside the dugouts all day, all night." At such a time elaborate funerals seemed not only inadequate but also callous, whereas attempts to contact the spirits made a certain amount of intuitive sense to many of those who mourned.[8]

As the number of Spiritualists in England increased, the focus of research into the paranormal shifted once again back to the nature of mediumship. A very public battle of wits and tests took place between two famous adversaries in the Spiritualist debate: the author Arthur Conan Doyle, creator of the master sleuth Sherlock Holmes, and the magician Ehrich Weiss, otherwise known as Houdini. Doyle's own son, Kingsley, had been wounded in World War I and died of influenza in 1919, not long after peace was declared. In September of that year Doyle heard Kingsley's ghostly voice say, "Forgive me," an event that transformed the author's faith in spirit communication into absolute certainty.[9]

Houdini's fascination with Spiritualism developed after his mother's death in 1913, but the seances he attended convinced him that mediums were not only frauds but something worse: inferior magicians. Since he knew how to accomplish by magic many of the manifestations attributed to the spirits, he exposed some of the most prominent mediums of his day.

Houdini's unlikely friendship with Doyle began in 1920 and quickly evolved into a race in which each strove to prove his point. Their friendship withered after Doyle's wife produced a message purportedly written by Houdini's mother. No one doubted Mrs. Doyle's sincerity; however, the magician protested that his foreign-born mother, who spoke no English in life, in death had produced a model of perfect English prose.

Houdini trapped many mediums in conscious or unconscious acts of fraud, but he was less successful in destroying the stubborn and age-old appeal of the supernatural. Older occult organizations persisted after World War I, some of them having splintered off from the Theosophical

Society or been influenced by it, others drawing on Freemasonry and Rosicrucianism for their ideas. New groups arose as well. Interest in alchemy and astrology and other bodies of esoteric lore were commingled, particularly in Austria and Germany, with a mythology manipulated to stress racial superiority, secret rites of initiation, and a millennial expectation of a new world order. Groups such as the Ariosophical societies, which proposed the existence of a psychic energy perfectly realized in what the organizations' members called the Aryan type, represented a small but significant factor in the rise of Nazi ideology.[10]

The desire to find scientific proof for psychic phenomena, one of nineteenth-century Spiritualism's major concerns, never entirely died out, and by the 1930s it had given rise to the new discipline of parapsychology, a field that attracted particular attention in the United States. Parapsychologists believed that if phenomena such as telepathy existed, incidents should be reproducible in a laboratory setting. Researchers turned to accumulating specific data on extrasensory perception, ESP, which the leading pioneer in the new field, Joseph Rhine, divided into three categories: telepathy, clairvoyance, and precognition. Rhine considered psychokinesis—PK, the movement of objects in the absence of any apparent force—a separate but equally vital subject for investigation. He grouped these various paranormal powers under the umbrella term *psi*.[11]

Both psychologists and parapsychologists at different times have entertained the theory that PK events such as poltergeistlike phenomena may be related to the release of unconscious psychic energies, particularly those produced by the stresses of puberty. Youngsters around the ages of Kate and Maggie at the time of the Hydesville raps, it's been suggested, are particularly prone to triggering plates flying in the kitchen, mysterious fires raging at the prom, or frogs falling from the sky.

The field of parapsychology to some extent has come full circle. Some scholars now question whether it's possible to conduct limited, controlled experiments within a laboratory setting. Perhaps, they say, there is no way to reliably test the powers that exceptional individuals may manifest spontaneously.

Psychologists as well as parapsychologists continue to try to find a framework for understanding phenomena such as trances, altered states of consciousness, and mystical visions. A new field of study, neurotheology, explores the possibility that certain religious and visionary experiences—for example, a sense of oneness with the universe or union with a greater power—may originate within a particular part of the human brain. Curiously enough, a phrenologist named Joseph Rhodes Buchanan posited a not dissimilar theory in 1841: he identified a specific spot on the human head that when stimulated, he wrote, produced visions of spirits.

Today the National Spiritualist Association of Churches claims fewer than four thousand members, but even nineteenth-century Spiritualists recognized that organizational membership isn't a reliable indicator of how many people believe in spirit communication.[12] Twenty-first-century Spiritualists say their influence is wider than ever before. They may be correct, if their impact on the rise of the so-called New Age in the United States is taken into account. The New Age, the name given to the efflorescence of interest in spirituality and the occult that began in the 1960s, draws on many traditions, both Eastern and Western. The movement is notable for the widespread belief it has fostered in faith healing, reincarnation, and channeling. But insofar as its benign, intimate, and affectionate spirit guides are its hallmark, the New Age is the legitimate heir to Spiritualism.

In 1904 schoolchildren playing around the Hydesville "spook" house ventured down into the dark cellar. A crumbling wall gave way: Eureka! a skeleton lay behind it. According to an article in the *Boston Journal*, a doctor was consulted who estimated that the bones were about fifty years old.[13]

The man who moved into the Hydesville house shortly after the Fox family left became a devout Spiritualist, as did his children. His greatgrandson, a stage magician named Gene Gordon, broke with the tradition yet helped keep the memory of Kate and Maggie alive by writing in his memoir about tales of the Hydesville rapper he had heard as a boy. The spirits may work in mysterious ways.[14]

In 1916 the Hydesville house was dismantled, loaded onto a barge, and floated west along the Erie Canal to the town of Lily Dale. After being reassembled, the house was inhabited by a medium who claimed to be in frequent contact with the Fox sisters, and some Lily Dale residents can still recall hearing the girls' spirits rap messages. Then, in the 1950s, the house burned to the ground in what was called a mysterious fire. A peddler's trunk, still on view at the Lily Dale Museum, was rescued from the remains, although skeptics question whether it actually belonged to the infamous Charles Rosna.

A decade later an enterprising Canadian bought the plot of land in Hydesville, and he erected a facsimile of the house. But it too was subsequently destroyed by fire. The National Spiritualist Association of Churches acquired the property, which had reverted to a wilderness of brackish weeds, in the last decade of the twentieth century, fittingly on the one hundred and fiftieth anniversary of the movement's birth.[15]

In tribute to the Fox sisters, Spiritualists also have created a memorial garden at Lily Dale, a peaceful circle of trees and flowers surrounding a small fountain. Two stone doves perch at the fountain's center, their beaks touching, their wings spread as though to soar to the reaches of another world.

Descendants of John and Margaret Fox have tended to guard their privacy, but a few matters are on public record. Kate's second son, Henry, died while still in his teens, most likely the same year as his mother. In 1899 the husband of Leah's deceased daughter, Lizzie Fish Blauvelt, sued his uncle, David Fox, in a property dispute and won.[16] Long afterward, in the 1950s, the wife of one of David's own grandsons wrote a book about the Fox sisters. A great-great-great-niece of the mediums is engaged in researching her famous family's background and is thinking about writing a new book today.

Ferdie Jencken, Kate's oldest son, died in his early thirties in 1908, his life a struggle with the same addiction to alcohol and possibly drugs that had afflicted his mother and his aunt Maggie. Although he had married and had children, by then he was living alone, having lost them perhaps to death or in divorce.

The stories of Ferdie's mediumship, while not widespread, never entirely disappeared. Kindhearted Titus Merritt sometimes visited him, helping him out financially and encouraging him to stay sober.[17]

During one meeting in 1903, Merritt wrote, raps were heard, and Ferdie instantly seized a pencil and paper. After writing out the alphabet, he pointed to individual letters to spell an affectionate message from his mother. There was nothing special about it, Merritt said, nothing that the medium himself couldn't have invented. But then Ferdie communicated an extraordinary message. Through Ferdie, the spirit of Maggie asked Merritt if he remembered the time she had knocked off his hat.

The astonished Merritt did indeed remember the moment. He had been taking her to Brooklyn two days before she died. She was too weak even to walk. She had needed to be helped off the carriage, through the door of Mrs. Ruggles's State Street home, and into a chair. But frail though Maggie was, Merritt recalled, she was mischievous enough to reach up and purposely topple his hat from his head.

Merritt declared that he had never spoken of that teasing exchange and had forgotten it entirely himself until reminded by Ferdie, or the immortal Maggie.

AFTERWORD

I HAVE NO DOUBT that the manifestations produced by the Fox sisters could have been created by magic tricks. The phenomena often occurred under cover of darkness or when a sitter's eyes were closed or after hours of patient waiting, prolonged periods that may have induced a sort of shared, waking trance. Visible apparitions were often the work of a magic lantern or a willing confederate. While no one could ever convince me to remain in a room where a mahogany table was drifting overhead, I know that magicians and psychologists have explanations for table levitations as well, ranging from hidden wires to the imagination of an unreliable observer—such as me.

Most nineteenth-century Spiritualists, of course, were as familiar with a range of explanations as we are. They understood that mediums sometimes worked with accomplices; they knew about techniques such as cold reading, gauging information from someone's facial expressions or body language; they were well aware of the capacity of the human eye to see, not what's there, but what the mind expects or hopes to see.

But believers—and an occasional scientist or philosopher such as William James—continued in the face of rampant fraud to pose questions. If a medium sometimes commits deception, does it mean that he or she always does? If most mediums are fakes, does it follow necessarily that they all are? Many books on psychic or Spiritualist phenomena—and now this one as well—at some point quote James's opinion on the investigation of "wild facts":

"If you wish to upset the law that all crows are black," he wrote, "you must not seek to show that no crows are; it is enough if you prove one single crow to be white."[1]

Kate and Maggie gave seances and made public appearances for forty years, sometimes when they were sick or drunk or in despair. In all those years the sisters were never exposed in outright trickery the way so many of their colleagues were. The two youngest Fox sisters confessed—Kate to Mrs. Norman Culver, Maggie to an audience of hundreds—and in substantial detail. Yet Kate went on to boast about the accomplishments of the spirits, and Maggie herself recanted her harsh words.

Although I can be accused of brushing aside the mediums' own explanations, I find it difficult to make all aspects of the Fox sisters' lives fit into an orderly pattern. As Spiritualists and skeptics well know, supposition in the absence of proof can lead in many different directions. Perhaps what matters, then, isn't the degree to which the Fox sisters did or didn't believe in the spirits, or what tricks the mediums may have used to create the manifestations, or whether the spirits themselves occasionally paid a visit, or even how much the sisters contributed to the rise of a movement. Consensus will probably remain elusive. Looking at the Fox sisters' story is like peering through a kaleidoscope: the configuration is never fixed; it changes depending on the angle of the prism and the way the pieces seem to fall.

And perhaps change itself is what makes the story resonate, at least for me: the devices we use or the faith we rely on to ease anxiety in periods of significant transition. Everyone in the saga of the Fox sisters was in motion in one way or another: progressing, passing from childhood to adulthood; from sinner to saint; from lower to upper class; from an agricultural society to a commercial and industrial one; from life to death to eternity. The children, Kate and Maggie, represented and embodied these many different and overlapping transitions, as did the spirits for whom they claimed to speak.

A time when I'm prone to seeing spirits is during moments of transition, when my own imagination has been freed by loss or change, or sometimes set wandering by as routine a passage as twilight. In the first decade of the twenty-first century the rate of change, we are told, is accelerating exponentially. Communications—only one example—has come to seem as miraculous in this new century as the telegraph did in 1850. One executive quoted recently in the *New York Times* described his vision of wireless technology as "a little bit like God. God is wireless. God is everywhere and God sees and knows everything." Soon all of us, he said, will be able to find "anything, anywhere, anytime."[2]

Perhaps it's not surprising, then, that as many as 40 percent of Americans have voiced a willingness to believe in the possibility of contacting the dead.[3]

I can't claim to be objective about the Fox sisters. I feel abashed and slightly guilty that I can admire three women who at the very least committed fraud part of the time. Whether they were nothing more than marvelous conjurers or (I am especially puzzled by Kate) something other, I enjoy the mediums too much to be critical of them: openhearted Kate, captivating Maggie, and bold Leah.

The fact that nineteenth-century America was rife with mesmerists, faith healers, and prophets of course doesn't excuse their dissembling. But the Fox sisters certainly fall within the American tradition of self-invented characters in literature and life. Like Benjamin Franklin, Barnum, Lily Bart, Gatsby, and even certain roguish past presidents of the United States, they were quintessentially American spirits. In the early twentieth century, a machine politician in New York City coined a credo with which any one of the Fox sisters might have agreed. "I seen my opportunities," observed the irrepressible Plunkitt of Tammany Hall, "and I took 'em."[4] To say that the Fox sisters seized their opportunities isn't to pass judgment on the role the spirits may have played in their lives.

Would popular belief in spirit communication have flourished in America without Kate and Maggie as its icons and Leah as its impresario?

Interest in spirit communication predated Hydesville, but the passion for it might not have spread so widely without someone coming along who telegraphed what these three sisters did. Splendid, noisy, tactile, amusing, theatrical, and enigmatic, their gatherings were filled with life, as were the sisters themselves. At a time when sound itself was in transition, the hoot of a locomotive echoing through the landscape, these three women turned unfamiliar noises into a provocative puzzle that drew national and international crowds.[5] Without doubt, a seance's countless questions, long silences, and hectic activities could be tedious, yet they were equally and paradoxically suspenseful: at any moment a spirit might speak or a fraud be unmasked.

The Fox sisters also had a genius for collaboration. With help from their mortal visitors and perhaps from immortal ones as well, the mediums constructed stories about the past, present, and future; they listened to voices from within and without and wove them into narratives in a process that—to use terms familiar today—was interactive and branching. They were storytellers who created an exciting, involving forum—the seance—in which all participants could tell themselves a different version of the tale.

And so can we. If exploring the Fox sisters' lives is a little like looking through a kaleidoscope, it's a lot like attending a seance. It's easy to catch oneself listening for spirits and watching for tricks, trying to deduce what's happening and how. After spending several years with Kate and Maggie, I still imagine different scenarios to explain the strange sounds that were heard one night in the little-known hamlet of Hydesville in Arcadia, that disrupted the sleep of two young girls' parents and changed how we think about immortality.

Mysterious Noises

1. Eleven-year-old Kate and fourteen-year-old Maggie lie in their bed together in the chilly dark, too sleepy even to whisper secrets. They hear soft taps, and they accuse each other of making the sounds. Neither one is doing so, but it's easier, less scary, for each child to believe that her clever sister has invented a game.

2. Maggie knocks lightly on the side of the bed, to annoy Kate for fun. Instead, she truly frightens her, so she guiltily confesses and stops. Just as her own eyes are closing: Bang! Snap! Her vengeful little sister startles her awake. The game widens to parents, then friends, and the challenge grows more elaborate, from apples to apparitions.

3. Kate has the nervous habit of cracking her knuckles. Almost silent in daytime, at night the hidden motion of the joints jolts like a rifle shot. The girls' mother, getting ready for bed, jumps like a rabbit; their father stirs from his bedside prayers. A compulsion. An amusement.

4. Sounds, more like humming vibrations, follow Kate, drape over her like a light quilt. Maggie decides to say nothing. She thinks Kate is somehow fooling her, and she wants to frustrate the little trickster. Kate, of course, knows differently, but for reasons of her own she also chooses not to speak. For the rest of the sisters' lives, Maggie devises ways to simulate the spirits, immersed as she is in sisterly competition. She never understands that Kate communicates with them day and night.

5. In the nineteenth century, two young girls with a bond between them like shining steel become mediums for the spirits, invisible beings who wish to announce to the world that death does not exist. The children do their best. Most mortals aren't ready to hear the news, and the spirits wisely retreat to bide their immortal time.

ACKNOWLEDGMENTS

I OWE A DEBT OF GRATITUDE to many individuals and institutions. The American Antiquarian Society funded my initial research through a Lila Wallace-Readers Digest Fellowship for Creative Artists and Writers, and it was a pleasure to work there. Ellen Dunlap, John Hench, James David Moran, Georgia Barnhill, Nancy Burkett, Joanne Chaison, Thomas Knoles, and Marie Lamoureux in particular were generous and creative advisers. A grant from the Parapsychology Foundation, the D. Scott Rogo Award for Parapsychological Literature, enabled me to complete the manuscript and to work under the guidance of the institution's dedicated directors, Eileen and Lisette Coly. My thanks extend as well to Richard Snow, the inspiring editor of *American Heritage,* for encouraging my interest in the Fox sisters.

Robert Hoeltzel, Arcadia town historian, was a lively guide through the early history of Spiritualism in upstate New York; Ralph and Frances Blauvelt of the Association of Blauvelt Descendants were skilled genealogical detectives; Celeste Oliver, a descendant of David Fox, graciously shared family anecdotes and documents; Neil Robertson, a descendant of Henry Jencken's brother, provided an unpublished biography of his family; John Catanzariti of the Underhill Society supplied background on Leah's husband. Alison Blank opened her extensive files on the Fox sisters to me; Jim Murphy helped guide me through the Civil War; Veronica Herndon introduced me to the resources of the Parapsychology Foundation; Anne Schaetzke conducted valuable research; and Joanne McMahon of the Higgins Center served the double function of scholarly consultant and cheerleader. Mary Huth of the University of Rochester Library not only helped with this project but also urged me on to the next.

I had the opportunity to spend hours in conversation with many people on the subject of the Fox sisters; I spoke only briefly to others. Some of those who graciously and without hesitation spent time with me in person or on the phone may disagree with much of what I say in this book, but I hope they won't regret assisting me in my honest effort. Wherever they may have objections to the material, the thoughts are mine and not theirs. I'm grateful to the following individuals for sharing information, thoughts, comments, documents, photographs, and fruitful suggestions for further research: Robert S. Cox of the American Philosophical Society, a historian whose recent book on Spiritualism is illuminating at every point; Patrice Keane of the American Society for Psychical Research; Christopher Densmere of the Friends Historical Library, Swarthmore College; Joyce LaJudice, chronicler of Lily Dale; the Reverend Cosie Allen, the Reverend Sharon Snowman, and Sylvia Kincaid of the National Spiritualist Association of Churches; Wayne Furman and Warren Platt of the New York Public Library; Leslie Price of the Society for Psychical Research; Kathy Hunt and Deborah Farrell of the Wayne County Historical Society; Simon Pettet of the Parapsychology Foundation; Valerie Scott of the Cobourg Library, Ontario, Canada; Elsa Dixler; Sarah Stage; Kenneth Silverman; Frank Dailey; Mark Salem; Joseph Gabriel; Richard Dreyfuss; and Michael Peterman.

The following organizations and institutions granted me access to their archives and in some cases gave me permission to quote from their collections: the American Antiquarian Society; the American Philosophical Society; the American Society for Psychical Research; the Friends Historical Library of Swarthmore College; the Eileen J. Garrett Library of the Parapsychology Foundation; the New–York Historical Society; the New York Public Library; the Department of Rare Books and Special Collections, University of Rochester Library; the National Spiritualist Association of Churches; the Wayne County Historical Society; the Society for Psychical Research Archive at Cambridge University; the Rauner Special Collections of the Dartmouth College Library; the Historical Society of Pennsylvania; and the Houdini Collection at the Library of Congress.

As I've tried to indicate in notes and bibliography, I've incurred a great debt to the authors of many books, articles, and pamphlets on American history in general and Modern Spiritualism in particular. If my understanding or interpretation of some of that material is mistaken, my apologies to the authors.

My thanks go to Miriam Quen Cheikin, Forrest Church, Judy Collins, Peter Coyote, Tom Gelinne, Lisa Gornick, Douglas Hatschek, Donald Johnson, Richard Lourie, and Joan Keiser for taking the time to read and comment on drafts of this manuscript. Miriam Cheikin gave exceptionally detailed and always astute suggestions. Joan, my sister, shares those early, childhood memories of secrets whispered in the dark. I'm grateful to all the Keisers, including Richard, Lauren, and Matt, for their support in good times and bad.

I'm indebted to Leo Ribuffo, Society of the Cincinatti George Washington Distinguished Professor of History, George Washington University, for his thought-provoking opinions and comments throughout this project. Anne Bianchi remained a relentless and perceptive critic; her example and love were inspiring. Joan Erle also contributed insights that helped at every stage.

In my agent, Mel Berger, I found a wonderful friend as well as an extraordinary advocate for this project and a perceptive guide for others yet to come. My editor, Renee Sedliar, knew exactly how to improve this book, from the first page to the last. Her creativity, wit, and wisdom made every aspect of the process of writing and revising more interesting and fun.

I'm lucky to live in a household of writers, always willing to read and contribute. My love and thanks to my family, David, Tobiah, and Susannah Black, with special appreciation to Susannah, who, like a magician pulling an endless silk scarf from a little hat, kept producing wonderful books for my research from her rich and eclectic personal library.

NOTES

EPIGRAPH

Eileen Garrett's statement comes from "Notes on New Insight in Psychic Research," a manuscript housed at the Parapsychology Foundation in New York City, quoted by Lawrence LeShan, *The Medium, the Mystic, and the Physicist: Toward a General Theory of the Paranormal* (New York: Viking, 1966), 73. Born in Ireland in 1893, Garrett became known as a medium for channeling spirits and also as clairvoyant, having predicted the crash of a British dirigible in 1930. Her powers were investigated at Johns Hopkins University in Baltimore and Roosevelt Hospital in New York. She became an American citizen in 1947 and founded the Parapsychology Foundation in 1951. The foundation's Web site, as of September 29, 2003, is http://www.parapsychology.org.

INTRODUCTION

1. Mary Redfield's reaction to news of the sounds and quotations from Margaret Fox, Mary Redfield, and one of the sisters are found in E. E. Lewis, *A Report of the Mysterious Noises Heard in the House of Mr. John D. Fox, in Hydesville, Arcadia, Wayne County, Authenticated by the Certificates, and Confirmed by the Statements of the Citizens of That Place and Vicinity* (Canandaigua, NY: E. E. Lewis, 1848), 29–31.

2. I've retained the original spelling in most letters and other documents, but I generally have regularized punctuation and capitalization.

3. Lewis, *Mysterious Noises*, 4.

CHAPTER 1:
"A LARGE, INTELLIGENT AND CANDID COMMUNITY"

1. The title of part 1, "Earth and the World of Spirits," comes from the subtitle of the book by the Spiritualist historian Emma Hardinge, *Modern American Spiritualism: A Twenty Years' Record of the Communion Between Earth and the World of Spirits* (1869; repr., New Hyde Park, NY: University Books, 1970). The title of chapter 1, "A Large, Intelligent and Candid Community," comes from E. E. Lewis, *A Report of the Mysterious Noises Heard in the House of Mr. John D. Fox* (Canandaigua, NY: E. E. Lewis, 1848), 4.

2. *Western Argus* (Lyons, NY), December 22, 1847, and January 5, 1848.

3. The children's ages at the time of the move to Hydesville are a point of controversy. Different authors cite different ages to suit their agendas. I have chosen to work with the dates inscribed on the two sisters' joint gravestone in Cypress Hills Cemetery, Brooklyn, New York, and to try to deal with the disagreement as the story unfolds.

4. Robert L. Hoeltzel, *Hometown History: Village of Newark, Town of Arcadia* (Newark, NY: Gene McClellan for Arcadia Historical Society, 2000), 72. I'm indebted to Robert Hoeltzel, Arcadia town historian, for sharing his knowledge about the community of Arcadia and his thoughts on the rise of Modern Spiritualism. His series of five articles on the origins of Modern Spiritualism, "Arcadia Earns a Place on the Map," was first published in the *Courier Gazette* (Newark, NY) in 1998, to coincide with Spiritualism's one hundred fiftieth anniversary. He later compiled many of his articles on Spiritualism and other subjects into his fascinating book, *Hometown History*, which can be ordered through the Arcadia Historical Society, PO Box 289, Newark, NY 14513.

Two other sources from the Wayne County Historical Society furnished valuable information on Wayne County's local history: George W. Cowles, ed., *Landmarks of Wayne County, New York, Illustrated* (Syracuse, NY: D. Mason, 1895), and a booklet by Irma Gallup Stroup, *Around the Town in By-Gone Days* (Newark, NY: Newark Courier Gazette, 1957).

5. This description is drawn from a letter by Joseph Post to Amy and Isaac Post, August 15, 1852, Department of Rare Books and Special Collections, University of Rochester Library, Rochester, New York.

6. Figures are based on those in Robert V. Wells, *Facing the "King of Terrors": Death and Society in an American Community, 1750–1990* (Cambridge: Cambridge University Press, 2000), 39, 291. Wells's figures refer specifically to Schenectady, a community in western New York, for the years 1883 to 1886. The author notes that reliable evidence wasn't available before then but that life expectancy in the early 1880s was "not appreciably better, and possibly worse, than what was probably the case a century before."

7. Herbert Jackson Jr., *The Spirit Rappers* (New York: Doubleday, 1972), 20. In this excellent biography, Jackson, who was a journalist and longtime resident of Wayne County, paints

a vivid portrait of the Fox sisters and has assembled a lively collection of articles about them, particularly from the mainstream press. He leans in the direction of what has been called "the tricky little boys or girls" theory on the origins of Spiritualism, a point of view often associated with Frank Podmore, a historian of Spiritualism whose two-volume work, *Modern Spiritualism: A History and a Criticism* (New York: Charles Scribner's Sons, 1902), reissued under the title *Mediums of the Nineteenth Century* (New Hyde Park, NY: University Books, 1963), helped shape later attitudes toward Spiritualism.

8. *Western Argus,* November 17, 1847.

9. *Western Argus,* March 8, 1848.

10. The comments of Margaret Fox quoted throughout this chapter are taken from the "Certificate of Mrs. Margaret Fox," in Lewis, *Mysterious Noises,* 5–9. Other comments made by specific individuals can be found, unless otherwise noted, in the following sections of Lewis's pamphlet: "Statement of David S. Fox," 27–29; "Statement of Wm. Duesler," 10–16; "Statement of Mrs. Elizabeth Fox," 22–24; "Statement of Mrs. Mary Redfield," 29–31; "Statement of John D. Fox," 9–10; "Statement of Mrs. Jane C. Lape," 35; "Statement of Miss Lucretia Pulver," 35–36.

11. As Jackson points out in *Spirit Rappers,* whether for the sake of tact or for fear of a lawsuit, Lewis left a blank for Bell's name in the body of the pamphlet and mentioned it only at the end, in the context of a petition signed by Bell's friends and supporters.

12. Andrew Soverhill is quoted by Hoeltzel, *Hometown History,* 80–81.

13. The doctor is quoted by Jackson, *Spirit Rappers,* 20.

14. *Newark Herald,* May 4, 1848, quoted by Jackson, *Spirit Rappers,* 17.

15. Several secondary sources were particularly helpful on the topic of what the historian Jon Butler calls "The Antebellum Spiritual Hothouse," and specifically on the historical context in which Spiritualism evolved. These sources, which have informed many of the chapters in this book, include Butler's own *Awash in a Sea of Faith* (Cambridge, MA: Harvard University Press, 1990); Sydney E. Ahlstrom, *A Religious History of the American People* (New Haven, CT: Yale University Press, 1972); Ann Braude, *Radical Spirits: Spiritualism and Women's Rights in Nineteenth-Century America* (Boston: Beacon Press, 1989); Bret E. Carroll, *Spiritualism in Antebellum America* (Bloomington: Indiana University Press, 1997); Whitney R. Cross, *The Burned-over District: The Social and Intellectual History of Enthusiastic Religion in Western New York, 1800–1850* (Ithaca, NY: Cornell University Press, 1950); Ernest Isaacs, "The Fox Sisters and American Spiritualism," in *The Occult in America: New Historical Perspectives,* edited by Howard Kerr and Charles L. Crow (Chicago: University of Illinois Press, 1983); R. Laurence Moore, *In Search of White Crows: Spiritualism, Parapsychology, and American Culture* (New York: Oxford University Press, 1977); Leo P. Ribuffo, "The Complexity of American Religious Prejudice," *Right Center Left: Essays in American History* (New Brunswick, NJ: Rutgers University Press, 1992); and Ann Taves, *Fits, Trances, and Visions: Experiencing Religion and Explaining Experience from Wesley to James* (Princeton, NJ: Princeton University Press, 1999).

16. Harold Thompson, *New York State Folktales, Legends, and Ballads* (New York: Dover, 1939), 432.

17. Dr. Charles J. Pecor, *The Magician on the American Stage, 1752–1874* (n.p., 1977), copy number 368, p. 85.

18. *Ventriloquism Explained: And Juggler's Tricks, or Legerdemain Exposed* (Amherst, MA: J. S. and C. Adams, 1834), 30.

CHAPTER 2:
"SOME FAMILY ANTECEDENTS"

1. John's date of birth is cited as 1787 by Mariam Buckner Pond, *Time Is Kind: The Story of the Unfortunate Fox Family* (New York: Centennial, 1947), 6. Pond was married to one of Kate and Maggie's grandnephews. Other family sources today cite 1789 as John's birth date and his place of birth as New York City. John's younger brothers, however, were born in Ramapo, Rockland County, New York, suggesting that John was raised there as well.

2. Wills A:30, *Rockland County Surrogate Court Records,* Rockland County Courthouse, New City, NY.

3. For Margaret's nickname, see John C. Smith's will, Wills B:120, *Rockland County Surrogate Court Records,* Rockland County Courthouse, New City, NY. The date of Margaret's birth is from "Kakiat or West New Hempstead Records," trans. Nicholas Gentzlinger Blauvelt (1933), Genealogical Collection of the Association of Blauvelt Descendants, Spring Valley, New York, ABD.05 Marriages, p. 79, hereafter cited as "Kakiat Records." Although some descendants of the family today cite Margaret's birth date as 1797 and the place of birth as Canada, she seems much more likely to be the "Peggy" named in John C. Smith's will. The date of her marriage to John David Fox is from "Kakiat Records," 17. Ralph and Frances Blauvelt of the Association of Blauvelt Descendants were an invaluable resource for wills, deeds, church records, and family trees from Rockland County. The Association's Website is www.blauvelt.org (accessed November 20, 2003). Celeste Oliver, a Fox family descendant, generously provided an alternative family tree, a wealth of anecdotes about the past, and helpful information about the present, all passed down through the family of Kate and Maggie's brother, David.

4. Leah, the oldest child of John and Margaret Fox, discusses her family's ancestry in A. Leah Underhill, *The Missing Link in Modern Spiritualism* (New York: Thomas R. Knox, 1885), 74–76 from which the title of chapter 2 is drawn. Although Leah says that John C. Smith was of English ancestry, he too, according to information furnished by the Blauvelt Family Association, was of Dutch heritage. The Blauvelts cite as their source the "Genealogy of the Smidt, or Smith Family," by George H. Budke (1912), Genealogical Collection of Association of Blauvelt Descendants, Rockland County, New York, ABD.34, no. 60.

5. For information on the Ruttans and on the Loyalist settlement of Upper Canada, see *Pioneer Life on the Bay of Quinte, Including Genealogies of Old Families and Biographical Sketches of Representative Citizens* (Toronto: Ralph and Clark, 190-?). See also James J. Keegan, *A Rutan Family Index* (Bowie, MD: Heritage Books, 1996).

6. Leah discusses her family's clairvoyance in *Missing Link,* 74–84.

7. Leah's baptismal date is from "Kakiat Records," 78. David's birth date is on his grave-stone in the Newark Main Street Cemetery, Arcadia.

8. Underhill, *Missing Link*, 74. Leah preferred to call her book a work about Spiritual-ism rather than an autobiography, but she includes a great deal of information in it about herself and her family. She has been criticized for her tendency to embellish material, par-ticularly seance phenomena where there is no corroborating testimony, and her dates for events are often inaccurate and confused. That said, she offers a wealth of anecdotes and a selection of letters that at times seem to evidence either surprising candor or emotional insight. Unless there is material that directly contradicts her stories or calls them into ques-tion, I have used her information to provide clues to actual events and the feelings that may have accompanied the circumstances.

9. The legend of Hydesville and the Erie Canal is told by Robert Hoeltzel, *Hometown History: Village of Newark, Town of Arcadia* (Newark, NY: Gene McClellan for Arcadia Town Historical Society, 2000), 24.

10. Statement made by Titus Merritt to James Hyslop, February 7, 1908, Archives of the American Society for Psychical Research, New York, New York.

11. John C. Smith's will (see n. 3).

12. Underhill, *Missing Link*, 85.

13. On age at marriage, see Thomas Hine, *The Rise and Fall of the American Teenager* (New York: Bard, 1999), 93.

14. Underhill, *Missing Link*, 30–31. As for Lizzie, Maggie would later claim that her niece was as much as seven years older than she. But other descriptions imply that they were closer in age.

15. For information on marriage and divorce, see Nancy Cott, *Public Vows: A History of Marriage and the Nation* (Cambridge: Harvard University Press, 2000), 30–40.

16. On John's alcoholism and subsequent sobriety, see Pond, *Time Is Kind*, 7–8. See also W. G. Langworthy Taylor, *Katie Fox, Epochmaking Medium and the Making of the Fox-Taylor Record* (New York: G. P. Putnam's Sons, 1933), 98.

17. Kate and Maggie's birth dates are found in a letter from Titus Merritt to Mrs. Mary T. Longley, National Spiritualist Association Secretary, February 14, 1903, Archives of the National Spiritualist Association of Churches, Lily Dale, New York. As mentioned earlier, there is controversy surrounding the girls' birth dates. Margaret's earliest mention refers to Kate as "about twelve" and Maggie as "in her fifteenth year." Merritt's dates, which are the dates inscribed on the sisters' gravestone, would mean that Kate had just turned eleven on March 31, 1848. Other estimates, including one put forth by Maggie in 1888, make the girls as young as six and eight in 1848. Merritt's figures at least have the virtue of some specificity, and they roughly coincide with some of the earliest existing descriptions of the girls.

18. On where Kate and Maggie were raised, see Pond, *Time Is Kind*, 8. Their father's having a farm in Prince Edward County is confirmed in a letter from John Moodie to Pro-fessor Gregory, June 22, 1857, in Susanna Moodie, *Letters of Love and Duty: The Correspon-dence of Susanna and John Moodie*, ed. Carl Ballstadt, Elizabeth Hopkins, and Michael

Peterman (Toronto: University of Toronto Press, 1993), 228. The area is described by Nick and Helma Mika, *The Settlement of Prince Edward County* (Belleville, Ontario: Mika, 1984), 154. For information on Canadian life at the time, see J. M. Bumsted, ed., *Interpreting Canada's Past*, vol. 1, *Preconfederation*, 2nd ed. (Toronto: Oxford University Press, 1993).

19. This and the next quote by Susanna Moodie are from *Roughing It in the Bush, or Life in Canada*, with a new introduction by Margaret Atwood (1852; repr., Boston: Beacon Press, 1987), 515, 501.

20. John's purchase of a burial plot is recorded in *Mt. Hope Cemetery, Internment Index*, Vol. 1, *1837–1860* (Rochester: Rochester Genealogical Society, 1996). John J. Smith's land deed appears in Land Records, Wayne County Clerk's Office, Lyons, New York, bk. 30, p. 414.

21. On Rochester street directories, see Jackson, *Spirit Rappers*, 23. For the deaths of Maria and Jacob Smith, see *Mt. Hope Cemetery Internment Index*.

22. For Charles Finney's impact on Rochester, see Paul E. Johnson, *A Shopkeeper's Millennium: Society and Revivals in Rochester, New York, 1815–1837* (New York: Hill and Wang, 1978).

23. For information on Rochester, along with Johnson, *Shopkeeper's Millennium*, see Blake McKelvey, *Rochester: The Water-Power City, 1812–1854* (Cambridge: Harvard University Press, 1945), and Nancy A. Hewitt, *Women's Activism and Social Change: Rochester, New York, 1822–1872* (Ithaca, NY: Cornell University Press, 1984), which provide illuminating descriptions of Rochester in the first half of the nineteenth century. Additional material may also be found in the journal *Rochester History*, published by the Rochester Public Library: see Martha Montague Ash, "The Social and Domestic Scene in Rochester, 1840–1860" (April 1956), 1–17; W. Stephen Thomas and Ruth Rosenberg-Naparsteck, "Sleepers' City: The Sesquicentennial History of Mt. Hope Cemetery" (October 1988), 2–23; Dorothy S. Truesdale, "The Younger Generation: Their Opinions, Pastimes, and Enterprises 1830–1850" (April 1939), 1–21.

24. Laborers' wages are from Harriet Sigerman, "An Unfinished Battle," in *No Small Courage: A History of Women in the United States*, ed. Nancy Cott (Oxford: Oxford University Press, 2000), 270.

25. For a vivid portrait of the Post family and an analysis of their beliefs in relationship to the rise of Spiritualism, see Ann Braude, *Radical Spirits: Spiritualism and Women's Rights in Nineteenth-Century America* (Boston: Beacon Press, 1989). Her book also pointed me in the direction of the Isaac and Amy Post Family Papers, Department of Rare Books and Special Collections, University of Rochester.

CHAPTER 3:
"VISIBLE AND INVISIBLE WORLDS"

1. On attitudes about teaching music, see Asa Fitz, introduction to *American School Songbook Improved* (Boston: William B. Fowle and N. Capen, 1844); Maxmilian Hall, introduction to *The American Preceptor for the Piano Forte, Containing the Elementary Principles of Music*,

and an Introduction to the Art of Playing on the Above Instrument (Boston: Henry Prentiss, 1839); William B. Bradbury, introduction to *Musical Gems for School and Home: A Rich Collection of Music for the Young, Original and Arranged; with Choice Selections from the Schools of Germany and Switzerland, Together with a New, Easy, and Progressive Course of Elementary Instructions and Exercises, Constituting a Complete Musical Manual for Teachers and Students* (New York: Newman and Ivison, 1849).

2. Fitz, *American School Songbook*, 11.

3. Leah told of her reaction to the news and her trip to Hydesville in A. Leah Underhill, *The Missing Link in Modern Spiritualism* (New York: Thomas R. Knox, 1885), 31–33.

4. The spirits' mobility compared to the preferences of the homebody ghosts of the old world is an insight I owe to Susannah Black.

5. Leah's account of the first visits of the spirits in Rochester are found in Underhill, *Missing Link*, 33–43.

6. The Reverend Clark's accounts of seances and the title of this chapter are found in Robert Sieber, Kathy Peterson, and Marjorie Searle, eds., "Fox Sisters in Action," *New York History*, July 1974, 304–18, and Wheaton Phillips Webb, "The Peddler's Protest," *New York History*, April 1943, 242–47.

7. For information on death and mourning, see Ann Braude, *Radical Spirits: Spiritualism and Women's Rights in Nineteenth-Century America* (Boston: Beacon Press, 1989), and Robert V. Wells, *Facing the "King of Terrors": Death and Society in an American Community, 1750–1990* (Cambridge: Cambridge University Press, 2000). For English rituals, see Pat Jalland, *Death in the Victorian Family* (Oxford: Oxford University Press, 1996), specifically chaps. 14 and 15. For information on cemeteries, see Garry Wills, *Lincoln at Gettysburg: The Words That Remade America* (New York: Touchstone, 1992), 64, 74. Wills's book, with its emphasis on the liminality of childhood, has been extremely influential in shaping my ideas about Kate and Maggie Fox.

8. Accounts of the mob are drawn from Underhill, *Missing Link*, 20–27; see also Webb, "Peddler's Protest," 248–50.

9. Underhill, *Missing Link*, 46; see also *Wayne County Vital Statistics, 1847–1850*, Wayne County Historian's Office, Lyons, New York.

CHAPTER 4:
"IT SEEMS TO SPREAD FAST"

1. Isaac Post's comments come from a letter by Isaac Post to "brother and sister," November 23, 1848, Friends Historical Library of Swarthmore College.

2. Published statement by George Willets, quoted by E. W. Capron, *Modern Spiritualism: Its Facts and Fanaticisms, Its Consistencies and Contradictions; with an Appendix* (Boston: Bela Marsh, 1855; repr., New York: Arno Press, 1976), 69–72.

3. George Willets to Isaac Post, 1848, Department of Rare Books and Special Collections, University of Rochester Library.

4. Published statement by George Willets, quoted in Capron, *Modern Spiritualism*, 72–74.

5. For the relationship between radical politics and Spiritualism as well as for the background of the Posts as described later in this chapter, see Ann Braude, *Radical Spirits: Spiritualism and Women's Rights in Nineteenth-Century America* (Boston: Beacon Press, 1989), 11–16, 57–61.

6. Willets's comments and the title of chapter 4 come from George Willets to Isaac Post, 1848, Department of Rare Books and Special Collections, University of Rochester Library.

7. Isaac Post to "brother and sister," November 23, 1848, Friends Historical Library of Swarthmore College.

8. Sarah Fish to Amy Post, September 19, 1848, Department of Rare Books and Special Collections, University of Rochester Library.

9. Isaac Post to "brother and sister," November 23, 1848, Friends Historical Library of Swarthmore College.

10. Isaac Post to Amy Post, May 22, 1849, Department of Rare Books and Special Collections, University of Rochester Library.

11. Isaac Post to "brother and sister," November 23, 1848, Friends Historical Library of Swarthmore College.

12. Capron, *Modern Spiritualism,* 75.

13. A. Leah Underhill, *The Missing Link in Modern Spiritualism* (New York: Thomas R. Knox, 1885), 54.

14. Isaac Post to Amy Post, May 15, 1849, Department of Rare Books and Special Collections, University of Rochester Library.

15. For a discussion of the contributions made by Fishbough and Brittan to the rise of Spiritualism, see R. Laurence Moore, *In Search of White Crows: Spiritualism, Parapsychology, and American Culture* (New York: Oxford University Press, 1977), 10–13.

16. D. M. Dewey, who soon would produce one of the earliest and best-known pamphlets on spirit communication, also issued a pamphlet on the Hardenbrook trial, with the unwieldy title *Trial of Dr. John K. Hardenbrook: Indicted for the Murder of Thos. Nott, by Administering Strychnine to Him in Sufficient Quantity to Produce Death, on the 5th of February, 1849, at Rochester, N.Y. Tried at the May Term of Oyer and Terminer, 1849, Hon. Judge Marvin, Presiding* (Rochester, NY: D. M. Dewey, 1849).

17. John S. Clackner to Isaac Post, July 7, 1849, Department of Rare Books and Special Collections, University of Rochester Library.

18. The cholera epidemic of 1849 is discussed by Robert V. Wells, *Facing the "King of Terrors": Death and Society in an American Community, 1750–1990* (Cambridge: Cambridge University Press, 2000), and by Joan D. Hendrick, *Harriet Beecher Stowe: A Life* (New York: Oxford University Press, 1994), 189.

19. Maggie Fox to Amy Post, August 21, 1849, Department of Rare Books and Special Collections, University of Rochester Library.

CHAPTER 5:
"A GREAT VARIETY OF SUPERNATURAL SOUNDS"

1. Description of Auburn seances is from E. W. Capron, *Modern Spiritualism: Its Facts and Fanaticisms, Its Consistencies and Contradictions, with an Appendix* (Boston: Bela Marsh, 1855; repr., New York: Arno Press, 1976), 100–112.

2. Comments and chapter 5 title are from *Auburn Daily Advertiser,* quoted by Herbert Jackson Jr., *The Spirit Rappers* (New York: Doubleday, 1972), 45.

3. Emma Hardinge, *Modern American Spiritualism: A Twenty Years' Record of the Communion Between Earth and the World of Spirits,* with new introduction by E. J. Dingwall (1869; repr., New Hyde Park, NY: University Books, 1970), 41–42; see also Capron, *Modern Spiritualism,* 87–91.

4. R. D. Jones, "The Rochester Rappings"; William F. Peck, *The Semi-Centennial History of the City of Rochester* (Syracuse, NY: D. D. Mason, 1884), 508–18.

5. Information in this chapter and the next about Corinthian Hall and the cultural and social side of life in Rochester comes from Martha Montague Ash, "The Social and Domestic Scene in Rochester, 1840–1860," *Rochester History,* April 1956, and also from George Ellwood, *Some Earlier Public Amusements of Rochester, Read Before the Rochester Historical Society, 1894* (Rochester, NY: Democrat and Chronicle, 1894), 44–48.

6. *Western Argus* (Lyons, NY), August 23, 1848.

7. *New York Weekly Tribune,* January 19, 1850.

8. Quoted by Jackson, *Spirit Rappers,* 48.

9. Jackson, *Spirit Rappers,* 48; see also Capron, *Modern Spiritualism,* 385.

CHAPTER 6:
"THREE DAYS OF THE STRICTEST SCRUTINY"

1. The description of Corinthian Hall comes from George Ellwood, *Some Earlier Public Amusements of Rochester, Read Before the Rochester Historical Society, 1894* (Rochester, NY: Democrat and Chronicle, 1894), 44–45.

2. There are many nineteenth-century accounts of the events at Corinthian Hall, including those by Emma Hardinge, *Modern American Spiritualism: A Twenty Years' Record of the Communion Between Earth and the World of Spirits,* with new introduction by E. J. Dingwall (1869; repr., New Hyde Park, NY: University Books, 1970), and E. W. Capron, *Modern Spiritualism: Its Facts and Fanaticisms, Its Consistencies and Contradictions, with an Appendix* (Boston: Bela Marsh, 1855; repr., New York: Arno Press, 1976). An excellent secondary source that details some of the more skeptical newspaper accounts of the day is Herbert Jackson Jr., *The Spirit Rappers* (New York: Doubleday, 1972), chap. 5, "Wonderful Phenomena at Corinthian Hall," 47–57.

3. Quoted in Jackson, *Spirit Rappers,* 51.

4. Two excellent treatments of the seance (I include public performances such as the one at Corinthian Hall) and the importance of both sound and mystery to the experience are

David Chapin, "The Fox Sisters and the Performance of Mystery," *New York History*, April 2000, 157–88; and Steven Connor, "The Machine in the Ghost: Spiritualism, Technology, and the 'Direct Voice,'" in *Ghosts: Deconstruction, Psychoanalysis, History*, ed. Peter Buse and Andrew Stott (New York: St. Martin's Press, 1999), 203–25. Another source of information on the Fox sisters' lives in general is David Chapin's "Exploring Other Worlds: Margaret Fox, Elisha Kent Kane, and the Culture of Curiosity" (PhD diss., University of New Hampshire, 2000).

5. A. Leah Underhill, *The Missing Link in Modern Spiritualism* (New York: Thomas R. Knox, 1885), 67.

6. Underhill, *Missing Link*, 67–68.

7. Hardinge, *Modern American Spiritualism*, 45.

8. Quoted in *Banner of Light*, April 1868.

9. Comments and the title of chapter 6 are from the *New York Weekly Tribune*, December 8, 1849.

10. Hardinge, *Modern American Spiritualism*, 46.

11. *New York Weekly Tribune*, February 9, 1850. There's some confusion about *which* Langworthy actually wrote the letter. Leah implies it was H. H., but the *Tribune* states that it was W. A. Langworthy, although he wasn't even a committee member. In addition to H. H., an E. P. Langworthy also sat on the committee.

12. Joseph or Isaac (?) Post to relatives February 8, 1850, Department of Rare Books and Special Collections, University of Rochester Library.

13. William Cooper Nell to Amy Post, December 12, 1849, Department of Rare Books and Special Collections, University of Rochester Library.

CHAPTER 7:
"GOD'S TELEGRAPH HAS OUTDONE MORSE'S ALTOGETHER"

1. For a discussion of the word *scientist*, see the *Oxford English Dictionary*, s.v. "scientist"; Patrick Brantlinger, "Introduction: Zadia's Method Revisited," in *Energy and Entropy: Science and Culture in Victorian Britain: Essays from Victorian Studies*, ed. Patrick Brantlinger (Bloomington: Indiana University Press, 1989), xi–xii; and Iwan Rhys Morus, *Frankenstein's Children: Electricity, Exhibition, and Experiment in Early-Nineteenth-Century London* (Princeton, NJ: Princeton University Press, 1998), 3. For an analysis of the relationship between science, empiricism, and the rise of Spiritualism, see R. Laurence Moore, *In Search of White Crows: Spiritualism, Parapsychology, and American Culture* (New York: Oxford University Press, 1977).

2. For information on the dinosaur and a discussion of its terrifying appeal, see Martin Rudnick, "Domesticating the Monsters," chap. 5 in *Scenes from Deep Time: Early Representations of the Prehistoric World* (Chicago: University of Chicago Press, 1992), 140–60.

3. Clare Lloyd, *The Traveling Naturalists* (London: Croom Helm, 1986), 66–67.

4. Eliab W. Capron and Henry D. Barron, *Singular Revelations: Explanation and History of the Mysterious Communion with Spirits, Comprehending the Rise and Progress of the Mysterious Noises in Western New York*, 2nd ed. (Auburn, NY: Capron and Barron, 1850), 35.

5. For a discussion of Barnum's mermaid, see A. H. Saxon, *P. T. Barnum: The Legend and the Man* (New York: Columbia University Press, 1989), 119–24. On the subject of the avid quest for knowledge and information that characterized this period, and in particular the relationship between this inquisitiveness and Spiritualism, see also David Chapin, "The Fox Sisters and the Performance of Mystery," *New York History*, April 2000, 157–88.

6. Ralph Waldo Emerson, "Ode Inscribed to W. H. Channing," *Ralph Waldo Emerson: Collected Poems and Translations*, ed. Harold Bloom and Paul Kane (New York: New American Library, 1994), 63.

7. This and following quotes come from Capron and Barron, *Singular Revelations*, 30, 7, 31.

8. On the affinity of spirits with mortals, see Andrew Jackson Davis, as quoted in Capron and Barron, *Singular Revelations*, 35.

9. Capron and Barron, *Singular Revelations*, 65–66.

10. *New York Weekly Tribune*, January 26, 1850.

11. For a discussion of the importance of a domestic setting to Spiritualist practice, see Ann Braude, *Radical Spirits: Spiritualism and Women's Rights in Nineteenth-Century America* (Boston: Beacon Press, 1989), 24.

12. A. Leah Underhill, *The Missing Link in Modern Spiritualism* (New York: Thomas R. Knox, 1885), 103.

13. Frederick Douglass to Amy Post, March 1850, Department of Rare Books and Special Collections, University of Rochester Library.

14. The experiences of Augustus Strong are described by Adelbert Cronise, "The Beginnings of Modern Spiritualism in and Near Rochester," read before the Rochester Historical Society, October 29, 1925, *Rochester Historical Society Publication Fund Series*, 1926, 12–14.

15. D. M. Dewey, *History of the Strange Sounds or Rappings, Heard in Rochester and Western New-York, and Usually Called The Mysterious Noises! Which Are Supposed by Many to Be Communications from the Spirit World, Together with All the Explanation That Can as Yet Be Given of the Matter* (Rochester, NY: D. M. Dewey, 1850), 36.

16. This and the following quote are from Capron and Barron, *Singular Revelations*, 84, 90.

17. This and following quotes about Hammond's experience are from Dewey, *History of the Strange Sounds*, 27–32.

18. Comments by John Robinson are quoted in Dewey, *History of the Strange Sounds*, 42, 44.

19. Capron and Barron, *Singular Revelations*, 87.

20. Dewey, *History of the Strange Sounds*, 55–58.

21. Jervis's experience and the title of chapter 7 come from Capron and Barron, *Singular Revelations*, 39.

22. The experiences of the Drapers and the following quotes are drawn from Capron and Barron, *Singular Revelations*, 91–95.

CHAPTER 8:
"THE KNOCKING SPIRITS ARE ACTUALLY IN TOWN"

1. E. W. Capron to M. Fox, February 10, 1850, Department of Rare Books and Special Collections, University of Rochester Library.

2. A. Leah Underhill, *The Missing Link in Modern Spiritualism* (New York: Thomas R. Knox, 1885), 116.

3. Leah's quotes about Albany and Troy come from Underhill, *Missing Link,* 116–120.

4. Some biographers of the Fox sisters, including Earl Wesley Fornell in his chapter "Gotham Spirits" in *The Unhappy Medium: Spiritualism and the Life of Margaret Fox* (Austin: University of Texas Press, 1964), have suggested on the basis of their reading of P. T. Barnum's *The Humbugs of the World: An Account of Humbugs, Delusions, Impositions, Quackeries, Deceits and Deceivers Generally, in All Ages* (New York: Carleton, 1866) that the sisters were exhibited in Barnum's Museum. Slater Brown, in a note on p. 130 in *The Heyday of Modern Spiritualism* (New York: Pocket Books, 1970), suggests instead that the confusion came about because the girls stayed at Barnum's hotel, owned by P. T. Barnum's cousin, and that the Fox sisters had no professional connection with the impresario.

5. Edwin G. Burrows and Mike Wallace, *Gotham: A History of New York City to 1889* (New York: Oxford University Press, 1999), 692. For my information on New York and New Yorkers at midcentury, I'm particularly indebted to this and three other books: David Black, *The King of Fifth Avenue: The Fortunes of August Belmont* (New York: Dial Press, 1981); Karen Halttunen, *Confidence Men and Painted Women: A Study of Middle-Class Culture in America, 1830–1870* (New Haven, CT: Yale University Press, 1982); and Catherine Hoover Voorsanger and John K. Howat, eds., *Art and the Empire City: New York 1825–1861* (New Haven, CT: Yale University Press, 2000).

Halttunen's work, *Confidence Men and Painted Women,* has had a larger influence on this book, as some readers will recognize. Her exploration of the meanings of respectability and insincerity in American culture provided a foundation for my examination of the Fox sisters and their world. In particular, the themes of liminality and transition (*Confidence Men and Painted Women,* 29–32) seemed to me to offer a rich perspective for seeing the Fox sisters in a new way, separate from the old controversy about whether they were frauds and mischief makers or saints. Indeed, the notion of liminality can be applied to the sister's lives whatever one may feel about the nature of their powers.

Other books that have helped me develop this idea include Lewis Hyde, *Trickster Makes This World: Mischief, Myth, and Art* (New York: Farrar, Straus, and Giroux, 1998); Robert Jay Lifton, *The Protean Self: Human Resilience in an Age of Fragmentation* (Chicago: University of Chicago Press, 1989), and Garry Wills, *Lincoln at Gettysburg: The Words That Remade America* (New York: Touchstone, 1992), particularly chap. 2, "Gettysburg and the Cult of Death," 63–89.

6. Halttunen, *Confidence Men and Painted Women,* 6. See also Burrows and Wallace, *Gotham,* 694.

7. Burrows and Wallace, *Gotham,* 681.

8. William Harlan Hale, *Horace Greeley: Voice of the People* (New York: Harper and Bros., 1950), 122. For a discussion of the impact of children's deaths on Spiritualist beliefs and hopes, see Ann Braude, *Radical Spirits: Spiritualism and Women's Rights in Nineteenth-Century America* (Boston: Beacon Press, 1989), 49–55. For an illuminating look at the suffering of Mary Greeley prior to her involvement with Spiritualism, see Barbara Goldsmith, *Other Powers: The Age of Suffrage, Spiritualism, and the Scandalous Victoria Woodhull* (New York: Knopf, 1998), 55–62.

9. Quoted by Ernest Isaacs, "The Fox Sisters and American Spiritualism," in *The Occult in America: New Historical Perspectives,* ed. Howard Kerr and Charles L. Crow (Urbana: University of Illinois Press, 1983), 90.

10. Titus Merritt, "Chronology of the Fox Family: Interesting Details of the History of the Celebrated Fox Family," in M. E. Cadwallader, *Hydesville in History* (Chicago: Progressive Thinker Publishing, 1917; distributed by the National Spiritualist Association of Churches, 1992).

11. Quoted by Isaacs, "Fox Sisters and American Spiritualism"; see also Allan Nevins and Milton Halsey Thomas, eds., *The Diary of George Templeton Strong: The Turbulent Fifties 1850–1859* (New York: Macmillan, 1952), 15–16.

12. On the *Home Journal,* see Burrows and Wallace, *Gotham,* 724.

13. Quoted by David Chapin, "The Fox Sisters and the Performance of Mystery," *New York History,* April 2000, 181.

14. Underhill, *Missing Link,* 129.

15. *New York Weekly Tribune,* July 6, 1850. For the discussion that follows on art, see Peter Gay, *Education of the Senses* (New York: W. W. Norton & Company, 1999), 392–402.

16. Quoted by Emma Hardinge, *Modern American Spiritualism: A Twenty Years' Record of the Communion Between Earth and the World of Spirits,* with new introduction by E. J. Dingwall (1869, repr., New Hyde Park, NY: University Books, 1970), 71–72.

17. On Greeley's relationship with Fuller, see Hale's *Horace Greeley,* chap. 7, "Lover," 108–26. On Fuller's death, see the *New York Weekly Tribune,* July 27, 1850. Greeley's association of Kate with Margaret Fuller (at least in the first year of his acquaintance with the young medium) is referred to by both Leah Fox Fish Underhill and Titus Merritt.

18. *New York Weekly Tribune,* July 13, 1850.

19. Kate Fox to "friend," October 26, 1850. The letter was most likely to Robinson because it is similar in tone to the emotional letters she wrote to and about Robinson at a slightly later date.

20. Horace Greeley to Thomas Kane, October 7, 1850, Horace Greeley Papers, Manuscripts and Archives Division, New York Public Library, Astor, Lenox, and Tilden Foundations.

21. A brief but lively section on the notion of celebrity and the success of Jenny Lind can be found in Burrows and Wallace, *Gotham,* 814–17.

22. Horace Greeley, *Recollections of a Busy Life* (New York, 1868), 237.

23. *Spirit Messenger,* August 24, 1850.

24. *Spirit Messenger,* September 21, 1850. For background on the case, see the *New York Daily Tribune,* July 3, 1850, and Karen Halttunen, *Murder Most Foul: The Killer and the American Gothic Imagination* (Cambridge, MA: Harvard University Press, 1998).

25. *Spirit Messenger,* December 7, 1850.

26. Mary Robbins Post to "dear relatives," October 1, 1850, Department of Rare Books and Special Collections, University of Rochester Library.

27. Underhill, *Missing Link,* 122–27.

28. Information on the New York Circle comes from the Charlotte Fowler Wells Papers, Carl A. Kroch Library, Cornell University, Ithaca, New York.

29. Hardinge, *Modern American Spiritualism,* 72.

CHAPTER 9:
"THE IMPUTATION OF BEING IMPOSTERS"

1. *New York Daily Tribune,* July 9, July 17, and July 26, 1850; see also Herbert Jackson Jr., *The Spirit Rappers* (New York: Doubleday, 1972), 73.

2. E. W. Capron, *Modern Spiritualism: Its Facts and Fanaticisms, Its Consistencies and Contradictions; with an Appendix* (Boston: Bela Marsh, 1855; repr., New York: Arno Press, 1976), 416.

3. Capron, *Modern Spiritualism,* 418.

4. Somewhat different versions of the doctors' letter appear in Capron, *Modern Spiritualism,* and Emma Hardinge, *Modern American Spiritualism: A Twenty Years' Record of the Communion Between Earth and the World of Spirits* (1869; repr., New Hyde Park, NY: University Books, 1970). According to Capron (309–19), the doctors themselves modified their explanation for the March 1851 issue of the *Buffalo Medical Journal.* The doctors' quotes, the Fox sisters' response, and the title of chapter 9 are found in George H. Derby, *Rochester Knockings! Discovery and Explanation of the Source of the Phenomena Generally Known as the Rochester Knockings* (Buffalo, NY: George H. Derby, 1851), 6–9, 36–38. See also Capron, *Modern Spiritualism,* 313.

5. Diary of Charles W. Kellogg, March 18, 1851, Kellogg Family Papers, box 2, folder 8, New–York Historical Society, New York.

6. A. Leah Underhill, *The Missing Link in Modern Spiritualism* (New York: Thomas R. Knox, 1885), 196.

7. *New York Weekly Tribune,* March 22, 1851. See also Capron, *Modern Spiritualism,* 186.

8. John E. Robinson to Leah, March 12, 1851, quoted in Underhill, *Missing Link,* 204.

9. Culver's statement is quoted in Capron, *Modern Spiritualism,* 421–23.

10. For the Posts' employment of a Dutch girl, see Isaac Post to "brother and sister," November 23, 1848, Friends Historical Library of Swarthmore College.

11. Hardinge, *Modern American Spiritualism,* 96.

12. Charles Partridge, *The Spirit Messenger and Harmonial Guide* 2 (November 18, 1851): 163.

13. Quoted in Charles Wyllys Elliott, *Mysteries; or, Glimpses of the Supernatural Containing Accounts of the Salem Witchcraft—The Cock-Lane Ghost—The Rochester Rapping—The Stratford*

Mysteries—Oracles—Astrology—Dreams—Demons—Ghosts—Spectres, &c. &c. (New York: Harper & Brothers, 1852), 165–68.

CHAPTER 10:
"MODERN SPIRITUALISM"

1. Quotes from John Gray of the *Cleveland Plain Dealer* are from Mariam Buckner Pond's *Time Is Kind: The Story of the Unfortunate Fox Family* (New York: Centennial, 1947), 88–94.

2. Pond introduces an alternate birth date for Kate into the record in *Time Is Kind*, 93, claiming that soon after the girls arrived in Cleveland the family celebrated her fourteenth birthday on June 6, 1851, rather than in March as Titus Merritt would have claimed. In either case, at the time of the Hydesville raps in 1848 Kate would have been around eleven or so rather than six or eight as has sometimes been claimed.

3. Quoted by Dr. J. B. Campbell, *Pittsburgh and Allegheny Spirit Rappings, Together with a General History of Spiritual Communications Throughout the United States* (Allegheny, PA: Purviance, 1851), 48.

4. Joseph Post to Amy and Isaac Post, June 17, 1851, Department of Rare Books and Special Collections, University of Rochester Library.

5. Amy Post to Leah, quoted by A. Leah Underhill, *The Missing Link in Modern Spiritualism* (New York: Thomas R. Knox, 1885), 246–47.

6. Leah to Amy Post, July 22, 1851, Department of Rare Books and Special Collections, University of Rochester Library.

7. Quoted by Leah, *Missing Link,* 229.

8. Kate Fox to Amy Post, October 30, 1851, Department of Rare Books and Special Collections, University of Rochester Library.

9. Kate Fox to Amy Post, November 1851, Department of Rare Books and Special Collections, University of Rochester Library.

10. Maggie Fox to Amy Post, undated, Department of Rare Books and Special Collections, University of Rochester Library. I'm grateful to David Chapin for calling my attention to this letter in "Exploring Other Worlds: Margaret Fox, Elisha Kent Kane, and the Culture of Curiosity" (PhD diss., University of New Hampshire, 2000), 155.

11. Underhill, *Missing Link,* 251.

12. The Reverend H. Mattison, *Spirit Rapping Unveiled!* (New York: Mason Brothers, 1853), 161.

13. Susanna Moodie, *Letters of a Lifetime,* ed. Carl Ballstadt, Elizabeth Hopkins, and Michael Peterman (Toronto: University of Toronto Press, 1985), 157.

14. In n. 5 of chap. 8, above, I commented on the girls as symbolizing liminality. Chapin, "Exploring Other Worlds," and Robert S. Cox, "Without Crucible or Scalpel: A Sympathetic History of American Spiritualism" (PhD diss., University of Michigan, 2000), both explore the unifying impulse of Spiritualism, with "the harmonial philosophy" of Andrew Jackson Davis a clear example. Bret E. Carroll deals extensively with the meaning of the

circle in Spiritualism in his book *Spiritualism in Antebellum America* (Bloomington: Indiana University Press, 1997), esp. chap. 6, "The Structure of Spiritualist Practice," 120–51.

15. *Spirit Messenger,* January 25, 1851.

16. *Heat and Light for the Nineteenth Century* 1, no. 1 (1851): 18–19.

17. An excellent and innovative work that deals, among other issues, with the topic of racism within the Spiritualist movement is Cox, "Without Crucible or Scalpel."

18. *New York Weekly Tribune,* May 15, 1852. Ernest Joseph Isaacs drew my attention to the origin of the words *Spiritualism* and *Spiritualist* in his work "A History of Nineteenth-Century American Spiritualism as a Religious and Social Movement" (PhD diss., University of Wisconsin, 1975).

CHAPTER 11:
"DOCTOR KANE OF THE ARCTIC SEAS"

1. Quoted in Margaret Fox Kane, *The Love-Life of Dr. Kane* (New York: Carlton, 1866), 35–36.

2. For information on nineteenth-century attitudes toward sex, courtship, and marriage, see John D'Emilio and Estelle B. Freedman, *Intimate Matters: A History of Sexuality in America,* 2nd ed. (Chicago: University of Chicago Press, 1997), 76–77. See also Karen Lystra, *Searching the Heart: Women, Men, and Romantic Love in Nineteenth-Century America* (New York: Oxford University Press, 1989), which is particularly illuminating on the subject of love letters.

3. The Kane Family Collection and in particular the Elisha Kent Kane Papers at the American Philosophical Society in Philadelphia house a large number of Kane's letters and papers, and the brief biography of Kane posted on the Society's Web site at http://www.amphilsoc.org is excellent (accessed October 30, 2003). Other secondary sources on which I've drawn for information about Kane's life include George W. Corner, *Dr. Kane of the Arctic Seas* (Philadelphia: Temple University Press, 1972); Herbert Jackson Jr., *The Spirit Rappers* (New York: Doubleday, 1972); Jeanette Mirsky, *Elisha Kent Kane and the Seafaring Frontier* (Boston: Little, Brown, 1954); and Margaret Elder Dow, "Advance on the Dark," Margaret Elder Dow Papers, Rauner Special Collections, Dartmouth College Library. More recent sources include three by David Chapin: "The Funeral of Elisha Kent Kane," *Pennsylvania Magazine of History and Biography,* October 1999; "The Fox Sisters and the Performance of Mystery," *New York History,* April 2000; and "Exploring Other Worlds: Margaret Fox, Elisha Kent Kane, and the Antebellum Culture of Curiosity" (PhD diss., University of New Hampshire, 2000). Two other recent and helpful sources are Edmund Blair Bolles, *The Ice Finders: How a Poet, a Professor, and a Politician Discovered the Ice Age* (Washington, DC: Counterpoint, 1999); and Mark Horst Sawin, "Raising Kane: The Making of a Hero, the Marketing of a Celebrity" (master's thesis, University of Texas, Austin, 1997), available at http://www.ekkane.org/sawin/sawin.htm (accessed September 18, 2003). In his footnotes, Sawin identifies an archive, newly opened in the spring of 2001 at Brigham Young University, that contains correspondence of the Kane family and a wealth of other Kane-related materials. This archive may shed some new light on the relationship between Maggie and Kane.

4. This and following E. K. Kane quotes are from Kane, *Love-Life of Dr. Kane,* 237, 54, 75.

5. Mariam Buckner Pond, in *Time Is Kind: The Story of the Unfortunate Fox Family* (New York: Centennial, 1947), suggests that the author is Joseph LaFumee; based on letters housed in the American Philosophical Society, Philadelphia, Chapin in "Exploring Other Worlds" makes a good case for Ellet.

6. Quoted in Mirsky, *Elisha Kent Kane and the Seafaring Frontier,* 110.

7. Quotes from Elisha and Maggie here and following are found in Kane, *Love-Life of Dr. Kane,* 28, 42–43, 46–49, 51, 55–56.

8. Kate's letter can be found in A. Leah Underhill, *The Missing Link in Modern Spiritualism* (New York: Thomas R. Knox, 1885), 271.

9. Quotes here and following are found in Kane, *Love-Life of Dr. Kane,* 62, 65, 64, 66–69, 70, 78, 106, 88, 92.

10. Maggie Fox to Elisha Kent Kane, undated, American Philosophical Society, Philadelphia.

11. Underhill, *Missing Link,* 253–54.

12. George shows up as three years old in 1850 and has vanished from the records by 1855; *Wayne County Vital Statistics, 1847–1850* and 1855 Census, Wayne County Historian's Office, Lyons, New York.

13. Elisha Kent Kane to Eliza Leiper, May 1, 1853, American Philosophical Society, Philadelphia.

CHAPTER 12:
"MY DREAMS ALWAYS PROVE FALSE"

1. M. Margaret Wilkinson, ed., *Autobiography of Emma Hardinge Britten* (London: John Heywood), 40. Hardinge also gives Kate's salary, which is cited by R. Laurence Moore, *In Search of White Crows: Spiritualism, Parapsychology, and American Culture* (New York: Oxford University Press, 1977), 108.

2. A Searcher After Truth, *The Rappers; or, The Mysteries, Fallacies, and Absurdities of Spirit-Rapping, Table-Tipping, and Entrancement* (New York: H. Long, 1854?), 138–40; see also *Spiritual Telegraph* 1 (1852).

3. Margaret Fox Kane, *The Love-Life of Dr. Kane* (New York: Carlton, 1866), 159.

4. Robert Patterson Kane to Cornelius Grinnell, American Philosophical Society, Philadelphia. David Chapin called my attention to this letter in "Exploring Other Worlds: Margaret Fox, Elisha Kent Kane, and the Culture of Curiosity" (PhD diss., University of New Hampshire, 2000).

5. Maggie Fox to E. K. Kane, undated, American Philosophical Society, Philadelphia. Maggie mentions the death of Samuel Leiper, which would date the letter sometime in the late winter or early spring of 1854.

6. Maggie Fox to Cornelius Grinnell, April 10, 1854, American Philosophical Society, Philadelphia.

7. Maggie Fox to Cornelius Grinnell, November 4, 1854, American Philosophical Society, Philadelphia.

8. Kane's accounts of his experiences with animal magnetism and his glowing hand can be found in the journal of Elisha Kent Kane, December 25, 1854, and January 1, 1855, Stanford University Library. Edmund Blair Bolles first called my attention to this passage in Kane's journal in *The Ice Finders* (Washington, DC: Counterpoint, 1999), 133. Mark Horst Sawin discusses the phenomenon of Kane's luminous hand in "Raising Kane: The Making of a Hero, the Marketing of a Celebrity" (master's thesis, University of Texas, Austin, 1997), available at http://www.ekkane.org/sawin/sawin.htm (accessed September 18, 2003), chap. 9, "Celebrity and the Collision of Spheres."

9. Emma Hardinge, *Modern American Spiritualism: A Twenty Years' Record of the Communion Between Earth and the World of Spirits* (1869; repr., New Hyde Park, NY: University Books, 1970), 96–98.

10. J. M. Rich to Isaac Post, April 9, 1854, Department of Rare Books and Special Collections, University of Rochester Library.

11. Emma Hardinge's *Modern American Spiritualism* details the events of this period, 128–133.

12. E. W. Capron, *Modern Spiritualism: Its Facts and Fanaticisms, Its Consistencies and Contradictions; with an Appendix* (Boston: Bela Marsh, 1855; repr., New York: Arno Press, 1976), 52.

13. Capron, *Modern Spiritualism,* 51.

14. Kate Fox to Amy Post, June 19, 1855, Department of Rare Books and Special Collections, University of Rochester Library.

15. Joseph Post and Kate Fox to Amy Post, August 5, 1855, Department of Rare Books and Special Collections, University of Rochester Library.

16. Quotations here and following are from Kane, *Love-Life of Dr. Kane,* 202, 258, 206.

17. Maggie Fox to Elisha Kent Kane, undated, American Philosophical Society, Philadelphia.

18. Quoted in Kane, *Love-Life of Dr. Kane,* 216.

19. Mrs. Margaret Fox to E. K. Kane, undated, American Philosophical Society, Philadelphia.

20. This and the next quote are from Kane, *Love-Life of Dr. Kane,* 210, 236.

21. Bolles, *Ice Finders,* 229.

22. Kane, *Love-Life of Dr. Kane,* 260.

23. This and following quotes come from Kane, *Love-Life of Dr. Kane,* 265, 268, 271, 277, 278.

24. The best treatment of the significance of Kane's death in the context of his time, with a focus on his funeral, can be found in David Chapin's "Funeral of Elisha Kent Kane," *Pennsylvania Magazine of History and Biography,* October 1999.

25. Mrs. Margaret Fox to R. P. Kane, undated, American Philosophical Society, Philadelphia.

26. Maggie Fox to R. P. Kane, June 1, 1857, American Philosophical Society, Philadelphia.

CHAPTER 13:
"SO MANY UPS AND DOWNS IN THIS WEARY WORLD"

1. Quotes from Strong here and following are from Allan Nevins and Milton Halsey Thomas, eds., *The Diary of George Templeton Strong: The Turbulent Fifties, 1850–1859* (New York: Macmillan, 1952), 93, 244, 390.

2. On the phosphorus episode and George Willet's move, see A. Leah Underhill, *The Missing Link in Modern Spiritualism* (New York: Thomas R. Knox, 1885), 282–92.

3. Information on Agassiz is drawn primarily from Edmund Blair Bolles, *The Ice Finders* (Washington, DC: Counterpoint, 1999).

4. Quoted by Linda Simon, *Genuine Reality: A Life of William James* (New York: Harcourt Brace, 1998), 93.

5. This and the following quote are from *Spiritualism Shown As It Is! Boston Courier Report of the Proceedings of Professed Spiritual Agents and Mediums, in the Presence of Professors Peirce, Agassiz, Horsford, Dr. B. A. Gould, Committee, and Others, at the Albion Building, Boston, on the 25th, 26th, and 27th of June, 1857, Now First Published* (Boston: Office of the Boston Courier, 1859), 10.

6. Emma Hardinge, *Modern American Spiritualism: A Twenty Years' Record of the Communion Between Earth and the World of Spirits* (1869; repr., New Hyde Park, NY: University Books, 1970), 187.

7. Maggie Fox to R. P. Kane, May 27, 1858, American Philosophical Society, Philadelphia.

8. Maggie Fox to R. P. Kane, September 2, 1858, American Philosophical Society, Philadelphia.

9. Quoted in David Chapin, "Exploring Other Worlds: Margaret Fox, Elisha Kent Kane, and the Culture of Curiosity" (PhD diss., University of New Hampshire, 2000), 273. Chapin points out that the newspapers disagreed on what her conversion meant and stresses the paternalistic influence of Catholicism.

10. This quote and the title of chapter 13 are from Maggie Fox to R. P. Kane, October 25, 1858, American Philosophical Society, Philadelphia.

11. Daniel Underhill was born in 1821 in Washington, D.C., and was a descendant of Captain John Underhill, who, according to John Catanzariti, the archivist of the Underhill Society of America in Oyster Bay, New York, was the progenitor of the principal American Underhill family. The captain accompanied John Winthrop to the Massachusetts Bay Colony in 1630.

12. Lillie was mentioned in Daniel's will.

13. Robert Dale Owen, *The Debatable Land Between This World and the Next with Illustrative Narrations* (New York: G. W. Carleton, 1872), 357–60.

14. Owen, *Debatable Land,* 354–55.

15. Maggie Fox to R. P. Kane, April 1860, American Philosophical Society, Philadelphia.

16. Maggie Fox to R. P. Kane, May 16, 1860, American Philosophical Society, Philadelphia.

17. Maggie Fox to R. P. Kane, September 13, 1860, American Philosophical Society, Philadelphia.

18. Owen, *Debatable Land*, 346–47.

· CHAPTER 14:
"A MEDIUM OF REFLECTING OTHERS"

1. Some of Livermore's letters to Benjamin Coleman, housed in the Houdini Collection in the Library of Congress, are written on the firm's letterhead.

2. An extensive description of Kate's sittings with Livermore, coupled with excerpts from his letters and diary, can be found in Robert Dale Owen, *The Debatable Land Between This World and the Next with Illustrative Narrations* (New York: G. W. Carleton, 1872), 385–401. Owen's version tends to support the one given by Livermore in his letters, although some of the dates vary and it's clear that Owen has edited and beautified Livermore's prose. Another description of the sittings, which also includes excerpts from Livermore's letters and diary, can be found in Epes Sargent, *Planchette, or The Despair of Science. Being a Full Account of Modern Spiritualism, Its Phenomena, and the Various Theories Regarding It. With a Survey of French Spiritism* (Boston: Roberts, 1869). Once again dates vary between his account and Owen's. Owen not only may have prettified Livermore's prose but may have censored it as well. See next note also.

3. This description of the forty-third sitting and the quotes are drawn from Owen, *Debatable Land*, 386–89. Sargent's version is more sensual. He adds the following, attributed to Livermore's diary: "I [Livermore] asked her to kiss me if she could; and to my great astonishment and delight, an arm was placed around my neck, and a real, palpable kiss was implanted on my lips, through something like muslin. . . . The kiss was frequently repeated, and was audible in every part of the room."

4. Owen, *Debatable Land*, 390.

5. Charles Livermore to Benjamin Coleman, July 21, 1861, Houdini Collection, Library of Congress.

6. Charles Livermore to Benjamin Coleman, October 20, 1861, Houdini Collection, Library of Congress.

7. Charles Livermore to Benjamin Coleman, November 3, 1861, Houdini Collection, Library of Congress.

8. Charles Livermore to Benjamin Coleman, November 21, 1861, Houdini Collection, Library of Congress.

9. This and following quote come from Sargent, *Planchette,* entry for 12/28/1861 and January 24, 1862.

10. Charles Livermore to Benjamin Coleman, November 20, 1865, Houdini Collection, Library of Congress.

11. Emma Hardinge, *Modern American Spiritualism: A Twenty Years' Record of the Communion Between Earth and the World of Spirits* (1869; repr., New Hyde Park, NY: University Books, 1970), 418.

12. Quoted in James M. McPherson, *Ordeal by Fire: The Civil War and Reconstruction* (New York: Knopf, 1982), 278.

13. Hardinge, *Modern American Spiritualism*, 493.

14. For information on Spiritualism and the Civil War, I'm indebted to John Buescher's wonderfully informative Web site, *Ephemera*, http://www.Spirithistory.com, accessed September 24, 2003. For further information on the Civil War, Gettysburg, and Lincoln's assassination, as these related to attitudes toward death, I've relied on Garry Wills, *Lincoln at Gettysburg: The Words That Remade America* (New York: Touchstone, 1992), chap. 5 in Robert V. Wells, *Facing the "King of Terrors": Death and Society in an American Community, 1750–1990* (Cambridge: Cambridge University Press, 2000), and suggestions by Jim Murphy, author of *The Boys' War: Confederate and Union Soldiers Talk About the Civil War* (New York: Clarion, 1993) and other award-winning books for children and young adults. There are conflicting opinions about Lincoln's interest in seances; I've been guided by the moderate position of Jean H. Baker in *Mary Todd Lincoln: A Biography* (New York and London: Norton, 1987), 218–22.

15. Maggie Fox to Susanna Moodie, Patrick Ewing Collection at the National Archives of Canada. This letter was generously sent my way by Michael Peterman, one of the editors of *Susanna Moodie: Letters of a Lifetime*, ed. Carl Ballstadt, Elizabeth Hopkins, and Michael Peterman (Toronto: University of Toronto Press, 1985).

16. Quoted in M. Margaret Wilkinson, ed., *Autobiography of Emma Hardinge Britten* (London: John Heywood), 275.

17. Charles Livermore to Benjamin Coleman, September 1, 1863, Houdini Collection, Library of Congress.

18. Information on the convention and its resolution comes from Buescher, *Ephemera*, "Spiritualists Endorse Lincoln for a Second Term," http://www.Spirithistory.com/lincln.html, September 24, 2003, quoting Charles M. Plumb, "The National Spiritual Convention," *Friend of Progress*, November 1864, 16–20.

19. Quoted in Wells, *Facing the "King of Terrors,"* 166.

20. Walt Whitman, "When Lilacs Last in the Dooryard Bloom'd," *Leaves of Grass*, ed. Harold W. Blodgett and Sculley Bradley (New York: Norton, 1965), 330.

21. In *The Missing Link in Modern Spiritualism* (New York: Thomas R. Knox, 1885), Leah says that her father died in January, and an obituary in the *Syracuse Journal* on March 7, 1865, states that he was seventy-six years old. Information on Margaret's death comes from the New York City Death Registry.

22. A brief, vivid overview of the Flash Age and the Belmont clique to which Clews belonged can be found in David Black, *The King of Fifth Avenue: The Fortunes of August Belmont* (New York: Dial Press, 1981), 271–77.

23. Quoted in Margaret Fox Kane, *The Love-Life of Dr. Kane* (New York: Carlton, 1866), 253.

24. *National Cyclopedia of American Biography* (New York: J. T. White, 1930), vol. 5. The best source for information on the doctor can be found in the books that his wife and his son produced: Sarah E. L. Taylor, ed., *Fox-Taylor Automatic Writing, 1869–1892: Unabridged Record* (Minneapolis: Tribune–Great West Printing, 1932), and W. G. Langworthy Taylor,

Katie Fox, Epochmaking Medium and the Making of the Fox-Taylor Record (New York: G. P. Putnam's Sons, 1933). These books are also the source for information on the family's sittings with Kate.

25. Rachel P. Maines, *The Technology of Orgasm: "Hysteria," the Vibrator, and Women's Sexual Satisfaction* (Baltimore: Johns Hopkins University Press, 1999), 14–17, 92.

26. S. Taylor, ed., *Fox-Taylor Automatic Writing,* 111–12.

27. The following quotations and the title of chapter 14 are drawn from a letter by Harriet Beecher Stowe to George Eliot, February 8, 1872, Berg Collection of English and American Literature, New York Public Library, Astor, Lenox and Tilden Foundations.

28. The culmination of the attempt to produce Frankie's picture is described in S. Taylor, ed., *Fox-Taylor Automatic Writing,* 22–23. The following three quotes are found on 26, 84, and 80.

CHAPTER 15:
"EACH HAD HIS SECRET HEARTACHE"

1. The quotes about Kate's departure and the title of chapter 15 are drawn from Sarah E. L. Taylor, ed., *Fox-Taylor Automatic Writing, 1869–1892: Unabridged Record* (Minneapolis: Tribune–Great West Printing, 1932), 276–80.

2. Blanche Ogden was a middle-aged relative of Livermore's, according to Herbert Jackson Jr., *The Spirit Rappers* (New York: Doubleday, 1972), 182.

3. There is an extensive literature on the rise and progress of Spiritualism in England. Accounts written by Spiritualists in the late nineteenth and early twentieth centuries include Emma Hardinge Britten's chapters on England in her survey of the worldwide movement, *Nineteenth Century Miracles* (1884; repr., New York: Arno Press, 1976), and Arthur Conan Doyle's chapters on Great Britain in *The History of Spiritualism* (1926; repr., New York: Arno Press, 1975). Another comprehensive survey with sections on England, written by a member of the Society for Psychical Research, is Frank Podmore, *Modern Spiritualism: A History and a Criticism,* 2 vols. (London: Methuen, 1902), reprinted as *Mediums of the Nineteenth Century* (New Hyde Park, NY: University Books, 1963). Podmore's work swings in the direction of skepticism, particularly where physical rather than mental phenomena were involved. A more recent scholarly work is Janet Oppenheim, *The Other World: Spiritualism and Psychical Research in England, 1850–1914* (Cambridge: Cambridge University Press, 1985).

4. E. E. Fournier D'Albe, *The Life of Sir William Crookes, O.M., F.R.S.* (New York: D. Appleton, 1924), 223–24.

5. Information on Jencken comes from his marriage certificate to Kate; his obituary in *Light,* December 3, 1881; Mariam Buckner Pond, *Time Is Kind: The Story of the Unfortunate Fox Family* (New York: Centennial, 1947), 251–54; and a letter from Kate Fox to Daniel Dunglas Home, February 17, 1876, Society for Psychical Research Archive, Cambridge University Library. The most useful background came from Neil Robertson, a descendent

through one of Henry's brothers, who lives in Australia and who provided a family tree and a fascinating unpublished biography, "Grandmother's Story," by Amalie Christine Jencken. Information on Charles Livermore's later life was found in the 1880 census, through the Web site of the Church of Jesus Christ of Latter-day Saints, http://www.familysearch.org, October 30, 2003.

6. Information on the church is drawn primarily from *A Short History of St. Marylebone Parish Church,* a pamphlet published by the church. The description of the marriage ceremony comes from an article that was reprinted both by Jackson in *Spirit Rappers,* 183–84, and by Pond in *Time Is Kind,* 268–69. They credit it to two different American newspapers, but the article most likely originated in England and was carried by papers in the United States.

7. Information on Stainton Moses himself can be found, among other sources, in Alan Gauld, *The Founders of Psychical Research* (London: Routledge & Kegan Paul, 1968), 78–79, and in Leslie Price, *The Mystery of Stainton Moses: An Address Given in 1992 on the Centenary of his Death* (London: Psychic Pioneer Publications, 1999). Information on and quotations from the Stainton Moses sittings are drawn from R. G. Medhurst, "Stainton Moses and Contemporary Physical Mediums: Kate Fox," *Light,* Winter 1963, 183–84.

8. Information on Crookes's sittings and quotations from his article are found in William Crookes, F.R.S., "Notes of an Enquiry into the Phenomena Called Spiritual, During the Years 1870–73," *Researches in the Phenomena of Spiritualism* (London: J. Burns, 1874), 81–102. Crookes's own objectivity has been called into question by several authors; see Ruth Brandon, *The Spiritualists: The Passion for the Occult in the Nineteenth and Twentieth Centuries* (Buffalo, NY: Prometheus, 1984), 77–97.

9. Information on Ferdie and Henry is drawn from W. G. Langworthy Taylor, *Katie Fox, Epochmaking Medium and the Making of the Fox-Taylor Record* (New York: G. P. Putnam's Sons, 1933), 101–2. But the 1881 British Census cites 1874 as Ferdie's birthdate. On Ferdie's mediumship, see A. Leah Underhill, *The Missing Link in Modern Spiritualism* (New York: Thomas R. Knox, 1885), 89–95, 464–70. As her sources, Leah cites the *London Spiritualist,* December 12, 1873, and the *Medium and Daybreak,* May 8, 1874.

10. See Reuben Briggs Davenport, *The Death-Blow to Spiritualism: Being the True Story of the Fox Sisters, As Revealed by Authority of Margaret Fox Kane and Catherine Fox Jencken* (New York: G. W. Dillingham, 1888; New York: Arno Press, 1976), 164–67.

11. This and following quotes are from S. Taylor, ed., *Fox-Taylor Automatic Writing,* 284, 282, 283.

12. A brief mention of Henry's epilepsy can be found in Pond, *Time Is Kind,* 286. The relationship between epilepsy and a form of religiosity that triggers dreams and voices was explored in *Newsweek,* May 7, 2001, 55.

13. Kate Fox to Home, February 17, 1876, Archives of the Society for Psychical Research, Cambridge University Library.

14. Henry Jencken to Edward Jencken, May 24, 1880, quoted with permission from Neil Robertson, descendant.

CHAPTER 16:
"I LEAVE OTHERS TO JUDGE FOR THEMSELVES"

1. A. Aksakoff to Kate Fox, January 2, 1882, American Society for Psychical Research. Sarah Taylor and Titus Merritt also refer to Kate's St. Petersburg visit: Sarah E. L. Taylor, ed., *Fox-Taylor Automatic Writing, 1869–1892: Unabridged Record* (Minneapolis: Tribune–Great West Printing, 1932); Titus Merritt, "Chronology of the Fox Family: Interesting Details of the History of the Celebrated Fox Family," in M. E. Cadwallader, *Hydesville in History* (Chicago: Progressive Thinker Publishing, 1917; distributed by the National Spiritualist Association of Churches, 1992).

2. Mrs. Henry Sidgwick, "Results of a Personal Investigation into the Physical Phenomena of Spiritualism with Some Critical Remarks on the Evidence for the Genuineness of Such Phenomena," *Proceedings of the Society for Psychical Research* 4 (1887): 46–47.

3. Quotations from the Seybert Commission and the title of chapter 16 are drawn from the *Preliminary Report of the Commission by University of Pennsylvania to Investigate Modern Spiritualism* (Philadelphia: Lippincott, 1887), 32–47, 42.

4. Quoted in Linda Simon, *Genuine Reality: A Life of William James* (New York: Harcourt Brace, 1998), 190.

5. Sarah E. L. Taylor, ed., *Fox-Taylor Automatic Writing, 1869–1892: Unabridged Record* (Minneapolis: Tribune–Great West Printing, 1932), 293.

6. A. Leah Underhill, *The Missing Link in Modern Spiritualism* (New York: Thomas R. Knox, 1885), 242.

7. S. Taylor, ed., *Fox-Taylor Automatic Writing,* 364.

8. Interview with the *World* is quoted in Herbert Jackson Jr., *The Spirit Rappers* (New York: Doubleday, 1972), 198–99.

9. Maggie recounts this story in the *New York Herald,* September 24, 1888.

10. "The Curse of Spiritualism," quoted in Reuben Briggs Davenport, *The Death-Blow to Spiritualism: Being the True Story of the Fox Sisters, as Revealed by Authority of Margaret Fox Kane and Catherine Fox Jencken* (New York: G. W. Dillingham, 1888; New York: Arno Press, 1976), 30–31.

11. Kate's seance at Carlyle's house is discussed in *Light* on September 22, 1888, 468–69, and on September 30, 1888, 482.

12. Davenport quotes this interview in *Death-Blow to Spiritualism,* 34–38. The *Herald* article itself ends with the phrase "Spirits, is he not easily fooled?" When Davenport quotes from the article, he adds several extra paragraphs that didn't appear in the *Herald* and that seem to represent his attempt to underscore his point in *Death-Blow to Spiritualism.* The section reads as follows, p. 38:

> Then I addressed certain suppositions to her. At last she said, "Yes, you have hit it. It is, as you say, the manner in which the joint of the foot can be used without lifting it from the floor. The power of doing this can only be acquired by practice begun in early youth. One must begin as early as twelve years. Thirteen is rather late. We children, when we were playing together, years ago, discovered it, and it was my eldest sister who first put the discovery to such an infamous use.
>
> I call it infamous, for it was.

CHAPTER 17:
"THE DEATH-BLOW"

1. Kate's interview is quoted in Reuben Briggs Davenport, *The Death-Blow to Spiritualism* (New York: G.W. Dillingham, 1888; New York: Arno Press, 1976), 54–58. Davenport, not always reliable, attributes it to the *Herald*, October 10, 1888.

2. Caroline Fraser, *God's Perfect Child: Living and Dying in the Christian Science Church* (New York: Henry Holt, 1999).

3. Davenport, *Death-Blow to Spiritualism*. Accounts of Maggie's appearance at the academy are drawn from the *World*, the *New York Herald*, the *New York Times*, and the *New York Daily Tribune*, newspapers that all reported the event on October 22, the day after it occurred.

4. R. Laurence Moore drew my attention to Emerson's categories in *In Search of White Crows: Spiritualism, Parapsychology, and American Culture* (New York: Oxford University Press, 1977), 104. See John B. Wilson, "Emerson and the 'Rochester Rappings,'" *New England Quarterly*, June 1968, 250.

CHAPTER 18:
"UNCOMMON POWERS"

1. *Banner of Light*, November 10, 1888.

2. *Banner of Light*, November 17, 1888.

3. *Banner of Light*, November 24, 1888.

4. *Banner of Light*, October 8, 1892.

5. Joseph Rinn, *Searchlight on Psychical Research: A Record of Sixty Years Work* (London, 1954), 64.

6. *Journal of the Society for Psychical Research*, January 1889, 15.

7. *Rochester Democrat and Chronicle*, July 4, 1892.

8. The yellowed, dog-eared document dated November 16, 1888, now at the American Society for Psychical Research Archives, was delivered to James H. Hyslop by Mrs. Henry Newton, according to Hyslop's signed statement dated November 19, 1919. Hyslop doesn't swear to the document's authenticity, but he says that there's no reason to doubt it. Excerpts from the statement also appear in Arthur Conan Doyle, *The History of Spiritualism* (1926; repr., New York: Arno Press, 1975).

9. *Banner of Light*, October 8, 1892.

10. Sarah E. L. Taylor, ed., *Fox-Taylor Automatic Writing, 1869–1892: Unabridged Record* (Minneapolis: Tribune–Great West Printing, 1932), 369, entry for April 6, 1890. They were joined as well that day by the spirits of William Henry Vanderbilt, now a longtime visitor, and Helen Hunt Jackson, an occasional visitor.

11. S. Taylor, ed., *Fox-Taylor Automatic Writing*, 400.

12. S. Taylor, ed., *Fox-Taylor Automatic Writing*, 400.

13. Information on Maggie's death comes from her death certificate and from two letters from Titus Merritt to Mrs. M.T. Longly, March 26, 1903, and March 31, 1903, Archives of the National Spiritualist Association of Churches, Lily Dale, New York.

14. *Banner of Light*, March 18, 1893.

CHAPTER 19:
"WE OF MODERN TIMES"

1. The chapter title comes from *Banner of Light*, March 18, 1893. For a lively and engaging portrait of the town of Lily Dale yesterday and today, see Christine Wicker, *Lily Dale: The True Story of the Town That Talks to the Dead* (San Francisco: HarperSanFrancisco, 2003). See also the *New York Times*, August 25, 1997.

2. The number of Spiritualists remains a point of controversy and to some degree depends on whether one is talking only about those affiliated with the church or all sympathizers with the movement. Emma Hardinge, in *Modern American Spiritualism: A Twenty Years' Record of the Communion Between Earth and the World of Spirits* (1869; repr., New Hyde Park, NY: University Books, 1970), estimated that by the 1850s there were 40,000 Spiritualists in New York City alone (101). The *Banner of Light* in 1888 put the number far higher, at between 8 and 11 million believers (November 24, 1888). These estimates may have included not only committed Spiritualists but also curious investigators who for a time took part in seances. R. Laurence Moore puts the number of Spiritualists who participated in the movement in an organized church form at about 35,000 at the end of the nineteenth century. However, he adds that the number does not represent individuals who may have expressed the thought that "there was something in" spirit communication; see *In Search of White Crows: Spiritualism, Parapsychology, and American Culture* (New York: Oxford University Press, 1977), 41, 68.

3. For information on life expectancy, see Robert V. Wells, *Facing the "King of Terrors": Death and Society in an American Community, 1750–1990* (Cambridge: Cambridge University Press, 2000), 172–79.

4. On the impact of electricity, see Alexander Murray, "Revenants from Darkness: Clergy, Community, and a Twelfth-Century 'Invasion of Ghosts,'" *Times Literary Supplement*, June 4, 1999, review of Jean-Claude Schmitt, *Ghosts and the Middle Ages: The Living and the Dead in Medieval Society* (Chicago: University of Chicago Press, 1998). On Thomas Edison, see Moore, *In Search of White Crows,* 176.

5. An excellent source on the history of medicine in nineteenth- and twentieth-century America, particularly as medical practice and drug therapy pertained to women's health, is Sarah Stage, *Female Complaints: Lydia Pinkham and the Business of Women's Medicine* (New York: Norton, 1979).

6. Sources on the later history of Spiritualism, the SPR, the ASPR, the Theosophical Society, and occultism include books already cited: Ruth Brandon, *The Spiritualists: The Passion for the Occult in the Nineteenth and Twentieth Centuries* (Buffalo, NY: Prometheus, 1984); Alan Gauld, *The Founders of Psychical Research* (London: Routledge & Kegan Paul, 1968); R. Laurence Moore, *In Search of White Crows;* Janet Oppenheim, *The Other World: Spiritualism and Psychical Research in England, 1850–1914* (Cambridge: Cambridge University Press, 1985); and Peter Washington, *Madame Blavatsky's Baboon: A History of the Mystics, Mediums, and Misfits Who Brought Spiritualism to America* (New York: Schocken, 1993). In addition, a remarkable biography, John Patrick Deveney, *Paschal Beverly Randolph: A Nineteenth-Century*

Black American Spiritualist, Rosicrucian, and Sex Magician (Albany: State University of New York Press, 1997), examines one man's spiritual journey. There is, of course, an extensive literature by and about Madame Blavatsky and Henry Steele Olcott for readers who wish to delve into the history and philosophy of the Theosophical Society.

7. For information on Yeats's occult associations, see Brenda Maddox, *Yeats's Ghosts: The Secret Life of W. B. Yeats* (New York: HarperCollins, 1999).

8. Information on World War I and the fragment of the Wilfred Owen quote come from Pat Jalland, *Death in the Victorian Family* (Oxford: Oxford University Press, 1996), 370–74.

9. For information on Kingsley's death, see Daniel Stashower, *Teller of Tales: The Life of Arthur Conan Doyle* (New York: Henry Holt, 1999), 345–46. For Houdini's and Doyle's divergent views of the Fox sisters, see Houdini, *A Magician Among the Spirits* (New York: Harper & Bros., 1924), 1–16, and Arthur Conan Doyle, *The History of Spiritualism*, vol. 1 (New York: George H. Doran, 1926), 61–118.

10. Nicholas Goodrick-Clarke, *The Occult Roots of Nazism: Secret Aryan Cults and Their Influence on Nazi Ideology* (New York: New York University Press, 1992).

11. There is an extensive literature on parapsychology; Richard S. Broughton, *Parapsychology: The Controversial Science* (New York: Ballantine, 1991), provides a good overview of the field. The Parapsychology Foundation's Web site, as of October 30, 2003, found at http://www.parapsychology.org, and the American Society for Psychical Research in New York are both excellent sources for more detailed and current information.

12. For membership in the NSAC within the last decade, see the *New York Times*, August 25, 1997.

13. *Boston Journal*, November 23, 1904. Another doctor refuted the findings in print five years later, in the *ASPR Journal*, March 1909.

14. Gene Gordon, *Magical Legacy* (Norcross, GA: David Ginn, 1980), 43–44.

15. The subsequent history of the house is taken from Arthur Myers, *Fox Cottage Burns, September 21, 1955* (Lily Dale, NY: Lily Dale Historical Society); from the *Wayne County Star*, November 19, 1983; and from the Internet newsletter of the National Spiritualist Association of Churches, http://www.nsac.org/newsletter, September 24, 1998.

16. *Syracuse Post Standard*, October 21, 1899, Wayne County Historical Society. Mariam Buckner Pond was married to a grandnephew of the Fox sisters. W. G. Langworthy Taylor, in *Katie Fox: Epochmaking Medium and the Making of the Fox-Taylor Record* (New York: G. P. Putnam's Sons, 1933), supplies the death dates for Henry and for Ferdie (158). However a Jencken family tree puts Ferdie's death date as 1914.

17. Titus Merritt to Mary Longley, March 27, 1903, Archives of the National Spiritualist Association of Churches.

AFTERWORD

1. James's evocative sentence, a portion of which Moore uses for the title of his book, can be found in "What Psychical Research Has Accomplished," an essay James wrote in 1897 and that can be found today in many anthologies of his work.

2. Quoted by Thomas L. Friedman, "Is Google God?" *New York Times,* op-ed section, Sunday, June 29, 2003.

3. According to the *Fortean Times,* July 1998, 6, a *USA Today* article (April 28, 1998) cited a Gallup poll that a belief in Spiritualism (defined as "mediums and ghosts") rose from 12 percent in 1976 to 52 percent in 1996. The *New York Times* referred to the same poll in an article titled "A Voice from the Other Side" (October 29, 2000). According to the *Times*'s interpretation, the Gallup poll found that 20 percent of the respondents believed in spirit communication, and another 22 percent believed that spirit communication might be possible.

4. Quoted by William Riordan, *Plunkitt of Tammany Hall: A Series of Very Plain Talks on Very Practical Politics* (1905; repr., New York: Dutton, 1963), 3.

5. R. Laurence Moore makes this point in *In Search of White Crows: Spiritualism, Parapsychology, and American Culture* (New York: Oxford University Press, 1977), 5. A last-minute rereading, on David Black's recommendation, of Leo Marx, *The Machine in the Garden: Technology and the Pastoral Ideal in America* (1964; repr., Oxford: Oxford University Press, 2000), left me listening for the train's whistle as I finished this book.

SELECTED
BIBLIOGRAPHY

PRIMARY SOURCES: BOOKS AND PAMPHLETS

A Searcher After Truth. *The Rappers; or, The Mysteries, Fallacies, and Absurdities of Spirit-Rapping, Table-Tipping, and Entrancement.* New York: H. Long & Bro., 1854?

An Impartial Examiner. *Mesmeric and Spirit Rapping Manifestations Scripturally Exposed as Neither from Electricity nor Spirits of the Dead but Rather from Infernal Evil Spirits.* New York: R. T. Young, 1852.

Barnum, P. T. *The Humbugs of the World: An Account of Humbugs, Delusions, Impositions, Quackeries, Deceits, and Deceivers Generally, in All Ages.* New York: Carleton, 1866.

Campbell, J. B. *Pittsburgh and Allegheny Spirit Rappings, Together with a General History of Spiritual Communications Throughout the United States.* Allegheny, PA: Purviance, 1851.

Capron, E. W. *Modern Spiritualism: Its Facts and Fanaticisms, Its Consistencies and Contradictions; With an Appendix.* Boston: Bela Marsh, 1855. Reprint, New York: Arno Press, 1976.

Capron, Eliab W., and Henry D. Barron. *Singular Revelations: Explanation and History of the Mysterious Communion with Spirits, Comprehending the Rise and Progress of the Mysterious Noises in Western New York.* 2nd ed. Auburn, NY: Capron and Barron, 1850.

Coggshall, William T. *The Signs of the Times: Comprising a History of the Spirit-Rappings, in Cincinnati and Other Places; With Notes of Clairvoyant Revealments.* Cincinnati: William T. Coggshall, 1851.

Davenport, Reuben Briggs. *The Death-Blow to Spiritualism: Being the True Story of the Fox Sisters, as Revealed by Authority of Margaret Fox Kane and Catherine Fox Jencken.* New York: G. W. Dillingham, 1888. Reprint, New York: Arno Press, 1976.

Derby, George H. *Rochester Knockings! Discovery and Explanation of the Source of the Phenomena Generally Known as the Rochester Knockings.* Buffalo, NY: George H. Derby, 1851.

Dewey, D. M. *History of the Strange Sounds or Rappings, Heard in Rochester and Western New-York, and Usually Called the Mysterious Noises! Which Are Supposed by Many to Be Communications from the Spirit World, Together with All the Explanation That Can as Yet Be Given of the Matter.* Rochester, NY: D. M. Dewey, 1850.

Doyle, Arthur Conan. *The History of Spiritualism.* New York: George H. Doran, 1926.

Edmonds, John W., and George T. Dexter. *Spiritualism.* 2 vols. New York: Partridge and Brittan, 1853, 1855.

Elliott, Charles Wyllys. *Mysteries; or, Glimpses of the Supernatural Containing Accounts of the Salem Witchcraft—The Cock-Lane Ghost—The Rochester Rapping—The Stratford Mysteries—Oracles—Astrology—Dreams—Demons—Ghosts—Spectres, &c. &c.* New York: Harper & Bros., 1852.

Haddock, Joseph. *Psychology; or, The Science of the Soul, Considered Physiologically and Philosophically; With an Appendix, Containing Notes of Mesmeric and Psychical Experience.* New York: Fowlers and Wells, 1850.

Hardinge, Emma. *Modern American Spiritualism: A Twenty Years' Record of the Communion Between Earth and the World of Spirits.* 1869. Reprint, New Hyde Park, NY: University Books, 1970.

Houdini. *A Magician Among the Spirits.* New York: Harper & Bros., 1924.

James, William. *William James on Psychical Research.* Edited by Gardner Murphy and Robert O. Ballou. New York: Viking, 1960.

Jung, C. G. *Four Archetypes.* Translated by R. F. C. Hull. 1954. Reprint, Princeton, NJ: Princeton University Press, 1969.

———. *Memories, Dreams, Reflections.* Edited by Aniela Jaffe. Translated by Richard and Clara Winston. New York: Vintage, 1989.

———. "On Synchronicity." *The Portable Jung.* Edited by Joseph Campbell. Translated by R. F. C. Hull. New York: Penguin Books, 1971.

Kane, Margaret Fox. *The Love-Life of Dr. Kane.* New York: Carleton, 1866.

Lewis, E. E. *A Report of the Mysterious Noises Heard in the House of Mr. John D. Fox, in Hydesville, Arcadia, Wayne County, Authenticated by the Certificates, and Confirmed by the Statements of the Citizens of That Place and Vicinity.* Canandaigua, NY: E. E. Lewis, 1848.

Mattison, H. *Spirit Rapping Unveiled!* New York: Mason Bros., 1853.

Owen, Robert Dale. *Footfalls on the Boundary of Another World, with Narrative Illustrations.* Philadelphia: Lippincott, 1860.

Owen, Robert Dale. *The Debatable Land Between This World and the Next with Illustrative Narrations.* New York: Carleton, 1872.

Page, Charles G. *Psychomancy: Spirit-Rappings and Table-Tippings Exposed*. New York: D. Appleton, 1853.

Pond, Enoch. *Familiar Spirits, and Spiritual Manifestations: Being a Series of Articles*. Boston: Bela Marsh, 1852.

Post, Isaac. *Voices from the Spirit World: Being Communications from Many Spirits by the Hand of Isaac Post, Medium*. Rochester, NY: Charles H. McDonell, 1852.

Sargent, Epes. *Planchette, or The Despair of Science. Being a Full Account of Modern Spiritualism, Its Phenomena, and the Various Theories Regarding It. With a Survey of French Spiritism*. Boston: Roberts, 1869.

Spiritualism Shown As It Is! Boston Courier Report of the Proceedings Of Professed Spiritual Agents and Mediums, in the Presence of Professors Peirce, Agassiz, Horsford, Dr. B. A. Gould, Committee, and Others, at the Albion Building, Boston, on the 25th, 26th, and 27th of June, 1857, Now First Published. Boston: Office of the Boston Courier, 1859.

Taylor, Sarah E. L., ed. *Fox-Taylor Automatic Writing, 1869–1892, Unabridged Record*. Minneapolis: Tribune–Great West Printing, 1932.

Taylor, W. G. Langworthy. *Katie Fox, Epochmaking Medium and the Making of the Fox-Taylor Record*. New York: G. P. Putnam's Sons, 1933.

Underhill, Leah A. *The Missing Link in Modern Spiritualism*. New York: Thomas R. Knox, 1885.

PRIMARY SOURCES: NEWSPAPERS AND JOURNALS

Banner of Light (Boston) 1857–1893

Christian Spiritualist (New York) 1854–1856

Heat and Light (Boston) 1851

New York Herald (New York) 1888

New York Tribune (New York) 1849–1855, 1888

Sacred Circle (New York) 1854

Shekinah (Bridgeport, CT) 1851–1853

Spirit Messenger (Springfield, MA) 1850–1853

Spiritual Telegraph (New York) 1853–1857

New York Times (New York) 1888

Western Argus (Lyons, New York) 1847–1850

World (New York) 1888

SECONDARY SOURCES

Ahlstrom, Sydney E. *A Religious History of the American People*. New Haven, CT: Yale University Press, 1972.

Aveni, Anthony. *Behind the Crystal Ball: Magic, Science, and the Occult from Antiquity Through the New Age*. New York: Random House, 1996.

Bednarowski, Mary Farrell. "Nineteenth-Century American Spiritualism: An Attempt at a Scientific Religion." PhD diss., University of Minnesota, 1973.

Black, David. *The King of Fifth Avenue: The Fortunes of August Belmont.* New York: Dial, 1981.

Bloom, Harold. *Omens of the Millennium: The Gnosis of Angels, Dreams, and Resurrection.* New York: Riverhead, 1996.

Bolles, Edmund Blair. *The Ice Finders: How a Poet, a Professor, and a Politician Discovered the Ice Age.* Washington, DC: Counterpoint, 1999.

Branch, E. Douglas. *The Sentimental Years 1836–1860: A Social History.* New York: D. Appleton-Century, 1934.

Brandon, Ruth. *The Spiritualists: The Passion for the Occult in the Nineteenth and Twentieth Centuries.* Buffalo, NY: Prometheus Books, 1983.

Brantlinger, Patrick, ed. *Energy and Entropy: Science and Culture in Victorian Britain: Essays from Victorian Studies.* Bloomington: Indiana University Press, 1983.

Braude, Ann. *Radical Spirits: Spiritualism and Women's Rights in Nineteenth-Century America.* Boston: Beacon Press, 1989.

Broughton, Richard S. *Parapsychology: The Controversial Science.* New York: Ballantine, 1991.

Brown, Burton Gates Jr. "Spiritualism in Nineteenth-Century America." PhD diss., Boston University, 1972.

Brown, Slater. *The Heyday of Spiritualism.* New York: Pocket Books, 1970.

Burger, Eugene. *Spirit Theater.* Washington, DC: Kaufman and Greenberg, 1986.

Butler, Jon. *Awash in a Sea of Faith: Christianizing the American People.* Cambridge, MA: Harvard University Press, 1990.

Burrows, Edwin G., and Mike Wallace. *Gotham: A History of New York City to 1898.* New York: Oxford University Press, 1999.

Cadwallader, M. E. *Hydesville in History.* Chicago: Progressive Thinker Publishing House, 1917. Distributed by the National Spiritualist Association of Churches, 1992.

Carmer, Carl. *Listen for a Lonesome Drum.* New York: David McKay, 1936.

Carroll, Bret E. *Spiritualism in Antebellum America.* Bloomington: Indiana University Press, 1997.

Chapin, David. "Exploring Other Worlds: Margaret Fox, Elisha Kane, and the Antebellum Culture of Curiosity." PhD diss., University of New Hampshire, 2000.

———. "The Fox Sisters and the Performance of Mystery." *New York History,* April 2000.

———. "The Funeral of Elisha Kent Kane." *Pennsylvania Magazine of History and Biography,* October 1999.

Christianson, Rupert. *The Victorian Visitors: Culture Shock in the Nineteenth Century.* New York: Atlantic Monthly Press, 2000.

Clark, Franklin W. "The Origins of Spiritualism in America." Master's thesis, University of Rochester, 1932.

Connor, Stephen. "The Machine in the Ghost: Spiritualism, Technology, and the 'Direct Voice.'" In *Ghosts: Deconstruction, Psychoanalysis, History,* edited by Peter Buse and Andrew Scott. New York: St. Martin's Press, 1999.

Corner, George Washington. *Doctor Kane of the Arctic Seas.* Philadelphia: Temple University Press, 1972.

Cott, Nancy F. *The Bonds of Womanhood: "Woman's Sphere" in New England, 1780–1835.* New Haven, CT: Yale University Press, 1977.

Cox, Robert S. "Without Crucible or Scalpel: A Sympathetic History of American Spiritualism." PhD diss., University of Michigan, 2002.

Cross, Whitney R. *The Burned-over District: The Social and Intellectual History of Enthusiastic Religion in Western New York, 1800–1850.* Ithaca, NY: Cornell University Press, 1950.

Deveney, John Patrick. *Paschal Beverly Randolph: A Nineteenth-Century Black American Spiritualist, Rosicrucian, and Sex Magician.* Albany: State University of New York Press, 1997.

Douglas, Ann. *The Feminization of American Culture.* 1978. Reprint, New York: Farrar, Straus, and Giroux, 1998.

Ehrenreich, Barbara, and Deirdre English. *For Her Own Good: 150 Years of Advice to Women.* New York: Doubleday, 1978.

Faivre, Antoine. *Access to Western Esotericism.* Albany: State University of New York Press, 1994.

Fornell, Earl Wesley. *The Unhappy Medium: Spiritualism and the Life of Margaret Fox.* Austin: University of Texas Press, 1964.

Foster, Lawrence. *Women, Family, and Utopia: Communal Experiments of the Shakers, the Oneida Community, and the Mormons.* Syracuse, NY: Syracuse University Press, 1991.

Fraser, Caroline. *God's Perfect Child: Living and Dying in the Christian Science Church.* New York: Henry Holt, 1999.

Frohock, Fred. *Lives of the Psychics: The Shared Worlds of Science and Mysticism.* Chicago: University of Chicago Press, 1999.

Gauld, Alan. *The Founders of Psychical Research.* London: Routledge & Kegan Paul, 1968.

Goldsmith, Barbara. *Other Powers: The Age of Suffrage, Spiritualism, and the Scandalous Victoria Woodhull.* New York: Knopf, 1998.

Graff, Harvey J., ed. *Growing Up in America: Historical Experiences.* Detroit: Wayne State University Press, 1987.

Hale, William Harlan. *Horace Greeley: Voice of the People.* New York: Harper and Bros., 1950.

Halttunen, Karen. *Confidence Men and Painted Women: A Study of Middle-Class Culture in America, 1830–1870.* New Haven, CT: Yale University Press, 1982.

Hine, Thomas. *The Rise and Fall of the American Teenager: A New History of the American Adolescent Experience.* New York: Perennial, 1999.

Hoeltzel, Robert. *Hometown History: Village of Newark, Town of Arcadia.* Newark, NY: Arcadia Historical Society, 2000.

Hyde, Lewis. *Trickster Makes This World: Mischief, Myth, and Art.* New York: Farrar, Straus, and Giroux, 1998.

Isaacs, Ernest Joseph. "A History of Nineteenth-Century American Spiritualism as a Religious and Social Movement." PhD diss., University of Wisconsin, 1975.

Jackson, Herbert J., Jr. *The Spirit Rappers.* Garden City, NY: Doubleday, 1972.

Jay, Ricky. "Introduction." *Many Mysteries Unraveled or Conjuring Literature in America, 1786–1874.* Drawn from the Collection of the American Antiquarian Society and the Mulholland Library of Conjuring and the Allied Arts. Worcester: American Antiquarian Society, 1990.

Johnson, Paul E. *A Shopkeeper's Millennium: Society and Revivals in Rochester, New York, 1815–1837.* New York: Hill and Wang, 1978.

Johnson, Paul E., and Sean Wilentz. *The Kingdom of Matthias: A Story of Sex and Salvation in Nineteenth-Century America*. New York: Oxford University Press, 1994.

Kaminer, Wendy. *Sleeping with Extra-Terrestrials: The Rise of Irrationalism and Perils of Piety*. New York: Vintage Books, 1999.

Kerr, Howard. *Mediums, and Spirit-Rappers, and Roaring Radicals: Spiritualism in American Literature, 1850–1900*. Urbana: University of Illinois Press, 1973.

Kerr, Howard, and Charles L. Crow, eds. *The Occult in America: New Historical Perspectives*. Urbana: University of Illinois Press, 1983.

Landay, Lori. *Madcaps, Screwballs, and Con Women: The Female Trickster in American Culture*. Philadelphia: University of Pennsylvania Press, 1998.

Lifton, Robert Jay. *The Protean Self: Human Resilience in an Age of Fragmentation*. Chicago: University of Chicago Press, 1993.

Lystra, Karen. *Searching the Heart: Women, Men, and Romantic Love in Nineteenth-Century America*. Oxford: Oxford University Press, 1989.

Maddox, Brenda. *Yeats's Ghost: The Secret Life of W. B. Yeats*. New York: HarperCollins, 1999.

Marx, Leo. *The Machine in the Garden: Technology and the Pastoral Ideal in America*. New York: Oxford University Press, 1964.

McDannell, Colleen, and Bernhard Lang. *Heaven: A History*. New Haven, CT: Yale University Press, 1988.

Mirsky, Jeannette. *Elisha Kent Kane and the Seafaring Frontier*. Boston: Little, Brown, 1954.

Moore, R. Laurence. *In Search of White Crows: Spiritualism, Parapsychology, and American Culture*. New York: Oxford University Press, 1977.

Morus, Iwan Rhys. *Frankenstein's Children: Electricity, Exhibition, and Experiment in Early-Nineteenth-Century London*. Princeton, NJ: Princeton University Press, 1998.

Mulholland, John. *Beware Familiar Spirits*. New York: Charles Scribner's Sons, 1938.

Nelson, Geoffrey K. *Spiritualism and Society*. New York: Schocken, 1969.

Oppenheim, Janet. *The Other World: Spiritualism and Psychical Research in England, 1850–1914*. Cambridge: Cambridge University Press, 1985.

Pearsall, Ronald. *The Table Rappers*. London: Book Club, 1972.

Podmore, Frank. *Modern Spiritualism: A History and a Criticism*. 2 vols. London: Methuen, 1902. Reprint, *Mediums of the Nineteenth Century*. New Hyde Park, NY: University Books, 1963.

Pond, Mariam Buckner. *Time Is Kind: The Story of the Unfortunate Fox Family*. New York: Centennial, 1947.

Randi, James. *Flim-Flam! Psychics, ESP, Unicorns, and Other Delusions*. Buffalo, NY: Prometheus, 1986.

Ribuffo, Leo P. *Right Center Left: Essays in American History*. New Brunswick, NJ: Rutgers University Press, 1992.

Rich, Frank. "American Pseudo." *New York Times Magazine*, December 12, 1999.

Sawin, Mark Horst. "Heroic Ambition: The Early Life of Dr. Elisha Kent Kane." *Bulletin of the American Philosophical Society Library*, Fall 2002.

————. "Raising Kane: The Making of a Hero, the Marketing of a Celebrity." Master's thesis, University of Texas, 1997.

Saxon, A. H. *P. T. Barnum: The Legend and the Man*. New York: Columbia University Press, 1989.

Schmitt, Jean-Claude. *Ghosts in the Middle Ages: The Living and the Dead in Medieval Society*. Translated by Teresa Lavender Fagan. Chicago: University of Chicago Press, 1998.

Silverman, Kenneth. *Houdini! The Career of Ehrich Weiss*. New York: HarperCollins, 1996.

Simon, Linda. *Genuine Reality: A Life of William James*. New York: Harcourt Brace, 1998.

Smith-Rosenberg, Carroll. *Disorderly Conduct: Visions of Gender in Victorian America*. New York: Knopf, 1985.

Somerlott, Robert. *"Here, Mr. Splitfoot": An Informal Exploration into Modern Occultism*. New York: Viking, 1971.

Stage, Sarah. *Female Complaints: Lydia Pinkham and the Business of Women's Medicine*. New York: Norton, 1979.

Stashower, Daniel. *Teller of Tales: The Life of Arthur Conan Doyle*. New York: Henry Holt, 1999.

Taves, Ann. *Fits, Trances, and Visions: Experiencing Religion and Explaining Experience from Wesley to James*. Princeton, NJ: Princeton University Press, 1999.

Thomas, Keith. *Religion and the Decline of Magic: Studies in Popular Beliefs in Sixteenth- and Seventeenth-Century England*. 1971. New York: Oxford University Press, 1997.

Voorsanger, Catherine Hoover, and John K. Howat, eds. *Art and the Empire City: New York, 1825–1861*. New Haven, CT: Yale University Press, 2000.

Washington, Peter. *Madame Blavatsky's Baboon: A History of the Mystics, Mediums, and Misfits Who Brought Spiritualism to America*. New York: Schocken, 1993.

Wells, Robert V. *Facing the "King of Terrors": Death and Society in an American Community, 1750–1990*. Cambridge: Cambridge University Press, 2000.

Wicker, Christine. *Lily Dale: The True Story of the Town That Talks to the Dead*. San Francisco: HarperSanFrancisco, 2003.

Wills, Garry. *Lincoln at Gettysburg: The Words That Remade America*. New York: Touchstone, 1992.

Winter, Alison. *Mesmerized: Powers of Mind in Victorian Britain*. Chicago: University of Chicago Press, 1998.

INDEX